Carole Landis

Hollywood Legends Series
Ronald L. Davis, General Editor

Carole Landis

A Most Beautiful Girl

Eric Gans

UNIVERSITY PRESS OF MISSISSIPPI • JACKSON

www.upress.state.ms.us

The University Press of Mississippi is a member of the Association
of American University Presses.

Photographs not otherwise credited are from the collection
of the author.

First printing 2008

Library of Congress Cataloging-in-Publication Data
Gans, Eric Lawrence, 1941–
    Carole Landis : a most beautiful girl/Eric Gans.
        p. cm. — (Hollywood legends series)
    Includes bibliographical references and index.
    ISBN 978-1-60473-013-5 (cloth : alk. paper) 1. Landis, Carole,
1919–1948. 2. Motion picture actors and actresses—United States—
Biography. I. Title.
    PN2287.L27G36 2008
    791.4302′8092—dc22   2007043588
    [B]

British Library Cataloging-in-Publication Data available

You've never seen such a kisser. And her figure, . . . I'd say Jennifer North is about the most beautiful girl in the world.

—Henry Bellamy, describing a character modeled on Carole Landis in Jacqueline Susann's *Valley of the Dolls*

I admit proudly of having carried her photo with me through the battle of France, Luxembourg and Germany. Carole was always an inspiration, a model, a guiding light beaming down upon us with her understanding, her brilliant mind, and her unswerving loyalty. To all of us, Carole Landis was beautiful within as well as without—she had beauty of mind as well as of body.

She was humble and proud of our affection, and always hoped to reward our faith in her. Her heart was far more beautiful than her face and figure.

—Two World War II veterans, in the posthumous final edition of *The Caroler*, Carole's fan magazine

CONTENTS

ACKNOWLEDGMENTS

Many people have been of great help to me in writing this book. Among those whom I especially thank for their contribution are the following:

First, my wife, Stacey, whose patience and support throughout this project make her a fitting candidate for sainthood;

Walt Ross, Carole's nephew, who generously gave me access to family materials and permitted me to use what I needed for this book;

Gwen Serna, who has shared with me her time and collections and whose sweetness and generosity make her Carole's true disciple as well as her most loyal fan;

Laura Wagner, who unselfishly provided valuable leads about Carole and invaluable publication assistance;

Ned Comstock of the USC Cinema-Television Library, who was unfailingly helpful during my many hours poring through USC's remarkable collection of old movie magazines and memorabilia.

Among the members of Carole's family with whom I have been privileged to come in contact, I am grateful to Carole's niece Lyn Saye and her husband, Henry, for much valuable information, including a copy of the memorial issue of Carole's fan magazine; to Carole's second cousin Diane Ledo Madir for much useful material about the family tree; to Carole's niece and nephew Sharon Ross Powell and Billy Ross for meeting with me in Utah; to Carole's nephew Bryan Ridste; and to Sharon's daughter Tammy for our conversation in 2003.

Among the many Hollywood personalities who generously responded to my request for information about Carole, I should first mention those who are no longer with us: Kurt Kreuger and Fayard Nicholas, who provided particularly valuable memories of Carole, as well as Vivian Austin, Oleg Cassini, June Haver, Frances Langford, and Martha Tilton. Special thanks to Jean Porter Dmytryk for inviting me into her home and telling me about Carole before stardom, to Olivia de Havilland for graciously writing from Paris, to Jane Withers for our dinner conversation, to Betty Garrett, June Lockhart, Tony Martin, and Martha Stewart for providing material for the book, as well as to David Brown, Kay Linaker Phillips, Cobina Wright Jr., and Richard Zanuck. I am also grateful for the useful information supplied by Robert Dahdah and Ken Richards, who worked with Carole in New York.

My grateful thanks go to those who met Carole during the war and their heirs, a number of whom were kind enough to send me photographs and other materials. Among these I particularly want to thank Philip Castanza, Ace Elliott, Merrill Hilton, Barry Kazmer, Mary Koji, Frank Packlick, Jim Salley, Steve Sarbaugh, Nancy Skrocki, James H. Smith, Robert Stava, and Col. Eugene Wallace.

Among the many fellow researchers who provided advice and assistance, James Robert Parish, the dean of Hollywood film writers, was consistently helpful and supportive, and Aubrey Solomon kindly provided me with Fox box office data. Thanks to Bryan Cooper for his friendly and generous assistance at Fox and in Hollywood; to Valerie Yaros for Carole's Screen Guild records and her own Wupperman stories; to Denny Miller for our companionable travels to San Bernardino and his information on Carole's auto racing connections; to Bob Hudson, who put me in touch with Carole's family in Provo; to Bobby Gulshan, who assisted me at the start of this project; to Phil Weiss for generously sharing his Pattarini notes; and to Paul Georges for his detective work on my behalf. Thanks are due as well to Patrick Agan, Larry Billman, Lisa Burks, Adrienne Childers, Noonie Fortin, Stan Goodrich, Ray Hagen, Marlys Harris, Lynn Kear, Scott O'Brien, Karine Philippot, and Stephen Silverman for sharing research findings and Hollywood knowledge. And thanks to Gary Hamann of Filming Today Press for solving the *Blood and Sand* mystery and for many other scoops from the Los Angeles news media.

I am also grateful to the librarians who provided me with invaluable assistance, particularly to Barbara Hall at the Academy of Motion Picture Arts and Sciences Herrick Library; Julie Graham and Lauren Buisson at UCLA Fine Arts Special Collections; and Haden Guest, curator of the USC Warner Brothers archives.

Finally, thanks to my fellow Carole fans: to Bill Gerdts for our email exchanges about Carole's and other films of the past; to Jerry Diekmann for caring for Carole's grave; to my old friend and Carole admirer Stephen Werner; to Kathlene Avakian, Jeff Bissanti, Gerard Dessere, Kevin Dodge, Rodger Garrett, Peter Goldman, Sergio Huni, Jim McMurphy, Earl Mabin, Carole Ledo Johnson, Trevor Merrill, Peter Nazaretian, Paul Reed, Madeleine Rickardsson, Betty Rooks, Matt Schneider, Bill Shuttleworth, Bob Siler, Edward Sisson, Mark Stevens, Hap Trout, and Michel Wiederkehr of the "Carole support group"; to Jennifer D'Aquino and Norman Wall; to Joe Admire, the opera glove fan; to Benny Drinnon, the living Landis fan; to David Nordenbrock, the Anne Shirley fan; to Darlene Garcia for delivering all those Carole materials; to Sam Chen, Kurt Kreuger's assistant; and to the many other friends and correspondents who have offered me their encouragement and support in the course of this project.

Carole Landis

Introduction

One evening in January 2003, my wife and I watched a film on Turner Classic Movies entitled *I Wake Up Screaming*, a 1941 adaptation of Steve Fisher's novel of the same name. The two female leads were played by Betty Grable, familiar from many 1940s musicals, and Carole Landis, who was merely a name, but whose beauty amazed us.

Seeing Carole for what I believe to be the first time, I could not have guessed that this classic film noir told, after a fashion, the story of her career. Like Vicki, the film's ill-fated heroine, Carole burned with the ambition to "be somebody"; like Vicki, Carole died before her time. Vicki was murdered in a single act; Carole's life exhausted itself more subtly over a decade.

When the film was over, I searched the Internet and the library to learn more about Carole Landis. As I pursued this research, I was struck by both the paucity of information about her and by the contemptuous tone of much of it. Little was said about Carole beyond her suicide, which, retrospectively, became her destiny, the necessary outcome of the pathetic failure of her life. The books about 1940s Hollywood that documented the studios where she had worked mentioned her at best in passing. Books about women in Hollywood failed to include her. Even the memoirs of Carole's Hollywood friends, when they mentioned her at all, included no more than a brief incident or two. It was as though, the obligatory words about her suicide once written, it became awkward to say anything else about her. There were one or two sympathetic biographical essays, but even they emphasized her tragic death more than her accomplishments.

Beyond the serious writing, there were a number of references to Carole as a figure of scandal. Some referred to her as the "studio hooker" at Twentieth Century-Fox; some suggested that she "prostituted herself" to studio executives to obtain movie parts. It was often asserted that her only talent was her physical beauty, which was sometimes reduced to her bosom: one source attributed her celebrity to "brassiere-worship."

Yet those who repeated these catchwords were seldom those who had known Carole in person. When I came to examine Carole's file at the Motion Picture Academy's Herrick Library, I was struck by how much she was loved and admired by her family and friends, and above all by her fans. This observation was more than corroborated when Carole's nephew Walter Ross was kind enough to let me examine the dozens of letters remaining in Carole's family collection—out of the many thousands that she received. When I was able to speak with a few people who had known Carole personally, they told me how sweet and caring she was, how they admired her intelligence and sense of humor. I found ample evidence of her lack of self-importance and racial prejudice, of her generosity and concern for others, of her democratic insistence on showing as much if not more respect to the least of her fans than to the Hollywood bigwigs—who were probably not amused. I learned about Carole's unselfish contributions to World War II, the thousands of miles she traveled to entertain the troops in bases throughout the country and in both the Atlantic and Pacific theaters, the hundreds of messages she conscientiously delivered on her return to the men's sweethearts and mothers, the affection she inspired in the servicemen she met, some of whom told me of theirs in person.

Sadly, this woman who overflowed with affection for others, who claimed to want nothing more than marriage and family—Carole could not bear children, but often spoke of adoption—was unable to establish a long-term intimate relationship. Five times married, she was unable or unwilling to live for more than a month or two with any man, whether husband or lover. Carole was not a successful wife or partner, but she was a wonderful friend. She was, above all, a public figure who made of her beauty of body and soul a gift to her fans and to her country.

Carole's distinctive appearance limited the roles she could play, but within those limits her talents were rarely given full rein. What Carole needed and almost never found was a producer and director willing to build a film around these talents: beauty, wit, athleticism, and an appearance of being in control that could be comically turned into its opposite, a gift she would best demonstrate in the murder-comedy *Having Wonderful Crime* (1944). But Carole's historical importance cannot be measured by the quality of the films in which she appeared. What I shall try to show is that although Carole's presence on the world stage was entirely the result of her modest success in Hollywood, she was more than what Hollywood made of her; the degree of this excess, unique and surprising in the controlled world of the studio system, was both her glory and her tragedy.

There have been many beautiful actresses in Hollywood, and many sexy ones, but few have combined the two qualities as powerfully and inextricably as Carole. Of the many tributes she received at her death, not the least significant was Walter Winchell's remark that "a well-known doctor" had described her in 1945 as "one of the most sexicological women in and out of show biz." The very silliness of the neologism betrays the difficulty of fixing the nature of what might be called Carole's *sexual beauty*: a desirability that inspires admiration, even awe, inseparably from desire. This sentiment was expressed more delicately in 1941 by artist James Montgomery Flagg, who declared, after sketching Carole's portrait, that she had a "physical silhouette that is startling, bordering on the magnificent." The guarantee given by Carole's "silhouette" that her body fulfilled the promise of her beautiful face was the key to her uniqueness. Carole is sometimes compared with Marilyn Monroe, the vastly more celebrated icon of the fifties; but Marilyn's is an adolescent sexuality deliberately emphasized to the point of camp, whereas Carole's is that of an adult who never needed to *act* desirable.

What continues to draw us to Carole's public persona is her unemphatic display of confidence that her beauty gives us pleasure. Her image conveys no false promise of sexual intimacy but an offer of friendship that hints at the unspoken knowledge that intimate life was not where Carole herself found happiness. This was a woman who had four husbands and many lovers, but it suffices to read the final, posthumous issue of her fan magazine or to go through a few of the letters in her family collection to be convinced that, except for her family and a few intimates, those who most authentically shared her love were not her husbands or her lovers but her fans, whom she treated less as admirers than as friends. Many of their letters gave evidence that Carole had responded in person to every one of the correspondent's previous communications; a surprising number apologized for answering Carole's letters less promptly than she did theirs.

The 1940s were the heyday of fan clubs, often attached not to the biggest stars but to those whose careers the fans had the illusion that they could help along. For Carole, the movie star–fan relationship was a paradigm of her relationship to her vast military audience of World War II and to the public at large. Carole saw her stardom as a wonderful opportunity to profit from the charisma it lent her by offering it as a personal gift to each member of her audience. There is a complementary relationship between the instability of Carole's intimate life and the drive to make and maintain personal contact with the servicemen and fans she encountered. Clearly, transforming her initially asymmetric relationship with her fans into one of evenhanded reciprocity was easier and more rewarding for Carole than maintaining the delicate symmetry of a love relationship.

Whatever impact Carole had on her fans and on the soldiers of World War II, we can share their experience only through the images she left us, her photographs and, above all, her films. Until the invention of photography and, particularly, cinema, we were obliged to accept on faith all claims of beauty we could not verify for ourselves; the beauty of a painting or a statue belongs to the artist as much as to his subject. Hollywood at the time of Carole's arrival in the late 1930s had reached the moment of its greatest impact on the world's imagination. Never had the power to create and project images to the entire world been concentrated in so few hands; never had so much publicity focused on so few faces. Carole's own film ambitions, like those of countless others, had been inspired by her avid childhood reading of movie magazines and daydreaming before the star photographs with which she covered her walls.

The postwar consumer society that the film industry did so much to promote could not help but outgrow the monopoly of the imagery that fueled it. The notion of Hollywood glamour as Carole understood and embodied it is incompatible with today's multiple competing sources of notoriety. The constantly changing imagery of today's popular culture privileges sensation over beauty and resentful fascination over worshipful admiration. Female sexual beauty remains the most potent force of attraction in publicity material addressed to either sex, but the images that display it have lost their serene self-confidence. The arrival in the 1950s of the Brigitte Bardot pout on top of Marilyn Monroe's campy sexiness reflected a new necessity to supplement the straightforward communication of desirability from bearer to observer with the playful archness of the junior femme fatale.

That Hollywood glamour reached its high point around Carole's time is hardly a controversial claim. What requires explanation here, if not proof—except insofar as the book's illustrations can serve as a demonstration— is that Carole herself occupies a unique place in the history of Hollywood glamour. The publicity that attaches to actresses newly appearing on the Hollywood scene tends, whenever possible, to emphasize their sexual attractiveness, and in most cases this attractiveness is real enough. Yet although Carole's beauty was the distinguishing factor that won her first job at Warner Brothers in 1937, her stint at Republic in 1939, her 1940 breakthrough with *One Million B.C.*, and her Fox contract in 1941, it soon became a source of problems, not merely in the world of Hollywood publicity but in the films themselves. A number of actresses, notably the ill-fated Barbara La Marr (who gave her name to the far more beautiful but untragic Hedy), have been spoken of as "too beautiful," but in Carole's case, excess of beauty became a theme of her films, posing a problem to which the solution arrived at was to limit its impact as much as possible. Yet, as Carole herself well recognized, if Hollywood frustrated her professional ambitions, it was Hollywood that gave her a profession in the first place. It would be fair to say that in the course of her twelve-year film career, Hollywood both did and did not recognize Carole's uniqueness. To define this uniqueness is the purpose of this book.

For two reasons, I have felt that it is useful to focus more on Carole's public persona as displayed in her films and other performances than on her personal life. In the first place, the beauty of Frances Ridste the San Bernardino housewife would not have had the means to touch the public in her own time, let alone today. Carole was surely one of the most generous and unassuming of all the Hollywood stars, but her generosity and unpretentiousness were those of someone who was able to display her public persona to the world even as she communicated on an equal footing with her fans in and out of the armed forces. Each of Carole's films reveals in its own way the evolution of this persona; each brings out facets of Carole's life and character that, put together, tell a more coherent and revealing story than the trivia of her daily existence.

The second reason, which does not make the first superfluous, is that nearly all the details of Carole's intimate world are lost beyond any hope of retrieval. Almost no personal materials—diaries, letters to family, friends, husbands, and lovers—survive; the many thousands of letters Carole wrote to her fans and friends are scattered or lost, almost entirely uncollected. Those who knew her well, and nearly all of those who knew her at all, are either dead or too old to remember. I would not minimize the precious tidbits of information I have obtained from a number of very gracious Hollywood personalities, some of whom are no longer with us, but the result of putting together these little anecdotes with the material found in gossip columns and movie magazines is not comparable to the story that might have been told had we had access to Carole's diaries or her intimate correspondence, or to one of the few persons who knew her intimately, such as her sister, Dorothy, or her longtime friend Florence Wasson. Since we can no longer know Carole's intimate life even at secondhand, we would do better to focus on the public materials that we do have, which provide insights not only into who Carole was "in herself" but, more importantly, into the persona she was able to create for and with her audience.

The era in which Carole flourished corresponds to the apogee of public beauty in Hollywood, American, and world history. The link between this high point and its setting in World War II—in a word, the "pin-up"—is more intimate even than Carole's USO tours make it appear. It is in conformity with human nature that the public manifestation of sexual attractiveness should reach its maximum power at the moment of humanity's greatest violence, on the eve and in the course of the war that made total war henceforth unthinkable.

Carole's personal tragedy both reveals the limits of the circulation of desire and entertainment in the studio system and presages its decline, precipitated in the year of her death by the Supreme Court's "Paramount ruling," which divested the studios of the theater chains that had bound the exhibition of films to their production. By ending her life before the age of thirty, Carole left the world at the beginning of the rise of television and just before the split between adult and adolescent sensibility opened in the 1950s and early '60s, the era of Doris Day and Marilyn Monroe, of Patti Page and Elvis Presley, when the forces catering to youth were growing in strength and self-confidence and would soon drive out the older adult popular culture, triumphing in the mid-'60s with the Beatles and the Berkeley Free Speech movement.

But although the youth culture has prevailed, adults have not disappeared, nor have all of them abdicated their cultural judgment. Whatever the verdict of the box office, adult sexuality trumps the infantile variety in the real world. The time has come to reintroduce Carole Landis to the general public as both a marvelous Hollywood singularity and the incarnation of a timeless ideal. Now that the moral basis of our civilization is once again called in question, it does us good to witness this living demonstration that, taken to its extreme, beauty is indeed truth, that our mimetic, "socially constructed" desires have an ultimate basis in nature. Carole reminds us of the reality behind the sign that the postmodern sensibility tries so hard to make us forget. It is because her warmth and generosity are visible in nearly every trace that Carole has left us, whether in her letters, her photographs, or her films, that this great beauty of film's golden age retains the ability to touch us today.

CHAPTER 1

Beginnings (1919–1935)

It is not to psychoanalyze Carole to point out that she came from a family without a father. Carole was not the first in her line to have problems living with a man.

Carole's mother was born Clara Sentek on May 11, 1894, on a family farm in Fairchild, Wisconsin, third of the eight children, two boys and six girls, of Louis/Ludwick and Frances/Franciska Sentek, both born in 1867. (At least six different spellings of the family name are found on official documents.) Fairchild, a small village in Eau Claire County in west-central Wisconsin (2000 population, 564), was, during the first quarter of the twentieth century, "a big railroad town . . . [that] served as a regional transfer center for lumber, cattle, grain, and potatoes. . . . In all, thirty trains a day passed through Fairchild."

Although both Clara's parents were of Polish stock, they had emigrated from Germany to the United States, presumably together, in 1888. In the 1900 census, Ludwick declared that he had been naturalized in Alabama and gave his profession as a "shingle sawyer." In the 1910 census, Ludwick was a "section hand" on the railroad, and Frances was a farmer on their "home farm." The couple must have prospered, for they were listed as renting their home in 1900 but owning it in 1910. The Senteks remained on their farm in Fairchild into old age. Their children and grand-children settled mostly in the upper Midwest, in Minnesota and in Wisconsin, where the bulk of their descendants live to this day.

To judge from the letters she wrote later, Clara's education must have been quite limited. She was a woman of some daring; in the last family photograph I have seen of her, which probably dates from 1964 and is cer-tainly not earlier, septuagenarian Clara is taking a ride on a snowmobile. She was also not without daring in her marital life. Marrying Alfred Ridste, whom she later characterized as "restless," at the age of seventeen was only the first of her conjugal adventures. Clara died in Los Angeles at the age of eighty-two, on August 9, 1976.

Carole's father, Alfred Ridste, was born on October 10, 1891, in Dawson, a small town in Lac Qui Parle County, Minnesota, about 150 miles due west of Minneapolis. He was the fifth of eight children of John Ridste and Gurine Herreid, the eldest of four sons but with four older sis-ters. The elder Ridste had come to the United States from Norway in 1889, one year after Clara's parents; his wife, Gurine, also of Norwegian ancestry, was born in Calmer, Iowa. John's original name was Andersen, but because there were so many other Andersens in his part of Minnesota he took the name of Ridste, presumably from his birthplace in Norway. In 1900, John lists his occupation as "carpenter." Although the family owned their own home, they could not have been very well off; their eldest daughter, Gina, seventeen years old, gives her occupation as "servant." They also had marriage difficulties. In 1910, there are no census records of John and Gurine, but in 1920, Gurine is listed as divorced and still living in Dawson with three of her children. She and her daughter list no occu-pation; two sons are listed as laborers engaged in "silo building." Meanwhile, in 1910, eighteen-year-old Alfred was lodging at 1518 Charles Avenue, Saint Paul, giving his occupation as "joiner, refrigerator fitting," presumably referring to railroad refrigerator cars. His two fellow lodgers were in the same trade, and most of the men living on his street, about half a mile from the railroad yards, worked on the railroad. It was probably Fairchild's importance as a railroad center that brought Alfred there; he most likely met Clara through her father, who was working at the time as a "section hand."

Alfred's wanderlust probably struck a chord in Clara, giving her an opportunity to escape her home town. Shortly after their wedding in Fairchild on June 19, 1911, the couple set off for Minnesota, where their eldest son, Lawrence, was born in Minneapolis on March 26, 1912, nine months and a week into their marriage, and thence to Denton, a small farming community (2000 population, 301) in Fergus County in central Montana, where they lived in an unincorporated area a mile or two to the northeast, known as Alton. Aside from its being on a railroad line to the nearby large town of Lewistown (2000 population, 5,813), we know nothing of the particular attractions of the place. In Denton, the couple had three more children, two boys, both ill-fated, and a girl. Lewis, born December 3, 1913, would die of a gunshot wound to the abdomen at the age of eleven; Jerome, born July 3, 1916, fell into water heated for the laundry and was scalded to death at the age of seventeen months, on December 20, 1917. Dorothy, born on July 8, 1917, would be Carole's closest confidante throughout her life.

Sometime after Dorothy's birth, and after March 1918 if we assume—as is not absolutely certain—that he was, indeed, Carole's father, Alfred Ridste left the farm in Denton to join the U.S. Navy, in which, however, he enlisted only in October 1919. The January 1920 census lists Alfred as an "aviation student" at the U.S. Naval Training Station in Great Lakes, Illinois, presumably being trained as a mechanic rather than an aviator. Despite the presence in Denton of a man who would soon become her second husband, Clara returned to her family home in Fairchild some time before Carole's birth, doubtlessly in order to bear her child in a supportive family environment and a more densely populated area. The influenza pandemic that ravaged the world in 1918 and 1919, causing twice as many deaths as the Great War, began in the Midwest in the spring of 1918, just at the time and place of Carole's conception. If we credit the story that Clara was afflicted by influenza that spring (in its earliest phase, the disease was less deadly than it later became), this would have given her an additional reason to return to civilization.

In her father's absence, Frances Lillian Ridste was born in Fairchild at 6 AM on January 2, 1919. Although Carole generally moved her birth date back a few hours to coincide with the New Year (identification with holidays led her to marry on July 4, 1940, and take her own life on the night of July 4, 1948), she used the correct date on most official documents, such as her marriage license with Horace Schmidlapp in 1945.

A few months after Carole's birth, Clara and the children returned to Denton, whereupon she divorced Alfred Ridste on December 19, 1919, and the very same day married Charles or "Charley" Fenner, who according to family accounts had been a hired hand on the family farm. Since Clara must have known Fenner before her departure for Fairchild, and since Alfred was away for some time before Carole's birth, it is certainly conceivable, as Landis biographer E. J. Fleming suggests, that Fenner rather than Ridste was Carole's father. It seems unlikely, however, that Fenner, who died in 1971 at the age of eighty-five, would never have revealed his status as the father of a famous movie star, nor could Clara have kept his paternity a secret from the man who served as Carole's stepfather a few months after her birth. There is no indication that Fenner maintained contact with Carole or anyone else in Clara's family after they left Montana in 1921. In the absence of family or other corroboration of Fenner's paternity, it remains unconfirmed speculation.

After Carole's birth, Clara became prone to short marriages and rapid divorces. Her second try at matrimony lasted less than sixteen months; she divorced Fenner in April 1921 and rejoined Ridste in San Diego, where he was working in the navy shipyards. Clara's divorce action, which was uncontested, claims that Fenner "inflicted and threatened to inflict grievous bodily injury" on her, that he "brutally" forced her to have intercourse while pregnant (presumably with his own child), resulting in a miscarriage, and that in addition he committed adultery on or about July 1 "with one Jane Doe." That Fenner appears to have been a highly sexed individual was not unlikely an important aspect of his attraction for Clara; this suggests in Clara a strong sexual temperament. Although, after divorcing Fenner, Clara changed her name back to Ridste, it does not appear that she and Alfred remarried.

At some time in 1922, when Frances was three, Clara moved the family to San Bernardino. Carole tells us that Alfred moved there at approximately the same time, but for "a job, not a reconciliation." Clara appears to have remarried between the 1930 census and 1937, perhaps while Carole was in San Francisco in 1935 and '36; Carole's payroll card at Warner Brothers in May 1937 gives her mother's name as Clara Sentek Dillon. Like the others, this marriage evidently proved unsuccessful, since once Carole's contract with Warner Brothers was signed in July 1937, she sent for her mother, and the two women lived together, off and on, for much of Carole's career, with Clara eventually adopting the name "Landis." As for Alfred, the 1930 census shows him remarried to Ann Lavery; left a widower in 1950, he married a third wife, Evadna Clifton Stone, in July 1952. Ridste died in Sonoma, California, on March 4, 1973.

In San Bernardino, Clara was faced with the unenviable task of bringing up four children on her own with no highly marketable skills. To support her family, she took on "cooking, cleaning, nursing, scrubbing, any kind of a job that would bring food for [her] children." Clara also waited tables; she listed her profession as "waitress" in the 1930 census. She must have been diligent, and possibly received help from her ex-husband, for in that same census she is recorded as the owner of her home at 175 Bryant Street, valued at $1,800.

San Bernardino was not a wealthy town, and the Ridstes were probably at least as well off as most in their neighborhood. Bryant is a modest street in the old, central part of San Bernardino, probably not very different in appearance today from the street Clara and her children lived on, except that the houses, new or close to it in the 1920s, have become rather run down; the *poor but respectable* appearance Clara describes has given way to a certain seediness. It's hard to imagine Clara tolerating the toys and other objects strewn casually about the spacious yard of the house that was most likely hers (the street number has been changed). This is a good-sized ramshackle stucco-frame dwelling whose projecting porch may have been added after the original construction. To the west, Bryant ends in two blocks and the view is blocked by a park, but to the east one can see the snowcapped mountains in the distance.

Carole attended Jefferson Grade School, which is still standing at Mountain View and Sixth Streets; Sturges Junior High School at Eighth and E Streets, now the Sturges Center for the Fine Arts; and San Bernardino High School, where she left no record in any yearbook and dropped out after her sophomore year. Carole was confirmed at Saint Bernardine's Catholic Church, a handsome building at 531 North F Street, completed in 1912. As its name implies, Saint Bernardine's is the founding Catholic parish of San Bernardino, dating from 1862; the original church went up in 1867. As a result of her confirmation, Carole's name is often cited as Frances Lillian *Mary* Ridste.

Clara describes Frances as a "happy outgoing child . . . trusting the whole world, loving it." Carole was beautiful from childhood, as her family photographs all suggest; the memory of her blonde hair as a child may have inspired her to lighten her naturally golden-brown color to blonde throughout most of her career. The family called Frances "Baby Doll," and Clara enjoyed dressing her up. Frances passed on the favor to her own dolls, which Dorothy remembers as always dressed more elegantly than her own; she also recalls that from early childhood Frances shared with others and never bore grudges. Frances also "had her little altar with Madonna and crucifixes"; all her life Frances/Carole wore a cross around her neck and considered herself a believing Catholic. Years after Carole's death, Dorothy and her husband, Walter Ross, joined the Church of Latter-Day Saints; their three surviving children live in Utah and continue to practice that religion.

The earliest remembered incident involving Carole is one that Clara recounts as taking place in San Diego in June 1921: Frances, eighteen months old, ran off by herself and was found five blocks away, surrounded by strangers, picking flowers. Since Clara mentions having "called her father home from work," she and Alfred must still have been together.

Another incident, in San Bernardino this time, appears to have occurred when Frances was about five or six; she got in a fight with Betty Watson, a girl a year older than she who lived next door at 159, because Betty had trampled Clara's flowers. Frances confessed to her mother that she had an "awful big problem"; ordered not to fight, she had slapped Betty because, she said, "Nobody can stomp on my Mommie's flowers." An elderly lady, described by Clara as "Grandma Brungalo" (actually Lucy Brumbelow, who lived across the street at 170 and was listed as seventy-seven years old in 1930), gave Frances a quarter despite her disobedience as a reward for defending her mother's flowers.

The unhappiest event in Frances's childhood occurred on July 15, 1925, when her eleven-year-old brother Lewis was shot in the course of a card game with friends at Harry Montgomery's house, just down the street at 160 Bryant. (The Montgomerys were no longer there in 1930, perhaps in part as a result of this unfortunate incident.) Although Carole's anonymous friend attributes Lewis's shooting to "a boy of 17 who had nurtured a mysterious grievance against him," the *San Bernardino Sun* confirms Clara's description of the shooting as an "accident." Apparently, the boys had placed a cartridge in the chamber of a revolver with the intention of using it to shoot tin cans in the nearby Santa Ana wash, then forgot about it; the gun had a hair trigger mechanism, and when someone picked it up, it fired a single bullet into Lewis's abdomen, puncturing his intestines in fifteen places. Despite attempts to save him, Lewis died two days later. According to Clara, Frances consoled her for being obliged to leave the children to fend for themselves. Dorothy, whose account of Carole's childhood is very brief, does not mention this incident.

As a little girl, Frances acted out plays, and Clara recalls that by the age of seven she had declared, "I'm going to be a movie star." She spent hours reading secondhand fan magazines and covered her walls with stars' photographs. Dorothy tells us that her favorite stars were Kay Francis and Mary Astor; Carole would later appear in films with both of them. Like other cities within an hour or two of Los Angeles, San Bernardino was frequently the site of film previews, the proximity of which might have fueled Frances's Hollywood ambitions.

An iconic incident recounted in nearly all Carole's capsule biographies is her spontaneous performance of the bouncy "That's My Weakness Now" in an amateur-night contest at the Strand Theatre. Although the age most commonly given for this presumably inaugural public performance is seven, the song, composed by Bud Green with words by Sam H. Stept and recorded, among others, by Boop-a-doop girl Helen Kane, dates from 1928, when Frances was nine, the year she claimed in the earliest version of the incident to have *stopped* singing it. As the story is usually told, Frances got her mother and older brother, Lawrence, who would have been sixteen in 1928, to take her to the amateur night, but gave no hint that she intended to perform. Yet when the contest began and the master of ceremonies asked for contestants, Frances called out that she wanted to sing, climbed onto the stage, and delivered. In many versions of the story, Carole claimed her performance was so embarrassing that her mother and brother were the only ones to applaud, but Clara's version, according to which she was so surprised and Lawrence so embarrassed that they were the only ones *not* to applaud, must be correct; what audience could resist a pretty nine-year-old girl with the courage to sing in public? The song itself, which begins, "Love, love, love, love, What did you do to me?" and speaks of the beloved's "eyes of blue" and "dimpled cheeks" as "my weakness now" is curiously prophetic of Carole's love life, in which she was called "a patsy for a handsome male."

A few years after this promising debut, Frances began competing on another terrain. The two beauty contests she entered at twelve and thirteen are another stock biographical element. Apparently, she won fourth prize and a pair of oversize stockings "with cotton tops" in the first contest and second prize and an electric heater in the second, for which she had prepared by purchasing a red bathing suit. One account adds that she entered several more times but was unable to win first prize. Clara's article claims mistakenly that Frances won both contests. This was well before the era of Jon Benet; in both these competitions, Frances was most likely the youngest contestant by a good margin. Under the circumstances, second place, even fourth, wasn't bad.

Although our picture of Carole's early life is spotty, these incidents of public competition not coincidentally touch on the two main factors that Carole counted on for success: the nerve to perform in public without formal training, relying solely on her natural ability to sing and dance; and her exceptional beauty, which she bore without embarrassment and displayed without shame. Stage nerve and beauty were the trump cards that Carole played to begin her career in San Francisco and to break into Hollywood. Carole's youthful exhibitionism formed the basis of her lifelong unself-consciousness. Always ready to strike a pose for the camera, she never seeks to invade our world but rather seems to welcome us into hers.

In a letter to Carole's fan club after her suicide, sister Dorothy, remarking on Carole's kindness to her school friend Peggy Freeman (who may be the anonymous "lifelong friend" who wrote about Carole in the November 1948 *True Confessions*), gives this lovely description of Carole's presence in early youth: "We three used to sit on the school lawn enthralled with Carole's singing, her grace and beauty."

Frances reached sexual and social maturity at an early age. Although she was quick witted, articulate, and gifted with an exceptionally good memory—in 1945 she impressed a columnist by learning in one shot the names of a tableful of people—she was unhappy in school. She cut classes and had Dorothy forge her mother's signature to excuses so she could drive around in her "old jalopy"; one source claims her teachers called her a "bad girl."

"She was a smart girl with a wonderful memory, but she learned from experience, not teachers." Frances went through many jobs; it is not specified whether some of them interfered with school attendance. Among these were working for a milliner, clerking in a dime store, ushering in a movie house, and "slinging hash" in a roadside diner where the "tired truck drivers . . . appreciated her curves even more than they appreciated the hash"—and where Carole complained that she could never make change properly and had to put half her tips into the till to make up for what she calls her "generosity to the customers." The one academic achievement Carole claimed was organizing a girls' football team, "but it didn't last long." She was more interested in boys' sports than girls'; she claimed to have broken both her nose and her arm on the athletic field.

Frances was also interested in boys, period. A fellow (female) high-schooler described her as "boy-crazy." She would develop crushes on older boys who, Carole claimed in sanitized movie magazines, ignored her presence. Clara, in contrast, emphasized Carole's attraction for the young men who frequented the diner where she worked as well as the fact that at the age of fourteen she was chosen to give out the prizes at a local air show.

We need not doubt the attraction in either direction. As an adult, Carole's confidence in her attractiveness to the opposite sex never prevented her from being vulnerable to desire. In 1941, at the height of her beauty, she declared that what she most demanded of men was that they not make her suffer. This is summed up in a capsule description of Carole by Phil Silvers, who met Carole during the war and worked with her in *Four Jills in a Jeep*: she "oozed sex appeal but was completely vulnerable." In sexual desire as in other domains, Carole, although no feminist in the ideological sense, refused to accept any form of feminine passivity despite the danger to her reputation occasioned by taking an active role. In life or in film (with the unconvincing exception of *A Scandal in Paris*), Carole was never the cold seductress who attracted desire by her lack of it; she seemed rather to have felt that her very desirability imposed on her the responsibility to desire no less than she was herself desired. As a consequence, the world of sexual desire, pleasure, and disillusion, however deeply she ventured into it, could not deform her into either an unself-respecting tramp or a vampish exploiter of her sexiness.

Clara had good reason to worry about her daughter's precocious, precarious mixture of desirability and vulnerability. At fifteen, abetted, she claims, by her father, Frances decided to marry. The chosen bridegroom was Irving Wheeler, "a nice-looking boy of 19 who had a crew haircut, a jaloppy [sic], and a terrific 'line.' [Carole] liked the way he danced and also the idea of being a married woman." So on January 14, 1934, pretexting a hike, the couple climbed into the "jaloppy" and drove the two hundred odd miles to the border town of Yuma, Arizona, where, giving their ages as eighteen and twenty-one, they were married. Aside from disguising her age, Frances spelled her name "Francis" as the family often did (for example, on both the 1920 and 1930 census records), no doubt recalling her grandmother's Polish name, Franciska. Big sister Dorothy and her future husband, Walter Ross, went along for the ride and served as witnesses—an extension of Dorothy's forgeries covering Carole's absences from school. The incident reflects their relationship throughout Carole's life: Carole living a life of adventure, Dorothy, one of domestic tranquility; one always there for the other. If one of the two was envious, it was rather Carole, who regretted her physical inability to have children and, probably still more, her psychological inability to find a stable love relationship like her sister's.

One probable reason for Frances's surprise elopement was to escape her childhood home; another was to get out of school, for Carole claimed to have been under the mistaken impression that married women were no longer obliged to attend. A third reason, not to be neglected, would have been to legitimize sexual relations; at this point in her life she no doubt preferred to become what used to be called an "honest woman." We may wonder whether Wheeler, who would later call himself a "writer" and seek bit parts in movies using the stage name "Jack Robbins," enticed Carole by claiming some connection with Hollywood.

On returning home from the Yuma excursion, Frances discovered that she would not only have to remain in school but also remain in her mother's home. Two or three weeks later (the exact date is unavailable), Clara went to the San Bernardino court to annul this marriage contracted under false pretenses. Frances finished out the semester at school, surely not improving her grades; when and where she continued to see Wheeler is unknown. But they must have remained in contact, for, having obtained her father's permission to marry before the normal age of consent, Frances was once again married to Irving in San Bernardino on August 25, 1934. This time the couple gave their correct ages; once again, the marriage was witnessed by Dorothy.

Mindful of the need to support his wife, Wheeler, who had obtained a job digging an aqueduct, listed his occupation on his second wedding certificate as "chuck tender." School being out, Frances went to live with Irving in his home town of Banning, about thirty miles to the southeast, where he resided with his mother. Life in these circumstances led to conflict, and the couple shortly moved to a boardinghouse, but separated after a few weeks; apparently, they quarreled over Carole's inability to cook potatoes and make coffee. In her divorce action four years later, Carole charged the customary "mental cruelty," complaining that "during their 25 days of wedded life [Wheeler] told her she was 'no good.' "

This marriage was a youthful fling, no doubt, but the pattern remained constant throughout Carole's life. Unable to apply her loving nature to conjugal existence, she seemed incapable of learning either to live with the men she married or to select a husband with whom she could live. In none of her five marriages (counting Wheeler twice) did she live with her husband for more than a month or two at a time; in each case, however profoundly she felt she was in love at the outset, she was quickly disillusioned. No doubt, had Carole been able to bear children, marriage would have acquired another dimension. She is said to have visited orphanages with both her third husband, Tommy Wallace, in 1944, and her fourth and last, Horace Schmidlapp, in 1946, in both cases without results. Clearly, domestic bliss was less a real goal than an ideal state that Carole was more able to envy in others than cultivate in herself. For the moment, the misadventure with

Wheeler left Frances as she was before: impatient with authority, disdainful of school, dreaming of stardom as a means of escaping her modest life in the flats of San Bernardino for the mountains beyond.

If Carole inherited anything from her parents, it was a restless openness to new experience. As someone who always believed in romantic love and who, despite her many failures, often dogmatically asserted that one "knew" when one had found the right person, Carole faced the world as someone always open to love but unable to share its intimacy. Party girl though she was from an early age, Carole was intensely reflective. Although the articles published under her own name in film magazines contain a large part of obligatory content and were surely not composed by her directly, and although even her unique volume of war memoirs, *Four Jills in a Jeep*, bears the imprint of a professional collaborator, the sheer number of first-person articles—at least thirty-seven in the seven years between 1941 and 1947, to which we may add another dozen or so autobiographical "told-to" articles—testifies to Carole's insistence on self-expression. In addition, Carole wrote (and usually typed) thousands of letters to friends and fans and composed diaries, sadly forever lost, that must have run to thousands of pages. But no man—and few women—fully shared her intimacy, neither her husbands nor even Rex Harrison, almost certainly the man with whom she had the fullest and most satisfying relationship. The "promise of happiness" that was Stendhal's definition of beauty was one Carole could keep to the world but not to any individual man.

CHAPTER 2

In Northern California (1935–1937)

We must presume in the absence of other evidence that the timing of Frances's departure for the Bay Area was determined by the state law that required school attendance until the age of sixteen, married or not. Thus, when she turned sixteen on January 2, 1935, she was free to leave school, and she did. Like Frances's rendition of "That's My Weakness Now," the financing of her departure is one of a number of often-told tales in which the data float from place to place. According to the most reliable account, the oft-quoted amount of $16.82 was the bus fare, not Frances/Carole's savings, which were given as about $100—a decent sum in 1935 ($1,485.39 in 2007 dollars, according to the consumer price index). But another source gives the less round and therefore more credible figure of $47 for Frances's total stake; still another makes it only $26.

Carole explains her choice of San Francisco by the fact that New York was too far and Hollywood too full of promising starlets. Although the first point is persuasive enough, the second is less so; what could a detour through the Bay Area offer a girl whose heart was set on Hollywood? Many young women of Carole's generation, such as Ann Sheridan and

Linda Darnell, both natives of Texas, had headed straight to Hollywood from places a lot farther away than San Bernardino. Although it seems unlikely that Wheeler was involved, could another man have been connected in some way with Frances's departure? Was the choice of San Francisco influenced by the city's fabled disdain for the Puritanism that no doubt stifled Frances in her home town?

There are other unanswered questions. Although the distance is not great, it does not appear that anyone from her past paid a call on Carole during the two years she spent in Northern California—years during which, if we can trust Clara's memory, Carole never communicated in any way with her family. For the details of Carole's childhood, there are several family sources and even some external corroboration; for her two years in the Bay Area, we must rely almost entirely on her own account. Although Carole unquestionably performed there as a singer, in particular as a soloist with Carl Ravazza's band, no record has been found in any newspaper or elsewhere of a contemporary reference to either "Frances Ridste" or "Carole Landis" in Northern California.

Some time after her arrival in San Francisco, Frances tells us she chose her stage name. Carole was her "favorite name," clearly borrowed from Carole Lombard, the first Hollywood star to spell her name that way, although Carole herself "never gave this story credence." Frances was surely aware that, like herself, her chosen namesake, née Jane Alice Peters, was born in the Midwest (in Fort Wayne, Indiana), the child of a broken home, had come to California as a girl, and had dropped out of high school to pursue an entertainment career; above all, Frances, whose best acting would be in comedy, must have admired Lombard's mastery of the screwball genre. Carole explained the choice of "Landis" as one of two hundred names she found in the San Francisco telephone directory; some writers claim that she made her selection on seeing the name of baseball commissioner Kenesaw Mountain Landis in a newspaper.

Carole says she had no contacts in San Francisco; she made the rounds of nightspots as a singer, including the St. Francis Hotel, but after an unsuccessful tryout with "The Way You Look Tonight," she was hired at the Royal Hawaiian as a hula dancer, more on the strength of her figure than for her knowledge of the hula, which she learned on the job after bluffing her way into the chorus.

The Royal Hawaiian, located at 960 Bush Street, about five blocks from Union Square, was a club with a notorious, not to say scandalous past. Formerly named the Kamokila Club, or hotel, it had been founded in 1933 by Alice Kamokila Campbell, a wealthy pineapple heiress on her father's side who claimed to be a Hawaiian princess on her mother's side. The institution, housed in a building that had begun as a Methodist church and subsequently become an exclusive speakeasy, was originally called Kamokila's Temple to Art. The "temple" auditorium was also used as and called a playhouse; November 22, 1933, saw a performance of *As You Like It*. But by 1934, it was simply the Kamokila Club, described as an "exclusive night life rendezvous."

The club was raided on January 27, 1934, for unlawful sale of liquor and remained in the headlines throughout the coming months. After a judge dismissed the charges, Campbell filed suit against the city, claiming that she had been "forced to pay police through intermediaries." Although a grand jury convened to investigate the scandal brought no indictments, the city continued its harassment by rejecting Campbell's application for a permit to allow public dancing. She finally closed the club on April 25, 1934, and on June 27 left San Francisco for her native Hawaii, leaving behind some minor legal loose ends. Shortly afterward, the club was taken over by an entity called the Kamehameha Corporation, after the founder of Hawaii's royal dynasty, and reopened as the Royal Hawaiian, a name it shared with a major Honolulu hotel.

How much Carole knew of this history when she arrived at the club is unknown, but she surely learned of it later, as well as of the Royal Hawaiian's somewhat unsavory reputation for drinking and "rendezvous." She tells us that she soon teamed up with fellow hula dancer Kay Ellis in a "sister act." Ellis was formerly a hat-check girl at a similar establishment, the Cairo Club, where in February 1935 she was a witness to the death of an army major allegedly pushed down a long flight of stairs by the club's bouncers, who were eventually acquitted of manslaughter. The specifics of the sister act have not been described. We only know that Carole sang at the Royal Hawaiian as well as danced—she claims she eventually convinced the manager to let her sing by giving a rendition of "My Man" in her sultry voice. Subsequently, Carl Ravazza (1912–1968), a former singer and violinist who was taking over the leadership of Tom Coakley's band, heard Carole's act at the Royal Hawaiian and hired her as his female vocalist. From references in Bay Area newspapers of the time, it appears that Ravazza often performed at the St. Francis Hotel, only a few blocks from the Royal Hawaiian, and he may have played the Hawaiian as well.

The following description of Carole's singing was given by her Royal Hawaiian employer or perhaps by Ravazza himself, who is quoted elsewhere as speaking of Carole "with affection": "He remembers that every time she came out to sing, the dancers would be jammed up in front, the men folk giving Carole the eye and their partners the go-by. He remembers, too, that he was sorry when she quit him for a job that opened up at the Rio del Mar Country Club at Santa Cruz." Indeed, Carole left San Francisco to accept a job singing for fifty dollars a week, room and board included, in the more elegant setting of the Rio Del Mar, where she particularly enjoyed swimming in the pool.

A picture in Carole's family collection shows her in her two-piece hula costume. The top is generously décolleté and visibly too tight, unsubtly displaying her breasts as she leans forward, with one leg raised, holding the edges of her diaphanous skirt to the sides with both hands as if executing a curtsy. Her expression is a rather blank smile, engaging but impersonal; her face is rounder than it would be later on and her body plumper than in her Hollywood years, displaying what in a sixteen-year-old girl could still be called baby fat. There is an earnestness in her look and a self-confidence that despite her awkward pose you will be pleased by what you see. This photograph is in itself a convincing piece of evidence that Carole made her way in San Francisco on her own. Another photograph of the same vintage shows just her face and shoulders, wearing what looks like a silk blouse tied around the neck with a bow and a black jacket or cardigan; no décolleté here! In this shot, Carole has penciled eyebrows and thinly reddened lips; her smile is sweeter and more open, and the overall effect is much prettier and more elegant. Yet this bright, confident face is that of a girl no more than seventeen years old.

As for Carole's activities other than singing and dancing during her two years in Northern California, all Carole tells us is that things were tough in the beginning but that with her fifty dollars a week Santa Cruz salary she would sing twice a night and just lie on the beach or sleep all day.

Ever since Carole came to Hollywood there have been rumors that she engaged in prostitution during her stay in Northern California. Following her death, an article by Florabel Muir claimed that Carole had paid off a blackmailer who threatened to reveal details of her activities in San Francisco. When Paul Georges, who runs a movie quiz show for retirees in New Jersey, asked his audience in 2004 for information about Carole Landis, the only two persons to respond were a gentleman who had heard she was a call girl and another who claimed that a friend had paid fifty dollars to spend a night with her some time in the 1930s.

The published but not widely read memoirs of Jimmy Starr, a gossip columnist of the 1930s and '40s, contain a graphic description of a night he claims to have spent with the then unknown Carole, introduced to him by San Francisco attorney Jake Ehrlich. The episode he recounts does not confirm the rumors that Carole was a "call girl," although this might seem to be implied by the nature of the situation. Ehrlich, who had served as Alice Kamokila Campbell's attorney during her altercations with police and city officials in 1934, tried a number of famous cases involving houses of prostitution. Might Carole have earned her living in this manner before breaking into the entertainment field? Was she between jobs, or just supplementing her income as a "semi-professional"? None of these possibilities imply in the least that Carole saw herself as a prostitute. She may well have conceived herself as a "good-time girl," a young woman who enjoys sex and is not averse to accepting "gifts" to supplement her income. This interpretation would explain why Carole was able to deny the nastier rumors about her early life while at the same time remaining afraid that the truth would surface—and perhaps paying blackmail as a consequence.

How could a woman who probably engaged in casual sexual relations throughout her two years in Northern California expect to keep all this a secret through ten years in Hollywood? Even if we assume that the encounters like that with Starr preceded her taking the name of Carole Landis in her role as an entertainer, she could hardly have kept her identity hidden from all her partners. Starr assures us that he didn't tell, but it is difficult to believe that the blackmailer referred to by Florabel Muir was the only other person in Los Angeles who was aware of Carole's "secret." Above all, one wonders how Carole's three post-San Francisco husbands were affected by this early experience. Almost certainly, she never spoke to them of her adventures in Northern California, but how could they not have heard the rumors and entertained suspicions? How could these suspicions not have been raised in marital quarrels? And even if none of them ever guessed the truth, the very necessity of hiding it from them must have exerted a psychological pressure on Carole that helps explain her inability to maintain a long-term intimate relationship.

In 1937, Busby Berkeley was taken with Carole and apparently proposed marriage, although their engagement was broken off. Of several extant photos of Carole with Berkeley, there is one in particular that shows her sitting on the floor of a sound stage in a dress that shows off her lovely figure. Carole's expression is radiant with something more than simple innocence: an acceptance of the human condition that transcends the dichotomy of innocence and experience. Carole was someone whom no sexual or other experience ever tarnished or cheapened; on the contrary, her attitude toward sexuality may explain how she was able to present herself frankly to the viewer of her films and photographs with neither perverse modesty nor brazenness. This is a subject I will have occasion to revisit in examining Carole's films, where we can tease out from our observation of her behavior in certain scenes a tentative understanding of what a philosopher might call her "being in the world."

Although Carole said, surely with tongue in cheek, that she was crazy to leave her soft life in Santa Cruz for the rough-and-tumble of Hollywood, this had probably been her plan, or at least her hope, all along. Among Carole's acquaintances in San Francisco were several young women who had worked in Hollywood and who gave her the idea that she might be able to get into the movies. Carole particularly mentions "one girl . . . willing to give [her] the names of some Hollywood people who might be able to help her"; this was almost certainly Evelyn O'Brien, who lived just below Carole in an apartment house on Bush Street (the street of the Royal Hawaiian), where she roomed for a time with Carole's "sister act" partner, Kay Ellis. According to O'Brien, Carole's own roommate, also a dancer at the Royal Hawaiian, was named Isabel Noonan but used the stage name "Gloria Martin."

O'Brien, who modeled hats in San Francisco, had previously worked for five years in Hollywood. She was primarily a beautician who worked with Perc Westmore, but she also served (uncredited) in Busby Berkeley's chorus for the Warners production *Wonder Bar* in 1934; Berkeley wanted her for other choruses, but O'Brien preferred the makeup department. O'Brien stayed in San Francisco from 1934 to 1936, at the same time as her sister Thelma. Some time after Thelma's death in July 1936, in the course of a minor operation, Evelyn returned to Hollywood, where for a time she shared a room with Carole. It is not unlikely that it was she who introduced Carole to Berkeley.

Probably in late 1936 and no later than January 1937, having by her own account saved $150 from her earnings (most accounts give $100, but the higher figure is more credible), Carole left the Bay Area and took the train to Hollywood, where she rented a flat for $5 a week. If we are to credit Clara's account, Carole, who had been out of touch for two years, contacted her family only half a year later, when she landed her Warner Brothers contract in July 1937.

CHAPTER 3

First Years in Hollywood (1937—1939)

Carole's beginnings in Hollywood were far from auspicious. After finding a five-dollar-a-week apartment, she did the rounds of the studios for a few months with no assurance of employment. Despite the contacts given her by Evelyn O'Brien, Carole had difficulty finding work; just as two years earlier in San Francisco, something like one hundred dollars was all that stood between her and destitution. After a few months, her circumstances may have become desperate; perhaps this is the period when Carole's anonymous friend says she and her husband put Carole up on their couch when her money ran out. Presumably O'Brien came to Hollywood during this period and shared the rent with Carole in the same or another apartment.

In a brief autobiographical article, Carole gives thanks to "the man upstairs," a dancer whose help led to a shot at a Warner Brothers role and, subsequently, to a contract. According to Kirk Crivello, Carole was an extra in the chorus of the Warner film *The King and the Chorus Girl*, in production between November and December 1936, although she cannot be identified on the screen. Her claimed appearances as an extra in Universal Artists' *A Star is Born* and MGM's *A Day at the Races*, also produced in late 1936 and early 1937, must also be taken on faith; there is no unambiguous sign of her in these films.

At Warner Brothers, Busby Berkeley was known for his preference for pretty girls. "He never made anyone dance. He never chose a girl on her dancing ability. Chose 'em purely on looks." As a Berkeley selection, Carole was given a spot in *Varsity Show*. Her first employment record, dated May 13, 1937, gives her birth date as January 1, 1916, in Chicago. Her attempt to make herself twenty-one and single was found out in mid-July when she was given, presumably at Berkeley's behest, a thirteen-week contract at fifty dollars per week. Because she was still a minor, a court judgment, rendered on August 2, was required to validate the contract. Ironically, it was Carole's nominal marital status that freed her from tutelage, a married woman of eighteen being deemed the equivalent of a twenty-one-year-old.

According to her mother, on signing the contract, Carole persuaded her to sell her house in San Bernardino and move to Carole's "homey apartment house in an unfashionable section of Hollywood." The "homey apartment house" was the Bronsonia Apartments at 1933 Bronson Avenue, north of Franklin, on the extreme northern border of Hollywood—an attractive building, built in 1927 and still standing. This is the earliest address we have for Carole in Los Angeles; her pre-contract five-dollars-a-week lodgings were presumably in a less attractive setting.

Berkeley was evidently uncommonly attracted to Carole, and their relationship soon became serious. The publicity attachments on a few 1937 photographs that show Busby and Carole together, to all appearances a happy couple, refer to him as her "fiancé." But the engagement was abortive. Kirk Crivello recounts that, much to Carole's disappointment, Berkeley's mother forced him to break it because of stories about Carole's "call-girl" activities in San Francisco. Or it may have sufficed for Berkeley and/or his mother to learn—surely with some surprise—that Carole was already married. Gossip columns refer to the romance as "running a temperature" in November 1937, note a breakup and reconciliation around New Year's Day 1938, and declare that by May of that year, when Carole left Warner Brothers, the relationship had again cooled.

It had surely become cooler on March 19, when Carole's still-husband Irving Wheeler, whose relationship with her since 1934 had presumably been inexistent, sued Berkeley for $250,000 for alienation of affection. Could this have been a publicity stunt carried out with Carole's complicity? The evidence suggests the contrary: Carole and Wheeler had long been estranged, and Louella Parsons claims that Carole told friends she would, if necessary, testify on Berkeley's behalf. The suit is more simply explained as a scheme designed to produce money for Wheeler rather than publicity for Carole. Yet although it succeeded somewhat in the latter, it failed dismally in the former; Wheeler's "love balm" suit was dismissed in August. Carole probably saw this as a wake-up call to end her non-marriage; in March of the following year, Frances Ridste Wheeler was granted a decree of divorce from her former first and presently second husband.

In 1940, Wheeler was reported attempting, apparently unsuccessfully, to sell the story of his marriage to Carole to a "pulp magazine." In 1942, Carole got him a job as a stand-in. Subsequently, he disappears from view, only to pop up as "Jack Robbins"—a name listed as having a bit part in *Citizen Kane*—when arrested on a marijuana charge in 1954. So much for marriage at fifteen.

As a result of Berkeley's "discovery" of her, Carole said a few words in *Varsity Show* (her dialogue was not retained in the final cut), was visible on screen throughout most of the second half of the film, and wound up dancing with the principals at the far left (from the audience's perspective) of the front row in the finale. This sequence gave rise to what appears to be Carole's first magazine appearance, a misspelled mention as "Carol Landis" accompanying a color photo of the ensemble number in the October 1937 issue of *Screen Book*. Sadly, as Carole could not have realized at the time, this was just about the high-water mark of her prominence at Warners, where she appeared in twenty-odd films in negligible parts, rarely remaining on screen for more than a few seconds, with never more than a peripheral role in the plot.

After *Varsity Show*, two other films stand out slightly. Carole's longest screen appearance comprised about four minutes (and a few lines of dialogue) in the October 1937 *Blondes at Work* as "Carol," a department-store model, a breezy showgirl type who makes a few wisecracks in the context of a murder investigation. This was the persona Carole displayed throughout her Warner films, to the extent that we can detect one at all. *Blondes* was the fourth of nine "Torchy Blane" movies, all but two of which starred Glenda Farrell as the brash star reporter who inevitably solves the cases of boyfriend Lieutenant McBride (Barton MacLane)—a not atypical example of the resourceful 1930s woman who can do everything better than her man while longing nevertheless to give it all up for matrimony and childrearing. This happy state finally arrives in the last film of the series, in which Jane Wyman and Allen Jenkins have replaced the two principals. And Carole's stint in the chorus line of *Gold Diggers in Paris*, shot during the first months of 1938, brought her first real movie publicity: a couple of solo photographs in the July 1938 issue of *Film Fun*. (There had been an earlier bit of exposure when two broken toes during the filming of *Hollywood Hotel* in the fall of 1937 won Carole a half-page shot on crutches in the February 1938 *Screen Guide*.) It was also during the shooting of *Gold Diggers* that fellow chorine Diana Lewis, the future wife of William Powell, gave Carole a chain with a small gold cross that she wore around her neck for the rest of her life.

As one of many Warner starlets, Carole was too tall and mature for an ingénue—a role she would come closest to as a foil to Joan Blondell in *Topper Returns*—yet too young and insufficiently "domestic" to play married women. Thus, she could follow neither the path taken by Lana Turner at MGM nor that of Betty Grable, who had kicked around several studios before her 1939 Broadway triumph in *DuBarry Was a Lady* landed her a contract with Fox as Alice Faye's musical-blonde successor—and Carole's permanent obstacle. In the Warner era, although Carole wore attractive clothes, she had not yet entered the life of glamour that began with her *One Million B.C.* buckskin costumes in late 1939 and her January 1940 nose job. What we see of Carole is charming, but in these trivial roles any display of intensity would have been out of place.

Carole's Warner films show her sunbathing on a roof (*She Loved a Fireman*, August 1937), as a gangster's girlfriend (*Over the Wall*, July–September 1937), secretary to Errol Flynn (*Four's a Crowd*, February–March 1938), disguised as a murder witness (*Missing Witnesses*, August 1937), as a hatcheck girl (*Hollywood Hotel*, September 1937), at a party (*When Were You Born*, February 1938), spinning a wheel (*Love, Honor, and Behave*, December 1937), answering a phone (*Boy Meets Girl*, March 1938), telling Pat O'Brien where to find his wife (*Women Are like That*, September 1937), asking about her sailor boyfriend (*The Invisible Menace*, August 1937), selling raffle tickets (*Penrod's Double Trouble*, December 1937–January 1938), riding a float in a leopard costume (*Torchy Blane in Panama*, January–February 1938), as a "school friend" (*Men Are Such Fools*, December 1937–January 1938), or just as a face in the crowd (*Broadway Melody of 1938*, February–July 1937; *Over the Goal*, July–August 1937; *Alcatraz Island*, August 1937; *The Patient in Room 18*, August–September 1937; *When Were You Born*, February–April 1938)—always an attractive addition to the cast, at times appearing to seek out the camera's attention (*A Slight Case of Murder*, October–November 1937), never more than peripheral to the story.

On April 24, 1938, as one of Warners' young hopefuls, Carole costarred with character actor John Ridgely in the radio play *Special Agent* on *The Warner Brothers Academy Theater*, the first of at least eight such plays Carole would do over the years. Most of these reprised and sometimes parodied popular films, generally with a different cast. *Special Agent* was a 1935 Warner production starring Bette Davis, whose acting skills Carole observed and hoped to emulate, and George Brent, who would play Carole's husband in her last American film nine years later. Carole played the role of a racketeer's secretary who cooperates with a crusading reporter to put her boss in jail. Her acting in this dramatic production is rather ten-tative at the beginning but more convincing at the end, when she conveys the emotions of fear and love quite effectively.

Sampling Carole's other radio performances, on February 16, 1941, already a seasoned radio actress, she spoke in a comical Brooklynese in Ann Sothern's moll role in a parodic *Brother Orchid*, with Pat O'Brien in the place of Edward G. Robinson; on April 10, 1942, she reprised her own per-formance in *I Wake Up Screaming*; on May 10, 1943, she took over Lana Turner's role in *Johnny Eager*, with John Garfield in that of Robert Taylor. Carole's last documented performance was on February 17, 1947, when she costarred with Don Ameche in *You Belong to Me*, based on a 1941 film starring Barbara Stanwyck and Henry Fonda. There are records of Carole's appearance in seventy-nine radio broadcasts, and she probably appeared in many more; her wit and warm voice made her particularly effective in this medium.

The one activity Carole was employed in extensively at Warners' was "leg art," a term of the era for what is better known as cheesecake photography. As Carole described her stay at Warner Brothers, perhaps a bit facetiously, "I couldn't act for sour apples . . . so all I was used for was 'leg art' publicity." There exist a good number of generally rather discreet "leg art," mostly bathing-suit photographs of Carole, from this period. There are also portraits in various poses and costumes, including shots from modeling jobs; after leaving Warners, Carole posed for a considerable number of fashion shots during the late 1930s. Many of these early photo-graphs of Carole reveal facets of her personality that would not reappear after she attained stardom: a romantic yearning that she would later hide behind a cheerful smile, and a certain wistful sadness.

Having begun at Warners in May 1937 and signed her first contract on July 17, Carole stayed on until May 1938, her original thirteen-week contract at fifty dollars having been extended to forty-three and a half weeks without the customary increase in pay. As for the circumstances of her departure, Carole claimed that she chose to leave to seek work elsewhere;

other sources state that she was let go. The latter alternative seems more likely; the Berkeley relationship had dissolved and, with it, any protection he might have afforded her at the studio. In June 1938, Carole appeared with Bob Hope in a week-long summer stock production of *Roberta* in which she played—ironically, given her singing background—the non-singing part of Sophie Teal. (Kirk Crivello states that Bob Hope's agent Louis Schurr took charge of Carole's career at this point; if so, it was a short-lived relationship.) Theatrical producer Lawrence Schwab then offered Carole a part in a Broadway production with Ken Murray entitled *Once upon a Night*. The play opened in September in Wilmington, Delaware (one source has Baltimore), but apparently never reached New York; Carole usually claimed that it folded after two days. Whatever the details, Carole quickly abandoned her unsuccessful attempt at a stage career and returned to Hollywood.

By this time, Carole's name had disappeared from the gossip columns. All we know of her activities between September 1938 and March 1939, when she obtained her first major movie roles at Republic Pictures, is that she attended one or more studio Christmas parties in December. She had most likely given up the Bronson apartment on the occasion of her trip east, if not before. A letter from Carole postmarked May 26, 1939, bears a return address in a modest Rancho Park neighborhood near the Fox studio in what is now Century City. Since by this time Carole had been working at Republic for two months, we may assume this was her own address.

Columnists identified Kenny Morgan as Carole's suitor in March 1939 (and again in 1940 and 1941); Carole's family photo album contains a number of shots of her and Morgan in casual settings such as parks and tennis courts. Carole's divorce from Irving Wheeler having been pronounced on May 10, 1939, this new relationship inspired a columnist in June to predict an "early wedding," which another columnist described as called off in November. Both journalists appeared unaware that the actual dissolution of Carole's marriage would occur only after the expiration of a

one-year waiting period, in May 1940. Morgan, who would serve with distinction in World War II, later married a close cousin of Lucille Ball and
was for a long time the publicity director of Desilu Productions.

By her own account, Carole learned at a Warners Christmas party
that Republic was hiring. But her actual introduction to the studio
occurred in March 1939, as recounted in colorful fashion by director
William Witney:

> The usual weekly get-together of our gang was at Ralph and Virginia
> Byrd's house. Although it was March, we'd had an early spring and a bad-
> minton game was in full swing. A car pulled into the driveway and a couple
> got out and walked across the lawn toward us. Ralph greeted the man. He
> worked for Mitch Gertz, Ralph's agent. He introduced us to the girl,
> Carole Landis. She was wearing a simple silk dress that clung to one of the
> most beautiful bodies I'd ever seen. When I got around to seeing if the
> body had a head, which it did, it was as spectacular as the body. . . . Carole
> was an actress trying to break into pictures. She also played a damn good
> game of badminton and mixed easily with our crowd, proving that she
> had to have a sense of humor to go along with her beauty.

Witney's story suggests that it was largely on the strength of her figure that
Carole was offered her first female lead, in *Three Texas Steers*, a Western
starring John Wayne, produced during the second half of March. The three
"steers" were, in fact, the leading actors in the film; this was one of fifty-
one "Three Mesquiteers" movies produced at Republic between 1936 and
1943. The personnel turned over rapidly. By the time of Carole's second
picture in this series in October, all three Mesquiteers had changed;
Wayne, who continued to make Republic Westerns into the 1940s, had
been replaced as the lead Mesquiteer, "Stony" Brooke, by regular Robert
Livingston, who played the role twenty-nine times between 1936 and
1941. Another stable factor was the director, George Sherman, who
directed a total of fifty-odd mostly Western movies, including twenty

Mesquiteers, in six years at Republic before moving to Columbia and Universal in the late 1940s.

Carole's first leading role finds her the owner of a circus, a credible casting for a tall, athletic girl who looks as though she can take care of herself, and which curiously would be repeated the following year in the Hal Roach comedy *Road Show*. The focus of the plot is a conspiracy directed against Carole by her traitorous manager, who wants to get hold of a run-down ranch she has inherited because the government needs the land to build a dam. (We are in the age of the New Deal.) The conspirators put financial pressure on Carole by sabotaging the circus, forcing it to close, then burning down her barn. But the Mesquiteers rescue the situation *in extremis* by entering a trick horse left over from the circus in a providential trotting race that pays just the amount of money both they (who own the ranch next door) and Carole need to avoid foreclosure.

On the whole, Carole acquits herself well of the limited displays of emotion required of her, although in the one sequence in the film where she is shown for any length of time in medium close-up, careful observation shows her trying to stifle a laugh when she is supposed to be feeling indignation. She is often shot unflatteringly in profile (as she will not be as a rule in her other Republic films), displaying her pre-nose-job nose and chin, like her mother's, pointing just a bit at each other.

Daredevils of the Red Circle, a twelve-part serial directed by John English and William Witney, was filmed in April and/or May and released on June 10, 1939; it is often considered one of the best serials ever. Like *Steers*, it stars a team of three men and also involves a circus, but no doubt for the sake of its youthful audience it excludes any hint of romance, including any allusion to Carole's attractiveness. Carole plays the granddaughter of Horace Granville, who is imprisoned and impersonated by an evildoer, a bitter man who seeks revenge on the one who sent him to prison. It is not clear how Granville, apparently still in his fifties, can have a twenty-year-old granddaughter, but were Carole Granville's daughter, we would expect her to be admitted into the hermetically sealed wing of the house in which the "ailing" ersatz Granville is confined.

Carole's part in the drama consists largely of surviving attacks on her life, although she helps out the Daredevils in several episodes and is ultimately revealed to be the mysterious figure who has nearly from the beginning left helpful notes for the Daredevils, marked with a red circle, as they gradually uncover "39013"'s fiendish plot. Thus, Carole had been on to the imposter all along but gave no sign of this, presumably to avoid endangering her captive grandfather's life—or the suspense—by revealing the plot. Carole's role in *Daredevils* is, like that in *Steers*, a credible piece of casting; a smaller or more obviously vulnerable young woman would have drawn too much attention to her plight. Carole's acting in this serial has been criticized, but the nature of the genre and of the ingénue's role in it precludes the subtle development of character.

Near the beginning of the first episode, there is a circus fire in which the Daredevils' kid brother is killed. During the filming of this episode on a closed set, kerosene vapors briefly burst into flame and lightly singed the players. William Witney tells the story: "Carole . . . had her dress pulled up and was beating at her panties. . . . I said, 'Carole, it's all over.' She stopped beating and looked at me. . . . She was still holding her dress under her chin. She looked down at her panties, then very ladylike, dropped her skirt. 'It could have ruined my little money maker.'" In another anecdote, Witney persuaded Carole to put on a brassiere—"She needs one like a hole in the head"—on a hot day by reminding her of the prudish Production Code. These amusing incidents give us a clear picture of Carole as both aware of and at ease with her attractiveness to the opposite sex.

In September, Carole found time for a bit part as a divorcing wife opposite Richard Dix in the RKO film *Reno*. She then returned to Republic for her second and last Western, *The Cowboys from Texas*, shot in a little over a week in October 1939. This time Carole is the daughter of a homesteader from Kansas, played by Charles Middleton, the villain of *Daredevils*. Again she is given a professional background, this time as a former secretary on a newspaper. On their first encounter with Carole, each of the three Mesquiteers is sufficiently smitten to recommend her individually to the local newspaper publisher; she lands a job with the paper writing on subjects of interest to women. But in contrast to her previous Mesquiteer outing, Carole is only peripherally involved in the plot. She tends to her little brother, who is shot—but this time does not die—during a raid on their farm by a gang of bad guys. The latter are seeking to foment discord between cattlemen and ranchers in order to buy up the land for themselves, a plotline with a clear family resemblance to Carole's earlier Mesquiteers outing. The conspiracy is expectedly foiled, and Carole briefly expresses her regret as the Mesquiteers depart for their next adventure.

The Carole we see in these Republic films is lovely but not yet glamorized, as she will shortly become with the marcelled hair of *One Million B.C.* In the Westerns, her hair is dark and her hairdo unelaborate; she wears plain, modest cotton dresses more historically plausible than the fancy duds worn in higher-budget productions. In *Daredevils*, which takes place in the contemporary world, Carole's makeup and hairdo are softened a bit, and her hair color lightened; throughout most of the episodes she wears a plain wool high-necked dress with a long coat for the outdoor shots and a cute little peaked hat. The paucity of eye shadow gives Carole's face a softness that one misses in the more extensive makeup jobs of her mature films. Not quite yet a celebrity, for all her sexual experience the heroine of these films is still a lovely young girl, as much Frances Ridste as Carole Landis.

CHAPTER 4

Ping Girl: At Roach Studios (1939–1940)

It was while working on her second and last Republic Western that Carole got her big break, the female lead in Hal Roach's eye-catching science-fiction tale, *One Million B.C.* The story has been told many times and is by all appearances authentic: D. W. Griffith, who was helping Roach cast the picture, chose the female lead by observing the candidates' running form. Hal Roach tells the story:

> *One Million B.C.* was a prehistoric picture, a figment of my imagination. D. W. came over to work for me, and I said, "Dave, I'd like you to cast the picture." They brought in girls. I wasn't paying any attention. He looked at them. We had already decided on Victor Mature as the man and Lon Chaney as the father. Every time these girls came in, he took them to the back lot. I didn't know what the hell he was doing out in the open spaces. Then one day he said, "I found your girl." It was Carole Landis. "Come out. I want to show you something." We went out on the back lot where there was street scenery and, on the corner, a telephone post. He looked at the girl and said, "Take your shoes off. Now run to that post as

fast as you can. Then run back to me as fast as you can." She did. I wasn't particularly impressed. That's a hell of a way to find a leading lady. We know she can run. He said, "I've had fifty girls run to that post and back. She's the only one who knows how to run. You're not going to make a believable girl in a picture of that kind who runs like an average girl. She's got to run like an athlete, a deer." And she did. Her rhythm was really beautiful. In the picture, you never noticed. But if she ran like most girls, you would damn well have seen the difference.

Indeed, Carole does quite a bit of running in *One Million B.C.*—and in a number of her other films as well. Although running is hardly a normal requirement for a glamour girl, not the least element of Carole's uniqueness is that she makes acts like running or ringing the bell on the strength test (*Road Show*) into a celebration of feminine gracefulness.

B.C., directed by Hal Roach Sr., with son Hal Roach Jr.'s assistance, was made during the last two and one-half months of 1939 and the first couple of days of 1940. Along with Carole's career, it launched the more successful one of Victor Mature. Much of *B.C.* was shot on location in the badlands of Logandale and Overton, Nevada, during the first two weeks of November.

In sister Dorothy's words, "I never saw such a happy girl as Carole was the night of the premiere in San Diego of her first picture, '1,000,000 B.C.'" There is a photograph of happy Carole showing the *B.C.* set to her mother, brother, and sister-in-law, along with an actor or crew member from the movie. To celebrate her triumph, Carole bought a Cadillac convertible in December 1939. She also began to be reported at nightspots at a far higher frequency than before; her escorts during the first four months of 1940 included regular boyfriend-publicist Kenny Morgan, gangster-producer Pat DeCicco, actor Harry Crocker, publicists Harvey Seymour and Alan Gordon, *Duffy's Tavern*'s Ed Gardner, and paper magnate Myron Kirk. By May, a gossip columnist reported that Carole, whose "beak" had been "done over twice," was "really going whacky with dates and drinks." But by the time this story was filed, Carole had already met and was more or less engaged to Willis Hunt Jr., a reportedly wealthy yacht broker and man about Hollywood, whom she would marry in July.

Taken on its own terms, the much-maligned *B.C.* is both entertaining and perceptive. The story is introduced by an archaeologist (Conrad Nagel) who is working in a cave where a group of hikers, including Carole and Victor Mature, take refuge during a rainstorm. The archaeologist invites the group to imagine the two as the young couple in the story he deciphers from hieroglyph-like drawings on the walls of the cave. Victor as Tumak, son of the chief of the Rock people (played by Lon Chaney Jr.), is injured in a fight with his father over a piece of meat and then knocked into the river by a marauding elephant. Victor floats downstream, where he is found by Carole in the role of Loana of the Shell people, a gentler and more technologically advanced tribe who have learned to make spear points, while the Rock folk have only clubs. Carole has a civilizing influence on Victor and the entire Rock tribe, and after a number of adventures with wildly anachronistic "dinosaurs," whose parts are played not by mechanical mock-ups as in *King Kong* but by real lizards and other small animals magnified to monstrous proportions—the major technical and budgetary innovation of the film—the couple go off together into the sunset with a little orphan girl to start a tribe of their own.

One of the curiosities of *B.C.* is that, as in *Quest for Fire* (1981) and *The Clan of the Cave Bear* (1986) many years later, the characters do not speak English but have their own prehistoric Rock and Shell "languages," glossaries of which were thoughtfully included in the press kit prepared by the studio publicity department. Hence, the dialogue is largely gestural, including occasional vocalized "words" but no apparent syntax. Within the limits of this constraint, the actors acquit themselves rather well. The outlandishness of the saurian fauna should not blind us to the film's insight into critical moments of communal interaction, such as dividing up the prey after the hunt or restoring tribal leadership after the former leader is injured (the new leader obliges the others to throw down their clubs as a sign of submission). The filmmakers could not be expected to know that hunter-gatherer societies never have a single authoritarian leader; permanent social hierarchy is an effect of economic surplus.

Thus, Carole's first high-profile film role is as an Eve figure who, in the inverse of the biblical story, exercises a positive moral influence on her Adam, teaching him to share and exchange with others rather than grabbing what he can for himself. For the first time, Carole is "glamorized," shot in soft focus with three-point lighting emphasizing her marcelled hair and pale skin; she wears a buckskin costume that shows off her legs and figure. More than any of her subsequent roles, that of Loana emphasizes Carole's natural sweetness; she never becomes angry or cynical as she is nearly always made to do in her later films. At this "prehistoric" dawn of her career, Carole incarnates an ideal very close to the one she lived by in the real world: caring and resourceful, sweet and strong, desirable and athletic, never happier than when she is bringing happiness to others. The reviews of the film were mixed, but "lovely, shapely and lightly clad" Carole made a strong impression.

Jean Porter, later the wife of director Edward Dmytryk of *The Caine Mutiny* and the Hollywood Ten—and who would direct Carole in *Mystery Sea Raider* at Paramount in May 1940—shared a dressing room with Carole while making *One Million B.C.* as a girl of fourteen. During this period, Carole lived a subdued life with her mother and often gave Jean a lift to the studio in her new car. Among the latter's recollections is a particularly ominous one: Carole, designating her bosom, said, "I really shouldn't get old!" This fear of losing her beautiful figure with age is a trait shared by Jennifer North, the character in *Valley of the Dolls* that Jacqueline Susann modeled on Carole. Thus, already at twenty-one, if not before, the fear that her beauty would not outlast her youth was a cloud in the back of Carole's mind.

Immediately after the shooting of *One Million B.C.* ended in early January 1940, presumably at the behest of Hal Roach or perhaps on the initiative of Kenny Morgan, Carole had cosmetic surgery to remove the tip of her

nose and a little piece of her chin. The successful results of the surgery are
in evidence in Carole's next picture, *Turnabout*, shot in February and March,
in which she stars with John Hubbard, who had played a secondary role in
B.C. In contrast to the earlier film, *Turnabout* shows Carole's face in close-
up several times as if to advertise the success of her operation. From a
Hollywood cutie in buckskins, Carole has become a glamour girl of breath-
taking beauty—so much so that in order to justify her anomalous presence
among the bourgeoisie, a line of dialogue had to be inserted in which
Carole explains rather implausibly that before marrying Hubbard she had
been a showgirl.

Turnabout, again directed by the older Roach, is a sadly neglected little
comedy—recently restored by the UCLA Film and Television Archive—in
which even the diversions from the plot are entertaining: butler Donald
Meek chasing and triumphantly catching a bear cub loose in the dressing
room; Adolphe Menjou and William Gargan trying to stop a radio from
playing a jazz tune by smashing its parts one by one; the byplay between
Meek and Marjorie Main, who delivers her lines in an excellent imitation of
W. C. Fields; Margaret Roach as a southern belle; Hubbard's office masseur
and jiu-jitsu teacher. Unlike *One Million B.C.*, *Turnabout* has dialogue,
a great deal of it. The plot, adapted from a 1931 novel by Thorne Smith,
the risqué sophisticate who gave us the *Topper* series, centers on a couple's
exchange of genders after a quarrel in which each expresses envy of the
other's role; the turnabout is effected through the power of a mysterious
animated bust from India (played by a Frenchman).

After the switch, Carole and John swap bodies with each other, but
strangely (and comically) keep their original voices, so that John's body
speaks with Carole's voice and vice versa. These voices, which they
attempt not altogether successfully to disguise, underline the fact that the
characters' souls remain unchanged in their new bodies. Thus, not only
does the new John take on Carole's intonation, he adopts her feminine
mannerisms, as, conversely, does she, although with a less potent comic
effect, a woman imitating a man being less stigmatized and, consequently,

less comical than the other way around. The homosexual angle is pointed up by having the "feminine" John, an advertising executive, develop an instant complicity with a client named Pingboom (a possible source of "Ping"?), played by Franklin Pangborn, classic Hollywood's most obvious gay; the importance of avoiding the least hint of "pansy flavor" in this relationship was the subject of an extensive correspondence between Roach Studios and Joseph Breen of the Production Code Office.

In a 1944 Fox publicity release, Carole named *Turnabout* the sole film in which "she had more than an even chance to demonstrate ability rather than matter." Indeed, Carole's acting, which includes supplying John's voice after the switch, is flawless throughout. She ranges effortlessly from petulant as the spoiled wife to magnificently seductive when, with the couple switched back to their original genders, she puts on her best dress and fur coat and goes off to patch up relations with a disgruntled major client. Whether speaking caressingly to her husband under the covers, only to react in horror on discovering he had put in his place a large dog, or wearing men's clothing, gestures, and faces during the gender switch, Carole displays considerable talent for comedy.

The reviewers called *Turnabout* "a far-fetched comedy of the screwiest nature, fantastic, ludicrous, completely off the beaten screen track." Carole, whose acting was praised even by reviewers who didn't care much for the film, was called "winning and alluring" and said to "[show] most attractive promise." The Hubbard-Landis pairing, too, received plaudits: "This cast extracts maximum comedy results from a script," "John Hubbard very capably handles the dual role. . . . Carole Landis was equally effective in adopting the male characteristics to the detriment of her own femme allure."

Turnabout is one of a number of Carole's films that have lost none of their freshness and are as watchable today as when they were made. The only regret an admirer takes from this film is the relative rarity of her presence. John Hubbard, who plays the more active role whether or not his body is inhabited by Carole's voice, has considerably more screen time, and the center of the action is less the Willows' living room than Hubbard's advertising agency office, which features alcoholic Adolphe Menjou, dimwitted William Gargan, sardonic Verree Teasdale, and an able supporting cast. At the end, the joke is on John; Carole was pregnant, but when the genie switched the souls back to their original bodies, he mistakenly switched the pregnancy from Carole's to John's body as well. Hubbard's horrified reaction to the news supplies the last shot of the film. This gender-bending finale was finally approved by the Hays office and granted a marginally acceptable "B" rating by the (Catholic) Legion of Decency only after Roach claimed insistently that test audiences disliked the film with the ending removed and that he lacked the financial resources to shoot another one.

Turnabout was filmed in four weeks, from February 19 to March 16, and released on May 17, 1940. Shortly afterward, Hal Roach invited Hollywood correspondents to a lavish afternoon reception at fashionable Ciro's for Tuesday, May 28, at which he was to introduce Carole to the press as the "Ping Girl," the silliest and most unsavory title of several during that era forged on the model of Clara Bow's "*It* Girl." In the best-known case, Warner Brothers a year earlier had made Ann Sheridan the "Oomph Girl"—"oomph" being a synonym for sex appeal.

The day before her scheduled reception, quarter-page announcements signed by Carole Landis appeared in *The Hollywood Reporter* and *Variety* proclaiming that she did not intend to be present at the press conference "to ping, purr, or even coo." In addition, Carole wrote to the editors of "100 of America's biggest newspapers" asking them not to break the Ping Girl story and to "consign all bathing suit photographs of her to the waste basket." The publicity, deliberate or otherwise, obtained by this incident swiftly provoked a spread in *Life* on June 17—the best coverage the iconic photo magazine would ever give her—entitled "Carole Landis Does Not Want to Be Ping Girl," which in turn made Carole a highly visible personality and, according to one source, earned her a raise from $75 to $750 a week—a figure that is surely exaggerated. Whether Carole herself or her studio offered a date with her to thank *Life* photo chief Dick Pollard depends on which book one reads.

The "Ping Girl" slogan was ostensibly adapted, almost certainly with tongue in cheek, from a motor oil ad that claimed to take the "ping" out of an engine and make it "purr." With dubious logic, Roach created the slogan, "The Ping Girl: She Makes You Purr." But for those in the know, *ping* had a less respectable meaning. Although the word does not appear in standard slang dictionaries, an Internet dictionary defines it as an exclamation accompanying an erection, as in, "I saw her, and *ping*." One can well understand why Carole, presumably aware of this usage, would have found the title unacceptable. At the same time, the fact that Roach was able to use the term in publicity suggests that its slang meaning was not widely known among the general public, who were expected to be duped by the motor-oil red herring. This is confirmed by an article on Carole a year later that states only that "ping" was a term of Hollywood slang, without proposing a meaning.

Although both the Roach studio and Carole herself always claimed that the protest was her own idea—its wording suggests her own witty style—and despite the apparent waste of "a consignment of Scotch whisky . . . and an order for 50 elaborate meals," the Hollywood press corps unanimously saw it as a publicity stunt. It is certainly unlikely that a young, scarcely established actress would take such a step without external guidance or, at the very least, prior approval; we may, if we like, see the hand of Kenny Morgan in some or all aspects of this affair.

As further proof that Carole meant business, on June 11, coincidentally or not, the bathing-suit manufacturer Calcraft Knitting Mills filed a $50,000 suit against her, claiming that she had signed a contract to be photographed for advertisements in October 1939—before or after her casting in *One Million B.C.*?—but subsequently had not only refused to pose for them but had written newspaper editors asking them to refrain from using pictures already sent out. If we are to believe Frank Smoot's well-researched but now inaccessible carolelandis.net Web site, Carole stopped writing the editors and Calcraft dropped the suit. At the very least, this suit, which was not covered by any Los Angeles newspaper, could not itself have been part of a publicity campaign, although Carole's attempt, sincere or not, to free herself from "leg art" was ipso facto an attempt to gain publicity of a different kind.

A 1946 Fox publicity release, Carole's last (she left Fox at the end of that year), claims that Roach's purpose in arranging for the Ping publicity was, unbeknownst to her, to "unload" Carole on another studio. If this was, indeed, the case, it was a successful strategy, since she obtained a contract with Twentieth Century-Fox at the end of the year. This should not, however, be taken to imply that Roach was dissatisfied with Carole's performances. Indeed, Roach was so insistent that Carole's contract with Fox contain a clause permitting her to do up to two films a year for his studio—a provision he never implemented—that the contract was finalized only in August 1942. But Roach's feature film production was winding down by the early 1940s, and he was not wont to keep rising young stars on his payroll, especially after a 900 percent (or even 400 percent) raise. Victor Mature made only one more film for Roach after *B.C.* In Carole's case, two Roach films for which she had been mentioned in the press, *Niagara Falls* and *Broadway Limited*, were both shot in 1941 with Marjorie Woodworth, Roach's new protégée, who would make eleven films for Roach Studios between 1941 and 1943.

The Ping incident signaled that sex-appeal titles had reached such a point of saturation that rejecting the appellation was a better publicity tool than flaunting it. The awkwardness of the episode, which would be writ large in the uneasiness of Carole's entire film career, is one more demonstration that the kind of overt sexual appeal that had flourished in the days of first Clara Bow and then Jean Harlow (who never needed a slogan to project it) was no longer possible. The 1930s image of the desirable woman had been divided between the ethereal sexuality incarnated by Greta Garbo and a pointedly sluttish style typified by Harlow and raised to the level of caricature by Mae West (who, we should not forget, turned forty in 1933). In contrast, 1950s sexuality, reflecting the budding postwar youth culture, would cater less to adult desires than to adolescent wet dreams. The sexuality of the 1940s was more restrained than either; more adult, no doubt, but also less explicit. Especially after the war, actresses such as Lana Turner and Rita Hayworth evolved a sexiness that was suggestive rather than direct. In *Gilda* (1946), under the direction of Charles Vidor, Hayworth inaugurated a new art of playing seductively to the camera—the implicit eye of the spectator—that in the following decade Marilyn Monroe would perfect and Jayne Mansfield parody.

None of these overt presentations of sex appeal create a relationship between spectator and character that is independent of the film; on the contrary, they are a tease that allows the spectator to share for a moment the desires of the film world. This is a perversity that Carole, as befitting her frank, adult attitude toward things sexual, never displayed in her films. Only in live performance and in the short song-and-dance films she made for wartime consumption, the best known of which is the charming *I'm Your Pin-Up Girl*, did Carole flirt with her audience; and this flirtation, in which Carole plays at eroticism far more than she exhibits it, is predicated on the audience's full complicity in the role she is playing. Carole is never either "poor little me" or a *femme fatale*. She told a reporter at just the time of her shift from Roach to Fox, "I think sex is definitely here to stay . . . so I don't see any necessity for throwing it in people's faces. I don't think a girl has to wear dresses cut down to her tummy to exhibit what is known as feminine allure. She can exhibit it in high-necked dresses, but subtly. . . . Heaven knows I want people to think I have sex appeal. But I also want them to think I have something besides sex appeal." While none of this prevented Carole from appearing in public in décolletés cut down, as one waggish reporter put it, "to customary Landis see-level," in her films Carole offers a sexual allure that is powerfully present without ever being deliberately emphasized. Carole's sex appeal was occasionally caricatured, nastily in *The Powers Girl* and affectionately in *Having Wonderful Crime*, where at certain moments she approximates a grown-up version of Marilyn Monroe. But the assurance her beauty nearly always gave of existing independently of the camera offered the spectator the subversive thrill, while watching Carole's character in the movie, of just watching Carole. A review of

Having Wonderful Crime reads, " It's my experience that when Carole Landis graces the celluloid, there's no need for the producer also to provide a photoplay to go with her, because who wants to take his eyes off Carole to look at the unfolding of a plot?"

That being "distractingly desirable" made Carole a challenge to casting directors was already remarked on in the June 17, 1940, *Life* spread that brought her to public attention: "Her exceptional physical attributes . . . proved an initial Hollywood drawback to Miss Landis. . . . Her directors sometimes complained that her curves interfered with their stories." Yet at the outset of her career, the radiance of a beauty that revealed itself without the need for emphasis is what gave Carole the chance to be seen in films at all.

After finishing *Turnabout* in March 1940, Carole, still under contract to Roach, was loaned out to Paramount to star in *Mystery Sea Raider*, a topical war film directed by Edward Dmytryk in his sixth outing. Dmytryk, whose career would be blighted by his "Hollywood Ten" jailing and subsequent testimony before the House Un-American Activities Committee (HUAC), is best remembered for male-centered dramas such as *Crossfire* (1947), *The Caine Mutiny* (1954), and *The Young Lions* (1958).

In his autobiography, Alfred Zukor, the head of Paramount on whose initiative the invitation was extended, paid Carole the compliment of designating her, along with Mabel Normand, Gloria Swanson, Clara Bow, and Jean Arthur, as one of the few "comediennes . . . lovely to look at and able to play dramatic roles." Zukor had an eye for female beauty, as the frequent appreciations in his book make clear; what is harder to explain than his hiring Carole for this film is why she was not invited back. With its tradition of worldly comedic elegance, Paramount might well have provided Carole with a more favorable environment than Fox. Be that as it may, both *Mystery Sea Raider* and Carole's acting were fairly well received, and it was during her association with Paramount that Carole, dressed by the screen's leading costume designer, Edith Head, posed for her most beautiful series of photographs.

Mystery Sea Raider, shot in May and the first days of June, is one of Carole's most tightly directed films. It allows her some scope of emotion and expression, even if her prominent role in the action is rather implausible. As in *Turnabout*, Carole/June McCarthy is a "showgirl," this time one still practicing her art—we see her in costume for a brief moment, although not on stage.

Given that Carole is portrayed as performing on several continents—at the opening of the film, she is returning from Europe on an ocean liner—her dependence on penniless shipman Henry Wilcoxon not merely for masculine companionship but for lodging on his old boat strikes us as bizarre. Indeed, her tepid love relationship with Wilcoxon does not prevent her from carrying on a shipboard flirtation with Onslow Stevens, a German secret agent posing as an import-export businessman, on whose instructions the Nazis torpedo the British liner. Having reached shore safely, in order to save Wilcoxon's boat from repossession, Carole innocently engineers its lease to Stevens, who, having manned the ship with his own crew of crypto-Germans, takes over the helm and converts the vessel into a "mystery sea raider," a decoy ship that feigns a fire on board to lure and capture enemy craft. But Carole ingeniously gets out floating S.O.S. messages, and a British cruiser comes to the rescue. Stevens, gallant to the end (although he had earlier ordered Carole killed), releases the allied naval officers he had held captive, then lets Wilcoxon and Carole jump overboard and swim to safety as he goes down with the ship.

As usual neither ingénue nor housewife, Carole/June has her own career and takes a crucial part in the action. As in many of Carole's films, her love relationship with Wilcoxon is without nuance, oscillating between the poles of trust and mistrust. Yet Carole expresses real emotions; both the world-weariness of the early scenes on the liner and her feelings for her lover are convincingly portrayed. There are also two swimming scenes in which she deports herself gracefully. There are no close-ups, scarcely even medium close-ups, of Carole or anyone else in this action film; throughout, she is nicely but not romantically photographed. A little soft lighting on her white dress in the early shipboard scenes with Stevens is about all the glamorizing Carole gets until the closing shot, where the reunited lovers' kiss is snapped by a newspaper photographer.

During the filming, Carole brought homemade cookies (baked by Clara?) on the set and showed off her physical strength by carrying both Dmytryk and the considerably bigger Wilcoxon on her back. There is an aura of happiness surrounding Carole in these early films that she would recapture only sporadically after moving to Fox in 1941.

Carole's second marriage to Irving Wheeler, the reality of which had been limited to a couple of weeks in 1934, remained on the books until May 1940. If Carole hadn't sought a divorce earlier, it was probably because she felt that marriage protected her, no doubt as much from herself as from anyone else. As if to demonstrate her need for this protection, the very month the divorce was made final Carole became engaged to yacht broker Willis Hunt Jr. During that same month of May, she was described by the always-friendly Louella Parsons as an everyday visitor at Hunt's hospital bedside during the filming of *Mystery Sea Raider*. And on July 4, 1940, Carole and Willis were married in Las Vegas. According to pilot Mendelssohn Mantz, the couple had first driven to Vegas on the preceding day, but Carole, apparently on the advice of her mother, decided at the last minute not to go through with the ceremony and flew back alone to Los Angeles. Hunt must have flown or driven back as well, for the couple, this time with Clara's blessing, flew off again to Vegas on July 4 and were married on their second try. Given Carole's penchant for doing things on holidays, it seems likely that they would have waited until then in any case.

But scarcely two months later, on September 17, Carole filed suit for divorce, alleging the customary "extreme mental cruelty"; according to a credible gossip item, she declined to ask for alimony. Carole alleged that Hunt refused to accept her life as an actress; he complained when she came home late from the studio and called her friends "damn fools, like everyone in the motion picture business," as if forgetting that for years he had been frequenting the same nightspots as movie people and was presumably making a living selling them yachts. Hedda Hopper, generally less friendly to Carole than her earthier rival Louella, claimed that Carole's chief motivation for leaving Hunt was her discovery that when she became a married woman her name appeared less often in the gossip columns. Another columnist, writing much later, claimed that Carole attributed the divorce to Hunt's continued attachment to his first wife, socialite Dolly Brewer, later the wife of Hal Roach Jr.

Describing her marital problems with Hunt in a perceptive autobiographical article written some years after the event, Carole empathized with the daily humiliations borne by the husband of a movie star, which would later be experienced virtually unchanged by her third husband, Tommy Wallace. Her analysis allows us a more sympathetic understanding of the grain of truth in Hedda's cynical crack: "I was invited to go on a premiere junket for the opening of *Kit Carson* in Wyoming. . . . [Carole is no doubt referring to the Denver opening on August 25, 1940.] When we arrived at the hotel, we found ourselves knee-deep in photographers and local big shots. *Before our marriage Bill and I had romance value and we were posed together at cafes and premieres. But now we heard the boys saying, 'Mr.—Uh, if you'll just step over there and let us get Miss Landis with this group'* [emphasis mine]." Hunt was reduced to holding Carole's coat while she posed with local dignitaries. Carole wrote, "At the end of the evening he said to me dryly, 'I'm not a husband. I'm a coat rack.' " This example suggests that the publicity value lost with her marriage was that of her new husband rather than her own.

Nonetheless, the bottom line of Carole's analysis is that had Hunt been more devoted to his own career he wouldn't have had to become "a spectator to his wife's." In a similar fashion, Carole later mistakenly thought that Tommy Wallace's heroic standing as a wartime aviator would protect him from this humiliating role. One of the great virtues she saw in her fourth and last husband, Horace Schmidlapp, was that his wealth and other interests put him above such concerns.

The divorce was granted on November 12, 1940, to become final one year later. Carole and Willis Hunt continued to see each other throughout the following year and seemed to maintain a tender relationship; Jimmie Fidler claimed that Carole was "mulling . . . Hunt's plea to reconcile," and Hedda Hopper, after blaming the separation on Carole's publicity hunting, suggested the same thing. Before Hunt departed for England in September 1941 with the intention of joining the Eagle Squadron—the same outfit that Carole's third husband, Tommy Wallace, was in, although the connection was not made either at the time or since—Carole dined with him regularly and even knitted him a pair of woolen socks. One gets the impression that before they married, neither Willis nor Carole—both of whom had nevertheless been previously wed—had given much thought to what married life together would be like. Hunt may well have expected Carole to abandon her career after marriage even if he protested to the contrary.

The upshot of the Hunt marriage and divorce was a gossip columnist's warning, anonymous but almost certainly meant for Carole: "Cal warns!!!!! . . . That blonde starlet who has already thrown a cog into her golden career by a hasty and silly marriage. She had better stop, look and listen; one more such step in the wrong direction and she's out." Strong words! In 1940 Hollywood, with morals clauses in actors' contracts, an inappropriate marriage was, indeed, a problem—not perhaps for Lana Turner, whose romantic tribulations only nourished her good-bad girl persona, but surely for Carole, who had too forceful a personality to attract pity and whose marriage to Hunt seemed less a heart-wrenching error than a "hasty and silly" act.

Carole's second failure in marriage was followed by another romantic disappointment. Carole met Franchot Tone in late October 1940, scarcely a month after the Hunt divorce hearing—and about eighteen months after Tone's own painful divorce from Joan Crawford. During the month of November they seemed inseparable, dining together at Ciro's night after night and apparently engaged in a passionate love affair—although this did not prevent Carole from appearing in public with other men, including attorney Bentley Ryan as well as Cedric Gibbons and Gene Markey, of whom there is more below.

It seems unlikely that Tone actually proposed marriage, but Carole appears to have said as much to her friends, despite denying it to Walter Winchell. Rumor had it that the couple had plans to elope on New Year's Day—which would have made Carole a bigamist. Louella Parsons, however, claimed on January 3 that Tone was "the least serious interest in her life" and that Markey and, above all, Gibbons were the real contenders. But Louella seems to have underestimated Carole's attachment to Franchot. As late as February 18, 1941, Sidney Skolsky reported, "Carole Landis tells friends that when her divorce is final she and Franchot Tone will get married," only to announce a mere six days later that "the Franchot Tone–Carole Landis romance is no more." On July 29, summing up Carole's amorous adventures in the previous months, *Oakland Tribune* columnist John Truesdell mocked what he interpreted as Carole's failed pursuit of Tone (and Markey as well), claiming that Carole was "stalking some nice game" but that Tone was "a pretty wary fellow"—although he would marry former model Jean Wallace on October 27 of that year.

Carole had explained to Skolsky in the cited column "why she loves Franchot. . . . 'Franchot is so polite. He lights my cigarets for me.'" The October 1941 *Screenland* article "What Carole Landis Demands of Men!" noted that what Carole admired in Tone—whose framed photograph adorns one of the article's illustrations—was his restraint and sense of humor, his lack of the "ear-marks of the Actor." In this article, based on an interview that probably took place no later than April, Carole goes so far as to say that "it would be very pleasant indeed to be married to Franchot." But by the time the interview that formed the basis of the December 1941 *Photoplay* article "Glamour Girls Are Suckers" took place, Carole's feelings for Tone, unnamed but fairly clearly indicated, had changed from admiration to wounded passion. Apparently, Tone liked Carole very much but considered her immature and coming on too strong, a fling rather than a serious romance.

Of all the men Carole was connected with between her divorce from Willis Hunt in 1940 and her love-at-first-sight meeting with Tommy Wallace in November 1942, only the relationship with Tone ever achieved anything like the intensity she describes in this article, even allowing for movie-magazine poetic license: "This went on for months. We were constantly together every possible moment. I felt this, at last, was it. I saw no one else, didn't want to see anyone else." But the man she cared for dropped her, she tells us, for "a nonprofessional, not pretty really," referring unflatteringly to Jean Wallace, whose earliest uncredited bit parts in Hollywood date from 1941. Ironically, Wallace's first fairly substantial film role would be opposite Carole in her last Fox film, the 1946 *It Shouldn't Happen to a Dog*.

The upshot of the Tone fiasco following hard upon the failure of her marriage to Hunt was that, although she had been and would again be too quick to marry, for the moment twice-bitten and thrice-shy Carole became overcautious about remarriage, passing over two choice suitors who might have had a beneficial influence on her both personally and professionally. Gene Markey, who remained one of Carole's more assiduous escorts through 1942 and was constantly spoken of as a potential husband, was a screenwriter, producer, and man-about-Hollywood, formerly the husband of Joan Bennett and Hedy Lamarr and later of Myrna Loy; in 1952, he left Hollywood to become, via a fourth marriage, the proprietor of the famous Calumet Farm Kentucky racing stables. Cedric Gibbons, whose relationship with Carole was confined to the October 1940–March 1941 period, was a pillar of Hollywood, a founder of the Motion Picture Academy who designed the Oscar statuette and won eleven of them, along with thirty-seven other nominations, in thirty-two years at the helm of the MGM Art Department; he was also the former husband of Dolores Del Rio.

Both Markey and Gibbons seemed quite taken with Carole; either would have brought her the benefit not merely of Hollywood savvy and influence but, above all, of maturity and stability, as well as the financial security to refuse the lackluster roles she felt obliged to accept as breadwinner of the household she shared with her mother. (This desire for financial independence from the studio would later contribute to the real, if clearly insufficient, attraction of her fourth husband, Horace Schmidlapp.) But unlike the younger, debonair Tone (born in 1905), Markey (1895) and Gibbons (1893) were in their late forties, doubtlessly too old to inspire in Carole the *"boom, boom, crash!"* that was for her the sign of true love. Caught up in the contradiction between her sense of independence and her desire to play the traditional woman's role, Carole seemed unable to become attached to a man who could be useful to her in her career.

In an article written shortly after Carole's death, Crawford Dixon, who had run into her in Beverly Hills just two days before her suicide, explains it as the effect less of a broken heart than of emotional exhaustion. Although he does not deny that Carole was deeply in love with Rex Harrison, he finds the motive force for her suicide not in a hypothetical decision by Rex to abandon their affair but in her despairing sense that it was the last and, paradoxically, the most successful of too many relationships. For Dixon, Carole "seemed to consider men a bunch of little boys she could amuse and entertain without too much effort. . . . She was jaded. She knew all there was to know about men." But the very idea of "knowing about men" is already a recipe for failure; in a good love relationship, one spends a lifetime learning about a single human being. Although we should not take Dixon's appraisal as the whole story, it gives us an insight into Carole's dealings with the opposite sex, one to which we can add our awareness of Carole's earlier activities in the Bay Area.

Aside from her four marriages, Carole dated dozens of men—she had at least seventy-nine attested escorts, or, as Dixon puts it, nearly every eligible bachelor in Hollywood, including over thirty publicly recognized names for 1941 alone. And aside from the relationships publicized in gossip columns, there were others mentioned only in books written after the fact. The best known of these is the "long-standing affair" with Carole that entertainer and Fox producer George Jessel refers to in his 1975 memoir, *The World I Lived In*; but casual relationships have been noted with such Hollywood figures as Spencer Tracy and Charles Boyer, and there is no reason to assume that the list ends there. We may balance Jean Porter's assertion that she didn't think Carole would ever sleep with someone to advance her career with her other statement that Carole "always had a guy" with her.

Carole may have "known everything about men," but to the last day of her life her cynicism was always superficial, her openness to emotion real. Not unlike Phil Silvers, who saw Carole as "utterly vulnerable," Jack Benny, who traveled with Carole to the South Pacific in July through September 1944, speaks of her as "a real human being [who] had a warm heart that spilled over with kindness." Carole's vulnerability is the secret of her special appeal; confident of our desire, but not of our love, and never quite able to distinguish one from the other, she was condemned to have her heart constantly "torn," until, in Benny's words, it "finally spilled over and drowned her."

Scarcely had Carole dried off from the swimming scenes of *Mystery Sea Raider* when in early July 1940—the very week of her marriage to Hunt—she returned to the Roach lot to begin filming *Road Show*, once more directed by Hal Roach himself, which remained in production until mid-August. As in *Three Texas Steers*, Carole, as Penguin Moore, is a circus owner, but this time Carole and her circus are at the center of the action; she is in charge from her first scene when, crossing a bridge in her circus truck, she gives a lift to costars John Hubbard and Adolphe Menjou, escapees from an insane asylum who snag the truck with a grappling hook just in time to stop their raft from going over the falls. Menjou as "Colonel" Carraway is really insane; Hubbard as Drogo Gaines was interned after feigning madness in order to avoid marriage to gold-digging Polly Ann Young (Loretta's older sister).

These old Roach comedies are always entertaining even if their plots seem to be held together with baling wire. Carole's traveling circus is forced to move from town to town, harassed by hostile sheriffs and rent-seeking proprietors. Carole's authority over the circus is unquestioned and never artificially imposed; she seems to have been doing this all her life. In the course of the action, Carole swings on a rope, then demonstrates to a customer how to ring the bell in the strength test. Her athleticism and physical presence well suit her for this role, which, however, like her other roles with Roach, affords little scope for the display of emotion. Penguin's somewhat hard-bitten persona, a model that we will see repeated with minor variations in a number of Carole's later pictures, has two chief modes of relating to the male lead, an ambivalence already noted in Carole's relationship with Wilcoxon in her previous film: either she has a chip on her shoulder and is wary of being taken advantage of, or she is all smiles and confidence, and it takes only a gesture from her partner to make her switch from one to the other.

Although the showgirl exoticism alluded to in *Turnabout* (and briefly on screen in *Mystery Sea Raider*) returns here in force and will recur in many of her twenty-one remaining film roles, *Road Show* gives Carole few opportunities to demonstrate her comic talents. *Turnabout* and the 1944 *Having Wonderful Crime* were Carole's only forays into the middle-class genre of screwball comedy, already in decline by 1940. Screwball comedy typically centers on a wackily rocky love relationship, whereas in *Road Show*, zany as it is, the relationship between the principals is played as straight romantic comedy. Responsible for her own livelihood and that of her employees, Carole is a figure of sanity to the point of exaggeration. It is her seriousness that permits the others, particularly Menjou, to pursue their antics; as Carole would complain in a January 1944 Fox publicity release, in nearly all her films, the object of her role was to "let other people score off her." However many lovely dresses she wears in *Road Show*, Penguin/Carole remains a professional all the way to the romantic conclusion; her final kiss rewards Hubbard for revealing to her the new, more luxurious circus he has secretly established in both their names.

Roach films abound in attractive women, and in *Road Show*, except for the fact that Carole is on screen more often, her spectacular looks are not foregrounded more than those of any other pretty player. If Carole is too attractive to be cast as anything but a showgirl, here she transforms this role into a profession by playing it seriously, combining her aerialist performance with running the circus. But if this refusal of any sign of complicity with the spectator is the price of "distractingly desirable" Carole's presence in the film, it is a price well worth paying. *Road Show*, in its very haphazardness, is one of Hollywood's more positive attempts to integrate Carole into its world as a beauty who not only works as an entertainer but manages her own life, finding employment for her brain as well as her body.

Although Carole was praised as "lovely" and "decorative," this film received tepid reviews for its "badly-constructed script." Carole was also praised for singing Hoagy Carmichael's romantic "I Should Have Known You Years Ago"; the voice we hear, however, is not Carole's but that of Martha Mears.

Topper Returns was the last of three films inspired by the Thorne Smith character famously created on screen by English actor Roland Young. It was also Carole's final picture for Roach, made during the last two months of 1940, when she and Roach were already negotiating her transfer to Fox. Of her four Roach films, it has the best production values, screenplay, and direction—by Roy Del Ruth rather than the producer himself. Yet instead of being an extension of Carole's current trajectory, *Topper* is a harbinger of her career at Fox; her role, secondary and passive, is a considerable comedown from the diverse individualized leads of the four preceding films. Carole plays a supporting role behind seasoned comedienne Joan Blondell, just as she would later play second fiddle to Betty Grable, Rita Hayworth, and Sonja Henie. Her *Topper* role as the dutiful daughter reprises her granddaughter part in *Daredevils of the Red Circle*. Once again, the parent she lavishes affection on turns out to be an impostor; this time her real father is dead rather than the imposter's prisoner. If in this film Joan gets to play comedy—although, arguably, chauffeur Rochester (Eddie Anderson) and, to a lesser extent, Billie Burke as Mrs. Topper steal the show—Carole's contribution is largely limited to screaming at the appropriate moments.

Daughter though she may be, Carole is no more a true ingénue here than in her other films. Although both Carole's filial roles exemplify feminine vulnerability—both young women are victims of attempted murder—neither embodies the normally associated promise of continuity with the next generation. The imposter's discomfiture leaves Carole with no remaining family to increase through marriage and no one to give her away. In *Topper* as in *Daredevils*, Carole has a male but no female relative; lacking organic connection with the family residence (to which she is returning from the "Orient" at the opening of the film), she functions merely as the intended victim of the murderous ersatz father, who makes a ghost of Joan by mistake. Thus, despite her nominal status as the young lady of the house, the film keeps her underplayed romance with taxi driver/rescuer Dennis O'Keefe at the narrative periphery; we are never invited to imagine Carole and Dennis marrying, let alone coping with the misalliance between an heiress and a chauffeur. Their departure from the "family home" at the very end of the film is scarcely noticed, our attention being focused on Blondell's welcoming the paternal impostor to the fraternity of ghosts.

The press praised *Topper Returns* as a whole, and to the extent that Carole was noticed, praised her too. But hindsight shows that this film was already the start of her career's downward slope, which her move to Fox in the new year, fraught with great hopes, would only intensify.

"Sex-Loaded": At Twentieth Century-Fox (1941)

Louella Parsons tells us that Carole's Fox contract, which she learned about on Christmas Day 1940, was no sooner signed than Carole had to rush to the hospital to visit her mother, who had been involved in an automobile accident. The contract began on the first of the year, with an opening salary of $400 per week, to increase in steps through $550, $750, $1,000, $1,350, and $1,750, ending at $2,000 in six years. (Carole went through the steps each year through 1945, when leaves of absence delayed her last increase, so that her final Fox salary in 1946 was at the fifth step of $1,350.) In consideration of Carole's relationship with Roach Studios, an understanding was included that permitted her to make two pictures per year for Roach. But since Fox was undertaking "at some considerable expense, to build Miss Landis into an important box office name," their legal department wanted to be sure that Roach's interest in Carole was subordinate to theirs. Contract negotiations between the two studios dragged on over Carole's head through August 1942, when Roach finally suggested a "lending or participation agreement" instead of "a separate employment agreement" with Carole, with "a minimum of one and a maximum of two films a year." All this, however, was so much legal hairsplitting for its own sake; Carole never made another film for Roach, nor does it appear that Roach ever so much as broached the subject.

In January 1941, Carole moved with her mother to a rented home at 12424 Sunset Boulevard in Brentwood. The five-bedroom house, built in 1933, was owned by Edna May Oliver, a New England character actress best known for her spinsterly roles in such films as *David Copperfield* (1935) and *A Tale of Two Cities* (1935); one of her last appearances was as Lady de Bourgh in *Pride and Prejudice* (1940). Oliver's house was a metaphor of her film persona; Carole pointed out to movie writers surprised at the bars on the windows that they had not been her idea.

When Carole gave offense, it was most often through the excess of her affections. In defiance of local zoning regulations, Carole, who loved dogs and "usually [had] an assortment of pooches which keep getting lost," insisted on keeping four that annoyed her neighbors with their barking. Carole was often photographed with dogs, most prominently, Donna or Donner, a Great Dane that had originally been a gift from Gene Markey to ex-wife Hedy Lamarr. On Donner's death, Carole published what was presented as an extract from her personal diary; still in mourning, she described finding a new puppy in a pet shop window: "So you see, I've done it again. I've given my heart once more 'to a dog, to tear.' " Unfortunately, Carole's wont to let her heart be torn was not confined to dogs.

By Carole's own account, Darryl Zanuck became interested in her not by seeing her films but by observing her social whirl. Zanuck told her, "I figured any girl who is so popular with men, whom so many men want to date, must have something we can use and need in our pictures." A third-party article tells the story a bit differently: Lew Schreiber, the Fox casting director, saw Carole in *One Million B.C.* and recommended her to Zanuck with the words, "she's got something." To sum it up, "Twentieth sure is going in for sex in a big way, what with Alice Faye, Betty Grable, Carmen Miranda, and now, Carole Landis"—"sex" in 1940 quaintly meaning "sex appeal." A more specific reason for hiring Carole was no doubt that Betty Grable, who had been brought on in 1940 to do backup for Alice Faye, had proved herself a solid box-office success requiring an understudy of her own. It suited Zanuck's formulaic production approach to keep his stars in line by having them always looking over their shoulders. "Teaming blondes is getting to be a habit at 20th Century-Fox. First, Betty Grable and Alice Faye battled for oomph honors in *Tin Pan Alley*, and now Betty's getting Carole Landis as her chief competition in *Miami*." Whereas Carole's Roach roles lack a common element, her first Fox role set a pattern that would prevail throughout her career at the studio: second leads in A musicals behind Grable, Hayworth, and, finally, Sonja Henie, along with female leads in B films.

Yet it would be difficult to draw this conclusion from the fall 1941 issue of the Fox publicity magazine *Dynamo*, which names (in this order) Gene Tierney, Carole Landis, and Anne Baxter as the female stars "sure of stardom" in 1941 and 1942. After describing Tierney's and Baxter's accomplishments, the article continues, "As for Carole Landis, the current season has left no doubt that she is star-stuff. In fact, her 'fan' mail has been growing to an extent where its volume is almost as large as that of much more seasoned feminine stars. Miss Landis' performances in *Dance Hall* and in *Moon Over Miami* spoke for themselves. She is now playing the feminine lead in *Cadet Girl*, a musical." (The lack of reference to *I Wake Up Screaming*, begun one week after *Cadet Girl*, permits us to date this passage during the third week of July.) After her first two Fox films, Carole's promise of future stardom appeared equivalent to that of actresses who had already starred in A pictures. The asymmetry is ominously apparent, however, from the fact that, whereas Tierney is cited for her title role in *Belle Starr*—a role that the January papers had rumored would go to Carole—and Baxter for her female lead in newly hired French master Jean Renoir's *Swamp Water*, Carole's major accomplishment is her fan mail, reflecting a connection with the public independent of the roles in which she appeared. As our examination of Carole's films will reveal, Fox was never able to reconcile her special appeal to the public with the narratives in which this appeal was supposed to be embodied.

A contemporary source has finally been found that clears up the mixture of fact and fiction in the oft-repeated tale that Carole turned down the role of temptress Doña Sol in the 1941 remake of the 1922 Valentino blockbuster *Blood and Sand*, a role that subsequently went to Rita Hayworth, because she refused to change her blonde hair color. This refusal was not picked up by the major syndicated gossip columns, *The Hollywood Reporter*, or other trade publications, nor was it ever alluded to in writings on or by Carole during her lifetime. The story reemerged in Gene Ringgold's 1974 *The Films of Rita Hayworth* in a reported interview with director Budd Boetticher, who had been a technical adviser on *Blood and Sand*; since then it has been dutifully repeated with various enhancements and inaccuracies by most writers on either Rita or Carole. It has been claimed, for example, that Carole staged the refusal as a pretext cooked up by the studio because the director, Rouben Mamoulian, wanted Rita Hayworth for the part. In some versions of the tale, Zanuck and/or Carole are supposed to have held a press conference—oddly, one never reported in the press—to announce Carole's real or spurious rejection of the role. This act of rebellion is sometimes given as the explanation for Carole's shabby treatment over a year later in *My Gal Sal*, where she plays a humiliatingly small role as second lead to Hayworth, appearing only in the first half hour of the film.

Our old friend Jimmy Starr is once again a source of enlightenment. He writes on January 9, 1941, in the *Los Angeles Evening Herald Examiner*:

> Flat refusal to dye her blonde hair black and affect a hairdo in the manner of Hedy Lamarr today cost Carole Landis one of Hollywood's most coveted roles—that of the seductive charmer in *Blood and Sand*, opposite Tyrone Power.

For weeks, 20th Century-Fox has been endeavoring to borrow the glamorous Hedy from MGM, but Miss Lamarr has been at odds with her home studio over salary and the number of pictures assigned her. This little difficulty put 20th Century-Fox on the spot for Tyrone's co-starring partner. Director Rouben Mamoulian got the bright idea of giving Carole Landis the role—if she would dye her hair. But Carole calmly chucked the plan with the line: "I made my reputation as a blonde. If I change now, people will dub me a copy-cat. That, I don't want."

So far, *Blood and Sand* is filming without its brunette vampire.

Starr's account allows us to understand why Carole was able to turn down the part with impunity, although she had just started working for Fox on January 1. In the first place, the idea came from Mamoulian, not from studio boss Darryl Zanuck, and, as Starr presents it, was more a tentative request than an order. It would be difficult to explain Carole's warm personal relationship with Mamoulian throughout 1942 had he expressed a preference for Hayworth over her for this role. More significant still, Rita, working at Columbia, had not yet been mentioned for the part; she would not be chosen until mid-February. Carole was not handing a role to a rival but refusing to become a "copy-cat" of established star Hedy Lamarr; the dye job requested of her was black, not red. One wonders how Carole would have reacted to Mamoulian's suggestion had she known that this star-making role would go not to Lamarr but to a fellow near-beginner.

Carole tended to sin more by an excess of audacity than of prudence; this ill-considered refusal had something of both. Seen in retrospect, it was a horrible mistake that aborted Carole's starring career at Fox before it began. Although there can be no direct connection between this decision and Carole's humiliating bit a year later in *My Gal Sal*, never again would she be offered a plum role in an A picture, nor would she ever play opposite Power, Fox's number-one leading man for a decade. Ironically, it would be following *My Gal Sal* that, according to studio publicity, Carole asked the studio for permission to return to her natural hair color, presumably as a symbolic contribution to the war effort. In her next film, *It Happened in Flatbush*, shot in March 1942, Carole had become the brunette she had refused to become when it might have made a difference.

It is difficult to imagine how Carole would have performed as femme fatale Doña Sol. Rita Hayworth played the part magnificently; although no fatal woman in real life, Rita convincingly conveys to the spectator the seductress's desire to humiliate her victim, as though avenging some long-ago seduction of her own. Carole never showed this edge, not even as the comi-tragic femme fatale Loretta in *A Scandal in Paris*, where she is more petulant than sinister. Carole was too confident of the other's desire and too generous with her own for the game of seduction to have been meaningful for her. Nevertheless, the variety of Carole's pre-Fox roles showed her to be quite adaptable, and she certainly had the wherewithal of a seductress. Had she been given the role and performed credibly in it, her movie career—and Hayworth's—might well have been very different.

There is another oft-told tale of Carole's early days at Fox. The following allegation by long-term Zanuck associate Milton Sperling appeared in Leonard Mosley's 1984 biography of Zanuck and has been repeated ever since:

> "I was a shy young man . . . but even I knew that every day at four o'clock in the afternoon some girl on the lot would visit Zanuck in his office. The doors would be locked after she went in, no calls were taken, and for the next half hour nothing happened. Headquarters shut down. . . . It was an incredible thing, but a girl went in through that door every day."
>
> It was usually a starlet who was chosen for this daily assignation, and it was rarely the same one twice. The only girl who ever seems to have been called in more than once was a Fox contract feature player named Carol [*sic*] Landis, who was casually referred to by Sperling as "the studio hooker." (She subsequently committed suicide after her name had been linked with a star, Rex Harrison.) Otherwise, any pretty (and willing) extra was picked for the daily session, and after her erotic (or therapeutic)

chore was completed, she departed by a side door with (or without) a little present or promise from her temporary lover. Only then would Zanuck's door be unlocked again, the telephone would begin to ring, work would be resumed, and conferences would be called.

As we see, Mosley knows so little of Carole that he misspells her name. Sperling certainly had the opportunity to observe the Fox boss's behavior; he was Zanuck's right-hand man at the time Carole came to Fox and produced *I Wake Up Screaming* with her in 1941. "Studio hookers," contract players who functioned as "escorts" for important visitors and clients, were, indeed, found at Fox and elsewhere during the studio era; Sperling's casual reference was doubtless intended as metaphorical rather than literal.

Sperling's or Mosley's allegations about Carole, whatever their basis in fact, are characterized by two major sins of omission. First, it strains credibility to claim that Carole was the "only" woman who visited Zanuck's office more than once—a pseudo-factoid from which a later writer extrapolates the absurd conclusion that on Carole's departure from Fox in 1946, "Zanuck freed her, probably with relief, and filled the role she had occupied in his office between 3.30 pm and 4 pm most days of the week without much trouble with other talent from the casting department," as though Carole, who, in the course of her Fox contract, had married twice and had been away from Los Angeles for a total of at least two years, had visited the boss's office "most days of the week" for six years running. Sperling's, or Mosley's, second, more serious omission is that, with one casual exception, they say not a word about either Carole's films or her wartime service, making the "studio hooker" tag sound reasonable to an uninformed reader. Even when Sperling refers later in the interview to Carole's casting in *I Wake Up Screaming*, he says that Zanuck "told him to find a role for Carole Landis," as though it were a bone thrown to the boss's sex partner.

A fact likely to have colored Sperling's disdainful attitude toward Carole is his friendship with Lilli Palmer at precisely the time of Carole's affair with Rex Harrison in 1947 and '48. Sperling not only produced Lilli's film *My Girl Tisa*, but delegated Lilli to receive an award for the film on his behalf from *Parents Magazine* as "the outstanding family picture for February [1948]." It does not strain credibility to assume that Lilli made Sperling aware of her quite understandable hostility to Carole. In Lilli's autobiography, she says she didn't want to know where Carole lived for fear that she would "pick up a kitchen knife some night."

Yet although Sperling's characterization of Carole is clearly exaggerated and slanted, this is hardly sufficient grounds to reject it altogether. Zanuck's sexual behavior has been convincingly attested elsewhere, and both Kirk Crivello and E. J. Fleming cite independent verbal confirmations of Sperling's claim that Carole was Zanuck's mistress. And as noted in the preceding chapter, there is no lack of evidence of Carole's casual attitude toward sex. The visible promiscuity of Carole's *social* life and the dubious reputation it earned her probably played at least a contributory role in Sperling's nasty characterization.

Whatever their precise nature, Carole's personal relations with Zanuck do little to explain either the good or the bad in her career at Fox. Zanuck was a businessman; had he thought Carole would be better box office than Grable or Hayworth, he would have used her in their place. Writers such as Crivello, Fleming, and John Austin, who have emphasized the personal angle with the laudable intention of defending Carole's reputation, are, in fact, confining her to the role she plays in Sperling's defamatory remarks. Carole was not a studio hooker tossed a few roles as a reward for services rendered; she was a talented actress whose extraordinary beauty, as analysis of her films reveals, didn't quite fit the mold of the Hollywood leading lady.

When we reflect on Carole's purported relationship with Zanuck or on her activities in San Francisco, what we should remember above all is that nothing in Carole's personal life ever affected the fundamental decency and graciousness toward others of the young woman described in April 1943 as "lovely, unspoiled Carole Landis, one of the most thoroughgoing right-guys in the picture business."

Moon over Miami was in production between early March and late April 1941. The director was Grable favorite Walter Lang, one of the chief architects of the Fox Technicolor musical style, slick and eye-catching but without the high-budget lushness of rival MGM. The previous fall, Lang had directed Grable in *Tin Pan Alley*; he would go on to direct her in four other musicals during the 1940s.

In *Moon over Miami*, Carole and Betty portray sisters working at the family's Texas hamburger stand. Recipients of a disappointingly small inheritance, they conspire with their aunt, comedienne Charlotte Greenwood, to seek their fortune in Miami by finding Betty a wealthy spouse. So Betty poses as an heiress, with Greenwood playing her maid and Carole her secretary. *Miami* sets a good Ralph Rainger–Leo Robin musical score to the plotline of *Three Blind Mice*, filmed just three years earlier from Stephen Powys's play of the same name. Fox would use this plot, suitably varied, for a third time in *Three Little Girls in Blue* (1946). A more complex variant, derived from Zoe Akins's similar (and previously filmed) play *The Greeks Had a Word for It*, gave rise to *How to Marry a Millionaire* (1953), with Marilyn Monroe in glasses playing a much juicier version of Carole's role and Grable herself playing Greenwood's. Zanuck had originally envisioned Carole's part in *Miami* for Alice Faye, who would probably have shared screen and performance time equally with Grable, as would be the case for June Haver and Vivian Blaine in *Three Little Girls in Blue*.

As things turn out, Betty finds not one but two suitors, played by Don Ameche and Robert Cummings; she prefers the more virile Ameche, but on discovering that he is broke, she switches her affections to Cummings, the scion of a great fortune. Yet Betty's heart remains attached to Ameche, while for his part Cummings shifts his attention to Carole. At the end, the deception is revealed, and the couples pair off (including Jack Haley as a waiter with Greenwood), the irony being that it is Carole rather than Betty who catches the wealthy man.

Within this hackneyed story line, the particular nuance of Carole's role is remarkable. Grable has the lion's share of screen time and all but monopolizes the song and dance numbers. (Aside from a few bars of the finale, Carole joins Betty only in a brief opening number at the hamburger stand, where she gets one chorus to Betty's two, and as backup along with Greenwood on "Oh-Me-Oh-Mi-ami!" in the hotel suite.) But not only are Carole's costumes, although less numerous, more attractive, Carole is designated throughout the film as the more beautiful of the two. On two occasions the two women are directly compared. When Betty is about to receive the young men for the first time, she tells "secretary" Carole to put her glasses back on so Carole won't look better than she does; later in the film, when Betty takes Carole out of wraps to distract Cummings while she is with Ameche (who she still thinks is rich), Cummings offers the joking accusation that Betty had kept Carole hidden in order not to be overshadowed. In a revealing shot, reproduced on one of the film's lobby cards, the two men stand between the two women, both facing and admiring Carole while turning their backs to Grable. And in a scene that follows Ameche's first meeting with Grable, he tells her that she isn't pretty and that although her figure is "almost perfect," it lacks "poetry."

In the most revelatory sequence of all, Cummings takes both sisters to meet his father, Betty as his fiancée and Carole still playing the secretary. Bob enters the room with Carole on his right and Betty on his left. His father jokingly asks if Bob is marrying both of them, and on Bob's answer that he is marrying only one, he turns without hesitation to Carole and exclaims, "And a very good one, too!" After Bob clears up the error, when the group sits down at the dinner table, the father asks Betty to sit next to him, but tells Carole, "Miss Sears," to sit opposite him so that he can look at her.

None of this foregrounding of Carole's attractiveness is a requirement of the plot. Even given that she is being set up to replace Grable as Cummings's fiancée, there is no need for invidious comparisons. By underlining Carole's beauty while leaving Betty to dominate the scene as the standard pretty girl, the film valorizes Carole's relatively small role while revealing a certain discomfort at her presence. In the less self-conscious environment of Roach studios, Carole's attractiveness had been taken for granted as the normal attribute of a leading actress. In *Miami*, by contrast, making the secondary but prestigious character of Cummings's father deliberately foreground Carole's beauty in a mini-judgment of Paris seems to acknowledge her beauty independently of the story. The face and figure that had hitherto opened doors for Carole in Hollywood had become at Fox the sign of a potential problem, one whose nature was no doubt still unclear to the film's creators.

Reviewers liked *Miami,* seeing it as a Grable picture but noting Carole's effectiveness in her role: "Carole Landis makes the most of a grand opportunity as the sister who must hide glamour under secretarial specs; naturally she can't"; "Miss Landis makes a fair vision when she removes her spurious secretarial spectacles." But that *Miami* was a modest box-office success (although it didn't make the list of Fox's twelve highest-grossing films of 1941) and that Carole fit smoothly into the story did not make her place at Fox less problematic. The problem posed by "distractingly desirable" Carole was compensated for but not resolved by her relative lack of screen time. Betty Grable, after her 1940 hits *Down Argentine Way* and *Tin Pan Alley*, where she displays great screen presence despite her second billing to Alice Faye, was an up-and-coming star; Carole was a relative beginner with no A-level hits to her credit. Between Faye and Grable, although Faye is superior in plastic beauty and singing ability, Grable comes out ahead as a box-office attraction because her personality is more dynamic and engaging. In contrast, *Miami*'s nervousness attests to a fear that Carole's sex appeal might distract from Betty's dynamism and, ultimately, from the filmic narrative that depended on it.

It is therefore easy to understand the "feud" the two actresses are said to have begun with this film, one that would be revived a few months later during their second and final collaboration, *I Wake Up Screaming*. Feuds make for good publicity. An "Open Letter To Betty And Carole" appeared in the February 1942 *Screenland* denouncing the "silly publicity" given the feud; included with the letter, signed by editor Delight Evans, was a reply from Carole categorically denying it. To the cynical eye, this is nearly as clever—or banal—an example of attracting publicity by denouncing publicity-seeking as the Ping Girl episode. Yet although both actresses denied the conflict and supposedly maintained friendly relations, more than one columnist of the day insisted on its reality. As for assigning blame, whereas E. J. Fleming credits a source with the statement that Betty was the "instigator," a contemporary columnist explained Carole's "flu" in early April by her desire for a "deluxe new dressing room," presumably rivaling Grable's.

Although it tempting to make this feud with a higher-ranked star a cause of Carole's later exclusion from A-level musicals, we should recall once again that in Zanuck's casting decisions box office was the all-important consideration. The Fox A musical formula, which fit Grable so well that it put her among filmdom's highest grossing female stars for a dozen years running and made her in 1947 and 1948 the highest-paid woman in the United States, had no real place for Carole. Although Carole sang in a sensuous contralto and had experience as a dancer, she was not and could never become a "hoofer" like Betty Grable or Betty's old Saint Louis acquaintance Emylyn Pique, later Carole's *Four Jills in a Jeep* cohort Mitzi Mayfair. In these Fox musicals, where the leading lady is almost constantly on camera, she is less a real woman than the performer of a rite of entertainment; it would not do for her to become an independent focus of desire.

Coincidentally, in early April 1941, during the production of *Miami*, the Production Code Office issued a ban on "sweater shots" in either films or stills. Both Carole and Betty expressed public dismay. A series of photographs made around this time of Carole in different poses wearing a blue sweater displays her unique fusion of beauty and sexiness; the effect of her sweet smile is to legitimize the sexual desire she inspires. As Sidney Skolsky would put it a few years later, "Carole Landis fills a sweater more naturally than any actress in town." It is not unlikely that this series of photographs was the catalyst that provoked the ban; a writer claimed later that year that "Carole Landis' publicity portraits have the highest mortality rate of those censored by the Hays Office."

If the spectator of Carole's early films could imagine that in seeing her he was getting something for nothing, it was becoming apparent that this gift undercut the system of Hollywood filmic narrative and would have to be reined in. This discovery, symbolically embodied in the Production Code Office's decree, would mark the downward turning point of Carole's film career. Ironically, April 1941 also saw the publication in *Screen Guide* of an article entitled "Landis versus Lombard," with full-page color portraits of both Caroles. This was the closest Landis would ever come to parity with her namesake.

In Carole's next three films, *Dance Hall*, *I Wake Up Screaming*, and *Cadet Girl*, Zanuck would experiment with different ways of using her, whether as the lead in B musicals, whose humdrum settings provide little opportunity for the fantasies inspired by the high-budget affairs, or once more as a second lead to Grable, again the beautiful sister but this time fated by her beauty to play the role of sacrificial victim. But Fox's B musicals were on their way out. During Carole's remaining five years at the studio, she would alternate between accessory roles in A productions and decorative female leads in male-focused B dramas. Her remaining interesting parts—in *Having Wonderful Crime*, *A Scandal in Paris*, *Secret Command*, the two British films, *Out of the Blue*, and *The Powers Girl*—would be created elsewhere.

Moon over Miami is Carole's sole decent role in a color film. Her only other color picture, *My Gal Sal*, made a year later, uses all the resources of costume, cosmetics, and cinematography to present Rita Hayworth as her superior in allure and beauty, ending any residual chances Carole may have had at Fox for genuine stardom. Although in some *Miami* scenes, for example during her conversation with Cummings at the night club where she encourages him to strike out for himself, Carole seems to be wearing more makeup than she needs, there is no more stunning footage of her than in this film, made at the height of her beauty.

Carole's second Fox film was in sharp contrast to the first. *Dance Hall*, made from a script that had been floating around the studio since 1933, had no

Betty Grable to outrank her, but neither did it have color or high production values. It was a B movie all the way, produced by Sol Wurtzel, the head of Fox's B unit, directed by Irving Pichel, one of its B directors, and shot on the B lot on Western Avenue rather than the Beverly Hills grounds that would one day give birth to Century City. After it had already been shot and released, *Dance Hall* was reportedly scheduled to receive A-level publicity, yet this had no obvious effect on the film's box-office receipts.

Carole is first billed above her longtime friend Cesar Romero, with whom she was to engage in similar sweet-and-sour relationships in *A Gentleman at Heart* (1942) and *Wintertime* (1943). But in *Dance Hall*, unlike these or any other of her Fox films after 1941, Carole is the dominant personality. This dominance is above all visual; Carole is almost constantly on screen, beautifully dressed and advantageously photographed.

The difficulty involved in fitting Carole into filmic narrative is mitigated in the B format. These films are not only considerably shorter than A films (*Dance Hall* lasts 72 minutes, *Cadet Girl*, 68, as opposed to 91 for the rather quick *Miami* and 103 for *My Gal Sal*), but create a far less powerful imaginary reality. If the A musical is a cultural rite in which the star is more officiant than desire-object, the B musical is simply a movie with music. B characters lack the depth and nuance of A protagonists; along with reduced time and budget comes a reduced biography and a cruder story line. In *Dance Hall* we know almost nothing about the characters' pasts, see only the plot-driven essentials of their present lives, and are given but a perfunctory idea of how they will pursue these lives when the film is over.

Carole is once more a showgirl, this time a singer who comes from New York City to a dance hall in "Stanton, Pennsylvania." For Carole's character, Lily Brown aka "Venus," a long-term contract singing in a cheap dance hall must represent a considerable come-down from the New York nightclub circuit, yet we hear nothing to suggest this, let alone explain it. The one thing Lily tells us about her past, in a conversation with two dance-hall girls, is that she spent three years on the dance floor before becoming a singer, a point with biographical resonances with both Carole's hula days in San Francisco and her early Warners career.

Dance Hall revolves around Carole/Lily's relationship with dance-hall owner Cesar Romero/Duke McKay, a romance in which the principals "play their parts in the jerky fashion of a tintype." Carole is natural and charming with the other two men in the film, a pianist-composer (William Henry), whom she admires and encourages without any romantic interest, and a middle-aged lingerie merchant, played sympathetically by J. Edward Bromberg, who falls for Carole and befriends her although he knows his love will not be reciprocated. In contrast, the romantic context with Romero finds Carole oscillating without transition from cynicism and insult to surrender, a pattern that will be repeated in many of Carole's other romantic screen roles.

No doubt in the Hollywood formula for romantic comedy, the initial contact between boy and girl is obligatorily hostile, but one expects to witness a growing tenderness that here remains almost entirely implicit. In the final sequence of the film, Carole gets Romero out of jail by returning $2,500 he had swindled from his customers to aid Carole's protégé, the pianist. But Romero insults her when he learns that the replacement funds came from Bromberg, and the couple go on arguing through the final shot, with Cesar walking down the street carrying Carole—who has twisted her ankle trying to escape him—in his arms. This conclusion is cute and original but resolutely unsentimental, a bittersweet harbinger of the couple's future that reflects their hot-or-cold oscillation throughout the film.

Dance Hall contains two symmetrical moments in which one of the Romero-Landis couple expresses a sincere emotion and the other exploits this sincerity as an opening to humiliation rather than reciprocity. After a drive to a romantic spot near a lake, Cesar hands Carole the line that he finds her different from "all the others"; yet after the couple exchange a kiss, Cesar laughs boastfully at having reduced Carole to the status of, precisely, "all the others." In the parallel scene, Carole gets Cesar to take her back to the very same spot, and when he begins a touchingly embarrassed marriage proposal, she jumps in his car and drives off, leaving him to walk the ten miles back to town.

The rockiness of the Lily/Duke love relationship reflects a telling ambivalence in Lily's character. Although she is presented as a successful professional making her own way in the world, when she needs money to get Romero out of jail, she must turn to her middle-aged admirer. At an earlier point in the film she asks Romero anxiously if he sees her as the kind of girl who will run after men, and the question of her sexual morality is still being raised in the final sequence—by which time Cesar's own amorous fidelity is no longer in doubt. These signs of uneasiness with Lily's role reflect, in more explicit terms than in *Miami*, the difficulty of situating Carole's unique blend of innocence and experience within Hollywood's cast of standard female characters.

Dance Hall's weak sense of closure—its failure to provide an emotional progression with which the audience can identify—was no doubt the reason for its mostly poor reviews: "Neither of the characterizations is convincing"; "neither Cesar Romero . . . nor Carole Landis is going to benefit by their showing in this picture." Only Carole's "deep-throated" singing and the generally "likeable" quality of the two principals was praised. Yet seen as a solution to the problem of integrating Carole into Hollywood story-telling, the film is a clear success. The Romero-Landis couple's emphasis on one-upmanship over romantic reciprocity encourages us to look at Carole less from Cesar's point of view than through the eyes of Bromberg, as someone divinely lovely precisely because he cannot hope to possess her. Nor is desire a prerequisite of friendship; the pianist whom Carole befriends so enthusiastically is in love with another woman—who trifles with his affection.

The high point of Carole's beauty in *Dance Hall*, perhaps of her entire movie career, is the sequence about twenty minutes into the film where she sings "There's Something in the Air" with the orchestra, then walks off the stage and out of the room. This concluding bit takes but a few seconds, as Carole moves quickly toward the door, escaping the clutches of the flirtatious Romero. This is the kind of scene that in the 1950s would have been slowed down and shot from closer in, accompanied by "sexy" music. Here it is given no buildup nor extended beyond its minimal necessity; yet Carole moves with such sensuous grace that for these few marvelous seconds, she truly is Venus herself.

Carole's first year at Fox was the year of her most intensive socializing. An unavoidably incomplete survey of sightings finds her several times a week at Ciro's, the Mocambo, the Rhum Boogie, La Conga, or in New York at the Stork Club or El Morocco, with a great variety of escorts, including several with whom she was linked romantically at one time or other. For example, in January, after a New Year's celebration with Gene Markey at Ciro's, we find her out with New York scion Phil Ammidon on January 2, with Greg Bautzer's law associate Bentley Ryan on the eighth, Ammidon again on the ninth, Cedric Gibbons on the eighteenth, dining with ex-hubby Willis Hunt (reportedly seeking reconciliation) at Victor's on the twenty-second, at a dinner party on the twenty-fourth with Gibbons, who accompanied her to Arrowhead Springs on Sunday and Monday the twenty-sixth and twenty-seventh, where she "swam all Sunday afternoon." During this same month, a columnist tells us she was also seeing actor Eddie Norris. The same pattern is repeated throughout the year, with actors Robert Stack and the much older Conrad Nagel in February, Charlie Chaplin, steel heir Alexis Thompson, and fellow Fox newcomer George Montgomery in March, producers Raymond Hakim and Matty Fox in April. It was common in those days for studios to assign stars to date each other, but few of Carole's escorts were fellow Fox actors; among those she dated in 1941 were Montgomery, whom it appears Carole took seriously, and the discreetly homosexual Cesar Romero, who had a deep friendship for Carole and much later told a Hollywood writer that he had even considered marrying her.

In the fall, Carole's New York mini-romance with Tony Martin made the movie magazines; *Modern Screen* published an extract of her September 1941 "diary" expressing her thrill at meeting Martin and included a shot of the crooner's picture on her desk. (Martin himself, with whom I spoke in February 2005, could or would recall only a single date with Carole, along with her infectious laughter.) Somehow, with all this going on, Carole found the time to take piano lessons; one wonders how many hours a day she was able to practice. As a likely sign of overexertion, Carole reported ill with the "flu" in April, September, and November 1941. Even if we assume the first illness was malingering designed to secure her a better dressing room in the context of her rivalry with Grable, the later bouts, the first of which kept her in bed for three days during her trip to New York and the second of which began when she collapsed on the set of *A Gentleman at Heart* and had to be taken home, appear to have been genuine enough. On the latter occasion, Carole was reported better after a day's rest, implying that the collapse was caused more by fatigue than infection.

Movie publications refer to Carole during this period as Hollywood's "most-dated starlet" and obtain from her such "told to" contributions as "Carole Landis Names Hollywood's Most Fascinating Men" (*Movie Stars Parade*, February 1941), "How to Handle Wolves with Kid Gloves" (*Modern Screen*, March 1941), "It's Out-Landis!—Intimate Close-up of that Gentlemen-preferred Blonde" (*Modern Screen*, October 1941), or the contrarily focused "I Don't Live in a Night Club!" (*Screen Guide*, July 1941). Two more substantive essays in this vein, both "told to" Gladys Hall, are discussed below.

How are we to interpret this near-frenetic social activity? In various places, Carole gives it a cynical spin: being seen in public is good publicity; knowing the right people in Hollywood is the way to get ahead; if the men think escorting her implies a promise of sexual favors, they are fooling themselves; and so on. This is the image of hard-nosed ambition that Carole would display in her next film, *I Wake Up Screaming*. Yet these cynical declarations have the ring of rationalizations. Even as Carole charmed and impressed others with her beauty, intelligence, wit, and *joie de vivre*, her playgirl image was damaging her Hollywood career.

Carole had in abundance two qualities that drove her to be in constant movement. On the one hand, she found pleasure in every aspect of
her night-clubbing life, eating ("Carole Landis, according to waiters, is a
terrific eater"), drinking, dressing up, being seen, dancing, joking and
laughing with others. On the other hand, her near-manic public activity
was balanced by a depressive side, and although she was unable to live
intimately with another person (even her mother apparently got on her
nerves), it seems likely that she indulged her manic tendencies for fear that
remaining alone would bring on depression. If we read between the lines,
Carole's oft-recalled phrase that she didn't want to end "her career in a
rooming-house with full scrapbooks and an empty stomach" reflects
greater fear of loneliness than of hunger.

Whatever might have been known or whispered about Carole's earlier activities in the Bay Area, all this socializing only confirmed her apparent
disdain for social norms. The reaction was not merely a matter of raised
eyebrows; Carole was creating for herself a public image that made her all
the more difficult to cast in leading roles. This situation was reinforced
even by the favorable publicity she elicited. An "anonymous admirer"
extols Carole's personality far more than her physical attractions: "Carole's
so frank and friendly that a man's carefully tucked away in the 'best pal'
category before he can plot a single pass. . . . She's almost unbelievably
cheerful. In all the years I've been associated with her I've never seen her
look 'beaten.' Not even two unsuccessful marriages have changed her dis-
position. . . . She is a completely natural person, interested in everyone
and everything about her." Naturalness and frankness are sterling qualities,
but the image the author gives us of an independent woman cheerfully
facing the world is not one that falls easily into the standard romantic plotline.
Someone so totally at ease with herself and others appears to lack problems
whose solution can provide dramatic material. This anonymous writer also
points out that other women naturally dislike Carole for the very reasons
men find her attractive. Here again, the significance of this hostility is less
in the gossip it might have inspired or the power and influence of "Hollywood

wives," of which some writers have made much, than in the doubt raised in the minds of the Hollywood powers-that-be about the feasibility of marketing Carole's image to the general public.

Despite Carole's marriages and her many hopeful declarations about raising a family, her persona never evoked domesticity. This lack of domestic credibility is reflected in the insubstantiality of most of Carole's "happily ever after" endings. In *Topper Returns*, Carole's romance with Dennis O'Keefe is far in the background; in *Dance Hall*, *Gentleman at Heart*, and *Wintertime*, Carole and Cesar Romero are a couple, but only in the first is the question of marriage even raised. *It Happened in Flatbush* has just barely a love relationship with Lloyd Nolan; the couple is warmer in *Manila Calling*, but they aren't expected to survive; the relationship with William Gargan in *Behind Green Lights* is perfunctory, and that with Allyn Joslyn in *It Shouldn't Happen to a Dog* is not much more intense. *Four Jills in a Jeep*, which is based on fact, is the only film in which Carole marries; and only seven films, *One Million B.C.*, *Mystery Sea Raider*, *Road Show*, *Moon over Miami*, *Secret Command*, *Dog*, and *Noose*, end with a clear anticipation of permanent union. In *Cadet Girl*, *My Gal Sal*, and *The Powers Girl*, Carole is abandoned by her lover; in *I Wake Up Screaming*, *A Scandal in Paris*, and *The Brass Monkey*, she is killed or arrested, and in *Turnabout*, *Orchestra Wives*, *Having Wonderful Crime*, and *Out of the Blue*, she is already married and does not change status. (To be complete, there is no romance at all in Carole's three Republic outings.) Interestingly, in not one of her films does Carole have children. In *Secret Command*, her most emotionally satisfying role, she and Pat O'Brien intend to adopt the two children they have been using for undercover work, a situation similar to Loana and Tumak's adoption of the little orphan girl at the end of *One Million B.C.*

Throughout Carole's career, her films, no matter how weak or conventional, grant us important insights into her public personality and the limits of her stardom; they also help us understand that Carole is memorable not despite but *because of* these limits. It is a reflection of Carole's greatness as a personality as well as of her limitations, less as an actress than as a *movie star*, that the spectator is always confident that there is more to her than her character on the screen.

I Wake Up Screaming, Carole's second turn as Betty Grable's sister, was not a film Carole claimed to have particularly enjoyed making, yet it is the most biographically significant motion picture of her career. Directed by versatile H. Bruce Humberstone—who went on from Charlie Chan films in the 1930s to turn out major musicals for Fox in the 1940s and Warner Brothers in the 1950s, ending his career with a few Tarzan pictures and some TV work—*Screaming* was shot from mid-July to late August 1941 and released on November 14. Vicki, Carole's character in *Screaming*, was almost certainly the inspiration for Jerome Charyn's obsessively counterfactual portrait of Carole in *Movieland* (1989): "almost pathological coldness . . . frozen beauty . . . coolness that was outside any art." This is 180 degrees from the way Carole is described by everyone who knew her, yet Charyn's is an understandable reaction to the eerie tale of Vicki/Carole's life and death.

The plot of *I Wake Up Screaming* follows fairly closely its source in the recently published Steve Fisher novel by the same name. No doubt because nothing in the story corresponds to the title, the film was originally entitled *Hot Spot*, a tough-guy term for the electric chair, with which the male protagonist is threatened in the opening scene; but it was ultimately found preferable to take advantage of the book's own modest notoriety. The action is moved from Los Angeles to New York, par for the course in the days when the movie audience was always presumed to be on the eastern seaboard. The story is told in flashback, with Victor Mature defending himself against the charge of having murdered Carole on learning that she had signed a movie contract and was about to leave for Hollywood.

Mature is a sports promoter who, on a dare, decides to transform Carole from a waitress in a cheap restaurant into a celebrity. He dresses her up, takes her to a chic nightclub with a couple of friends, an old-time actor (Alan Mowbray) and a columnist (Allyn Joslyn), and introduces her to the glamour world. Vicki is a big hit and immediately begins getting modeling and advertising offers, leading eventually to a screen test and the fatal Hollywood contract. When Mature is accused of Vicki's murder, her sister Jill, Grable in a non-singing role, falls in love with him and helps him prove his innocence. Mature is harassed and harried by the head detective on the murder case, powerfully played by Laird Cregar. Finally, the murderer turns out to be the desk clerk in Carole's apartment building (Elisha Cook Jr.), the most insignificant male in the story. It emerges that Cregar had known the clerk was guilty all along, but kept this to himself in order to torment Mature, whose real crime was lifting Carole into a higher sphere; at the end of the film, Cregar reveals that when she was a waitress, he had watched over her and nourished hopes of eventual marriage.

Vicki, the beautiful murder victim, remains the film's focus throughout. All the male principals are obsessed with her, Mature somewhat less than the others, which ironically explains why he is charged with the murder; conversely, the insignificance of the real perpetrator is a sign that he acts as the representative of them all. Although the Landis:Grable::beautiful: pretty paradigm had been marked in *Moon over Miami*, it was incidental to the substance of Carole's role, merely a way of justifying and mitigating her presence on screen. *I Wake Up Screaming* does something different, and rather daring: it foregrounds Carole's beauty not simply as an empirical reality of the fictional world but as a transcendental difference reflected in the formal structure of the narrative.

The first shot of the film tracks in on Carole's face on the front page of a newspaper under the headline, "Beautiful Model Found Murdered." It is the face of a dead woman, an image that haunts the fictional world that she could not enter alive. In the symmetrically themed climactic scene, Victor Mature slips into the ailing Cregar's room in his absence, then watches him enter with a fresh bouquet with which, in what appears to be a daily ritual, he replaces the flowers on the mantelpiece beneath Carole's portrait, as if making an offering to a goddess. The walls of the room are covered with Carole's photographs and posters. Cornered by Mature, Cregar, seated at a table, takes poison and dies before still another image of Carole.

Cregar's worship is repeated in less intense form by every one of the other principals. Both Grable and Mature have Carole's photograph in their apartments, and we never enter either without seeing it. We also see Carole in flashback with Mature's two friends, both of whom were in love with her; she appears in a film clip singing "The Things I Love," ominously interrupted when Mowbray bangs on the door of the screening room as if to escape a ghost.

If the chief formal innovation of the film is the opposition between living Grable and dead Carole, too desirable to inhabit the world of the story, it includes an equally significant advance in assimilating the story line to Carole's life. For the first time, the showgirl persona is given a past. Carole/Vicki is not, like Venus or Penguin, to the manner born, but a working-class girl to whom show business offers an escape route from mediocrity, just as Carole herself had waited tables in San Bernardino six or seven years earlier in preparation for her chance at stardom. Carole's cinematic hardness, which in *Dance Hall* is presumed to reflect the showgirl's sexual disillusionment, is here given a deeper source in the fierce ambition of a beauty from the wrong side of the tracks. When Jill cautions the headstrong Vicki against letting herself be tempted by Mature's promises of success, we imagine we hear Carole's own sister; only the narcissistic coldness that so impressed Charyn belongs to the character and not the player.

Not surprisingly, Carole, although less prominent in the reviews than either the two principals or Cregar, was uniformly praised for her performance, diversely characterized as "always pleasing and appealing" and "properly hard and brittle." "Carole Landis does a grand job in a glamorous part"; "Miss Landis is given every opportunity to register the fatal beauty and charm which in the story is supposed to enslave a columnist and passé actor."

Seven years later, Fox remade *I Wake Up Screaming* as *Vicki*, with Jean Peters in the title role and Jeanne Crain as her sister. Here the opposition between the sisters is not beautiful versus pretty, but delicate versus coarse; Crain is the lovelier of the two, but Peters has a tough sex appeal that fits the story line better than Carole's exquisite voluptuousness. Peters is a credible choice as a manufactured glamour girl; Carole's stunning appearance even in her waitress uniform—the second scene in the restaurant, where the camera follows Carole cleaning off a few tables while Betty waits for her, is one of the high points in Carole's display of beauty on screen—takes the edge off Mature's boast to his friends that he can make a celebrity out of a "hash-slinger." *Vicki* has also the advantage of not being a star vehicle. Fearful that the story line gave Grable and Mature insufficient opportunity for sex appeal, Zanuck added a gratuitous sequence in which the pair go for an evening swim together in order to show off their physiques. By the criterion of narrative coherence, *Vicki*—with Richard Boone doing a credible reprise of Cregar's performance—is a better movie than *Screaming*, yet it lacks the transcendental dimension of its predecessor. In the second film, the heroine's death is an ironic payback for fortuitous fame; in the first, it is retribution for the tragic flaw of excessive desirability.

Gene Tierney said that she was less remembered for her acting in *Laura* than as the woman in the painting; but in that film, abstracting from the far better screenplay and production values, the heroine is not really dead, and nowhere are we given the impression that her presence as anything but a ghost would be too powerful for the screen. By a terrible irony, when Carole committed suicide in July 1948, she was scheduled to star in a stage version of *Laura* the following week. We may also contrast Vicki/Carole's fate with that of Mary Astor-Brigid O'Shaughnessy in John Huston's *The Maltese Falcon*, also filmed in 1941. Huston's femme fatale, guilty of murder, will presumably be punished, but only after the film is over. Astor is alive and present in both her film's first and last sequences; in both of Carole's, she is present and dead.

On the final pre-shooting script of *I Wake Up Screaming* in the Fox archives at the University of Southern California, one of Darryl Zanuck's thick-penciled notes describes the still uncast character of Vicki Lynn as "sex-loaded." Whatever the truth about Zanuck's 4 p.m. trysts, it could not have escaped him that no one on the Fox lot fit that description better than Carole. But a woman whose sex appeal is so excessive that she must be expelled from the film before it begins is not compatible with very many movie plots. In Carole's Fox career, *Screaming* was in the nature of an exorcism. Henceforth, even as a B female lead, she would be increasingly cast in decorative roles; the solution for her beauty would be to marginalize it, if not to dissimulate and humiliate it.

In the script conferences on *Screaming*, various names had been suggested for both roles: Rita Hayworth or Gene Tierney as Jill, Lucille Ball as Vicki. Zanuck's choice of Carole for this "sex-loaded" role had been an afterthought. In contrast, the lead in *Cadet Girl* was never in doubt; it was just where one would expect to find Carole after *Dance Hall*. In the earlier film, she sang two numbers (plus a few bars of a third); in this one, she sings three—one more than the total of her singing performances during the entire remainder of her Fox career. Carole began work on *Cadet Girl* on July 14, 1941, one week before *I Wake Up Screaming*, and worked on both films simultaneously until *Cadet Girl* was completed on August 11. Not atypically, this film, whose first screenplay, entitled "Band Story," dates from May 1940, was originally conceived as an A musical with Alice Faye in the title role. The director was Ray McCarey, whose career, which included a stint with Roach in the 1930s, was overshadowed by the glory of his multi-Oscar-winning brother, Leo. McCarey, Carole's most frequent director at Fox, would direct her in two more films in 1942.

    Cadet Girl is a sweetly patriotic film reflective of prewar 1941, when Carole and other stars were visiting military bases and the war in Europe was on everyone's mind, but the nation was still at peace. Pearl Harbor, coming just nine days after the movie's November 28 release, would make it a stillborn anachronism. It is the only one of Carole's films that has never been available for purchase on the open market, nor is it listed in the Library of Congress catalog; to my knowledge, the only copy available to the public is in the UCLA Film Archive repository in Hollywood.

    Once more, Carole is a nightclub singer, this time in a sophisticated New York ambiance. Although she is first-billed, it can scarcely be a coincidence that her character's name, Gene Baxter, is composed from the names of the two other promising Fox actresses of 1941, both destined for Fox's A list. John Shepperd (who would be known from 1948 on as Shepperd—occasionally Sheppard—Strudwick) is Bob Mallory, the band-leader; his brother Tex, Carole's costar, is played by George Montgomery. Montgomery, who grew up in Montana, had played bit parts in dozens of Republic Westerns in the late 1930s, then moved on to Westerns at Fox, where he was being built up to bigger roles; after *Cadet Girl* he would co-star with Ginger Rogers in the satiric comedy *Roxie Hart*.

Tex is a West Point cadet who comes to New York over summer vaca-tion to play piano with his brother's band and falls in love with singer Carole. Their love affair and his musical success tempt him to leave the academy to marry her, despite her own and his brother's admonitions. Carole, herself in love, tentatively accepts his proposal, but when the cou-ple visits an army camp where Carole sings to the troops (the location shooting at Camp Hahn reprises an actual camp show she had put on shortly before), she realizes that he belongs to the army. A patriotic concert organized by his brother makes George/Tex realize it too; he kisses his erst-while fiancée goodbye and goes off with his West Point buddies, leaving a tearful Carole to find possible consolation in his brother's tenderness. We are not invited to ask ourselves why, if George and Carole are so much in love, they could not postpone their marriage until after his graduation; military officers do not take a vow of celibacy.

As in *Dance Hall*, Carole again has first billing in a B musical, yet this time Carole's role has no special charge. Despite otherwise modest production values, *Dance Hall* glamorized Carole in flattering dresses and poses. In *Cadet Girl*, although Carole is attractively made up and clothed, her glam-our is considerably restrained. From her halo-like hairdo on down, an effort seems to have been made to give her a more clean-cut appearance in keeping with the film's urbane and patriotic atmosphere, which contrasts with *Dance Hall*'s dubious milieu. These conditions give Carole little chance to transcend the mediocrity of the production. She is lovely as always, but her beauty is not foregrounded as it was in the three previous films, nor does it make her situation in the plot in any way problematic.

Gene Baxter in *Cadet Girl* has none of the brittleness of "Venus"; womanly tenderness dominates over cynicism, and for the first time, Carole sheds tears on screen. Carole's personal style is graceful and understated; she doesn't have the bounce and sparkle of Betty Grable, whom we could imagine without much difficulty in a splashier color version of this musical. This last of Carole's films released before Pearl Harbor marks the beginning of her normalization as a B-movie leading lady. The reviews ran hot and cold, less about Carole than the film; one publication affirmed, "There are a number of people who will be able to date their upward climb from advantageous appearances in *Cadet Girl*," but another declared that the film "will have no appreciable meaning at the box-office."

There is, however, a transcendent moment in *Cadet Girl* that is of great biographical resonance. On her visit to the army base, Carole, wearing a fantasy uniform, sings a cute, ironic number, "I'll Settle for You (You'll Do)," before an audience of real army trainees. In contrast with the rather subdued performances of her two other songs, here she seems fully in her element; we imagine that every soldier can feel himself to be the one that Carole has "settled for" and that her charisma is freely given here in the service of her country.

Pearl Harbor marked Carole's transformation from a woman kind and generous but focused on her own life and career into one selflessly and tirelessly devoted to a cause that became more important to her than success in Hollywood. Many other entertainers gave generously of themselves to the war effort, but few sacrificed personal ambition to it as much as Carole did. It is sadly ironic that *Cadet Girl's* unfortunate release just before this life-changing event led to its relative lack of success, which put an end to Carole's B-musical stardom. As Carole multiplied her "I'll Settle for You" performance hundreds of times in dozens of places throughout 1942, her roles on the Fox lot would dwindle in importance. Even her five-month voyage with the "Four Jills" to England and North Africa would earn her only one-fourth of a starring role in the black-and-white musical about the trip.

As early as June 1941, Carole had visited the central California bases, Camp Hunter Liggett and the now-defunct Fort Ord, where the soldiers gave her a puppy in appreciation; later in the year she attended the American Legion convention in Milwaukee, participated in a program at the New York Naval Training Station, and hosted soldiers and officers at dinners and parties on several occasions. Entertaining the troops and otherwise devoting herself to the Allied cause during World War II became the chief focus of Carole's energies at what would prove the high point of her life. To quote Walter Winchell, "No actress is doing more for the war effort than Carole Landis, who, in addition to her defense work, also makes personal appearances at camps. . . . Carole, probably more than any other actress in the movie capital, is bending every spare moment to the war effort . . . [and] in her wardrobe closet are two uniforms, one as Commander of the First Division of the Aerial Nurse Corps of America, the other as a Storekeeper, Third Class, in the Bundles for Bluejackets organization."

Beginning in late 1940, by which time her films and her June *Life* spread had given her a certain notoriety, Carole frequently supplied autobiographical material to movie magazines, often in the form of "told to" articles written in the first person, with or without supporting comments by the magazine professional. Although the articles include only what the principal (or her studio) wishes to tell us, we should nonetheless not read them with excessive cynicism. Just as her true self was the one Carole could not hide from the camera, so in these publicity pieces she reveals herself as both what she thought she was and what she hoped her self-depiction would make her become. Two articles referred to in the previous chapter, published in the latter part of 1941, offer complementary versions of Carole's self-awareness. The first, "What Carole Landis Demands of Men!" appeared in *Screenland* in October; the second, with the seemingly contradictory title "Glamour Girls Are Suckers," came out in *Photoplay* in December.

Despite the ostensible incompatibility between making demands and being a "sucker," the difference between the two articles is more one of pose than of substance. The first begins with the line, "MY FIRST demand . . . is that men do not make me suffer!"—an unexpected beginning unlikely to have been conceived by the Fox publicity department. We learn that Carole's subsequent list of demands—for attentiveness, considerateness, intellectual and cultural maturity—have not been met by the majority of her escorts, who were interested only in exploiting her visibility. The men she cites as exemplary: Gene Markey, Cedric Gibbons, Cesar Romero, and Franchot Tone, all described as gallant and cultivated, are also considerably older than she. Carole expresses distaste for "youth" and vows that her next husband will be at least fifteen years her senior. In reality, the oldest of Carole's four husbands was the already-divorced Willis Hunt, with a difference of eight years; of the two men she married after making this statement, Horace Schmidlapp was four years older and Tommy Wallace only one.

The curious air of sexual innocence in this text suggests that Carole had excluded from her publicly avowed persona any element of her own desire. She speaks pointedly of the importance of getting to know a man by visiting his home and dining with him there, as if in total disregard of the connotations of an attractive young woman's doing such a thing and of the gossip such activities would naturally inspire. Despite Carole's penchant for low-cut gowns, modesty was an important trait of her character; she loved to tell jokes, but according to at least one credible witness, these were never off-color, nor was she known to use foul language—in contrast to her notoriously salty-tongued namesake, Carole Lombard.

The impression left by this article is that, even if Carole knew what would be good for her, she was unlikely to follow her own advice, if only because she needed to formulate it so explicitly. Carole was intelligent and resourceful and had a charmingly persuasive personality in addition to her beauty, but these traits, which facilitated the attainment of immediate goals, only made it harder for her to acquire the self-discipline to follow a long-term plan. In a word, *Carole was all tactics and no strategy*. If this statement might be qualified with respect to her professional career, it is true without qualification of her love life. Whatever the effect of Carole's absent father on her basic emotional makeup, it was her desirability that defined her place in the world. Supremely confident of her beauty, Carole was unable to control in her own interest the desires it put into circulation.

The second article, "Glamour Girls Are Suckers," begins with an account of an unhappy love affair with an actor who was almost certainly Franchot Tone. It contains an oft-quoted passage that complements the strident line cited earlier about not ending life in a boardinghouse with a full scrapbook and an empty stomach: "Every girl in the world wants to find the right man, someone who is sympathetic and understanding and helpful and strong, someone she can love madly. Actresses are no exceptions; glamour girls are certainly no exceptions. The glamour and the tinsel, the fame and the money mean very little if there is a hurt in the heart." No doubt a star indifferent to the needs of love and family would be unlikely to say as much in a publication whose very raison d'être was to attach the reader to the "star system" by negotiating the interface between stars-as-actors and stars-as-people. But Carole's goes farther than expected in the other direction because she seems to have been qualitatively less able than most other stars to compartmentalize her personal and professional lives. Lana Turner surely suffered from her failed marriages and love affairs, but, if only for fear of Louis B. Mayer, she would be unlikely to sign her name to a paragraph like the one above.

Carole's celebrity status was all-important to her because it multiplied her ability to touch the lives of others, but at the expense of the domestic intimacy that she experienced as an always-shattered utopia rather than a genuine goal. Carole does not let us feel her pain the way we feel, or think we feel, Marilyn Monroe's, which explains why the latter is the incomparably bigger star. What we see and appreciate in the place of Marilyn's tortured self is Carole's openness to other people, even at the expense of her own well-being. Contemplating Carole's suicide, her sister wrote, "She gave so much of herself so unsparingly that when finally she needed great strength it had gone to others."

CHAPTER 6

B Actress and Patriot (1941–1942)

After completing her double assignment of *Cadet Girl* and *I Wake Up Screaming* in September 1941, Carole traveled to New York, where she stayed for a month, attending all or part of the "subway" World Series between the New York Yankees and the Brooklyn Dodgers. Carole attended the marriage of her friend Florence Heller (later Wasson) to Albert Lary on September 9 in Los Angeles, was in Milwaukee for the American Legion convention around the twentieth, and reached New York by the twenty-third. She appeared on the Eddie Cantor radio show with Joe Dimaggio on the twenty-fourth, did the town with Burgess Meredith and Tony Martin, and came down with the "flu" in the process. Carole went back to Los Angeles on October 8 to feed Donner, who "had refused to eat for a week," then returned to New York, attending a Fight for Freedom rally in Madison Square Garden on October 15. On the thirtieth, back in Los Angeles, Carole was escorted by Martin to Charlie Foy's Café.

Although, from the standpoint of stardom, the second phase of Carole's career at Fox was a year of disappointment, Carole was never kept busier, both on and off the set. Beginning in November 1941, she worked almost without a break on six films, including a loaner to Charles Rogers/United Artists.

Production on the first of these, *A Gentleman at Heart*, occupied Carole from early November until the twenty-ninth. *Gentleman*, like so many B films, had once been an A project. Dating back to 1937, it was originally titled "Masterpiece" and set in Italy; Simone Simon, Tyrone Power, Loretta Young, Henry Fonda, and Don Ameche had been thought of for the cast at one time or another before the story was moved to the United States and the B lot and assigned to Carole, along with Cesar Romero, her most frequent leading man, and her most frequent director, Ray McCarey.

If *Cadet Girl*, the beginning of Carole's "normalization," had left her in the foreground, in *Gentleman* Carole is little more than a female ornament in a masculine plot. The most obvious sign of this process is that she has become "respectable." The quasi-biographical resonance of *I Wake Up Screaming* that lent depth to Vicki's showgirl persona would be much less prominent in Carole's remaining Fox films. In *Gentleman*, all we know about Helen Mason's past is that she is a failed painter who went to work at an art gallery.

As the story goes, bookie Cesar Romero takes over a bankrupt gallery inherited by Milton Berle in payment of the latter's gambling debts. Struck by Carole's beauty, he takes interest in the gallery and gets her to teach him the rudiments of art history. Meanwhile Cesar and a master art forger, played with verve by J. Carrol Naish, concoct a plot to forge and sell a long-lost Velasquez painting. Coincidentally, a Spaniard gets Cesar to buy what he claims to be this very same painting. But when federal experts begin to examine it, it is revealed as a crude fake. In the nick of time, Naish substitutes his superior forgery and it passes the official inspection undetected. The government buys the painting from Cesar, but for less than he had paid for the supposed Spanish original.

The final sequence of the film takes place at a race track. Cesar is consoled for his loss when Berle reveals that the money given the Spaniard was just as phony as the painting. Meanwhile, in the romantic side plot, while Carole has been instructing Cesar about art, he has been teaching her about his own area of expertise. When in the final moment Carole joins Cesar and Milton at the track and begins vigorously cheering on a horse, we sense that she has put aside high-cultural snobbery for popular culture and true love; the movie ends with a kiss.

During their first encounter, Cesar tells Carole he intends to sell the gallery; Carole becomes upset at his crass materialism. But when he calms her down by expressing interest in getting the gallery back on its feet, her suspicions instantly evaporate; she asks him brightly, "You mean you're interested?" and unhesitatingly accepts his invitation to lunch. In contrast to *Dance Hall*, however, irrespective of his cynicism in seeking to profit from the sale of forged paintings, Cesar's interest in Carole never expresses itself with hostility or sarcasm. When in a rooftop scene she tells him she's fallen in love with him, far from using this confession to gain the upper hand, Cesar replies that he hasn't had the courage to tell her of his own feelings because he has placed her far above himself.

Paradoxically, however, this emphasis on Carole's transcendent status is just one more sign of her normalization. What was curious about *Dance Hall* was the film's reluctance to show, even at the end, a condition of trust between the two principals. Venus is too alluring for a stable reciprocal relationship; either the man resents her desirability and tries to humiliate her, or she suspects that he is attracted only to her body. Cesar's declarations of love may well be sincere, but how can a mortal show proper respect to Venus? In contrast, in everyday romance, the man's idealization in "putting the woman on a pedestal," as Cesar confesses to Carole in their rooftop declaration of love, is compensated by the woman's consent to share his social identity. *A Gentleman at Heart* ends as a romantic comedy should.

Gentleman received good reviews as a "very amusing, exciting and unpredictable yarn," "one of those cleverly written, smartly directed and alertly performed modest scale productions that Hollywood calls sleepers." Carole was praised for her "charming dignity" in "the most lady-like role in which she has so far appeared."

The coming of war impinged on Carole's life from day one. The grounding of all commercial aircraft following the attack on Pearl Harbor left her and Linda Darnell stranded in Los Angeles, forced to wait twelve hours before departing for a victory rally in St. Louis on December 8. On their way back the next day, their plane was grounded in Wichita, so they caught a train back to Los Angeles. It was full of soldiers and sailors delighted to find themselves eating and playing cards with two of Hollywood's loveliest stars.

Carole took the declaration of war as a call to action. She quickly assumed the responsibilities of commander of the First Division of the Aerial Nurse Corps of America, including undergoing basic nurse's training, and volunteered for work as a storekeeper (and fund-raiser) for the Bundles for Bluejackets organization that supplied extra comforts to navy personnel. At night, Carole patrolled the Santa Monica beach by her house at 703 Ocean Front (now Palisades Beach Road), where she had moved with her mother in February 1942—and where soldiers passing through the area were regularly invited for meals and weekends. Carole often joined with other Hollywood celebrities in taking groups of GIs out to dinner, or did it on her own. In March 1942, Carole was one of five Hollywood women (the others were Judy Canova, Hedda Hopper, Dorothy Lamour, and Jane Withers) commissioned as honorary colonels by Hollywood Post 43 of the American Legion. Throughout the year, Carole made several cross-country trips to entertain soldiers and sell bonds, notably, a two-week trip with USO's "Crazy Show" through Texas in late July and early August, during which she played to over thirty thousand men, among whom four thousand were in hospitals. Twice she auctioned off personal property, including a $1,500 opal ring, for the bond drive.

Carole threw herself into war work with such intensity that a number of Hollywood writers as well as Carole herself described it as a veritable conversion experience. After her return from the Four Jills tour in March 1943, a movie writer described the change Pearl Harbor had wrought in the woman he speaks of as "Body Landis": "The Cinderella was beginning then to discover that whatever it was she had that brought her a movie contract, her energy and enthusiasm added to it could mean something to the morale of a fighting man. . . . [W]hatever she had done for publicity's sake in the past, her work since has been a simple and wonderful mixture of humanity and humble patriotism."

An exemplary moment in which Carole's desirability was dedicated to the soldiers overseas provided a well-remembered incident in wartime broadcasting. In a letter dated May 4, 1942, a sailor at Pearl Harbor submitted a request to *Command Performance*, the wartime radio program broadcast exclusively to the military overseas. "The single most famous request [of the war] involved film star Carole Landis, who was requested to 'step up to the microphone and sigh. That's all brother, just sigh!'" A second letter, submitted with the first, added that "we could whip the Japs with our bare hands if [Carole] was around"; this was softened on the air to "we can win the war single-handed." And so on June 11, Carole stepped up to Don Wilson's *Command Performance* microphone and, in the words of the request, "just sighed." As an acknowledgment of the unfulfilled sexual yearnings of the soldiers overseas, Carole's sigh embodied "what they were fighting for" in the form of a biological imperative, synthesizing in a few seconds both unsatisfied female desire and its satisfaction. The sigh would become a standard element of Carole's wartime performances.

It would be an exaggeration, however, to conclude that Carole's devotion to the war effort meant an end to her intense social life. Walter Winchell's assertion, in the article quoted in the previous chapter, that Carole could no longer be found in Hollywood nightspots should be taken with a grain of salt. Throughout 1942 Carole continued nearly unabated the frenetic dating of the previous year. January saw her at night clubs with Cary Grant and Tony Martin; February, with Charlie Chaplin and "ardent" radio commentator Robert Arden; March, with Rouben Mamoulian, Anatole Litvak, Martin again, Huntington Hartford III. When Carole flew to Washington, D.C., on March 30, several newspapers erroneously claimed she was going there to marry Gene Markey, stationed there as a lieutenant commander in the navy. A Winchell column called the Markey story a "smokescreen. It's another lad"—perhaps referring to Hollywood lawyer-playboy Greg Bautzer, also in the navy at the time, whom Carole also visited in Washington.

Carole married no one, but continued dating. The list of sightings, which included such well-known playboys as "Wooley" Donohue in May and Brazilian Jorge Guinle in July, goes on through August with Arden and publicist Alan Gordon, and tapers off only in September, when Carole began preparing for her USO tour abroad. To top off her already-full plate, Carole, a loyal member of the Screen Actors Guild, served as an alternate member of its board of directors between August and October 1942.

One gets the impression that a combination of patriotic fervor and growing disappointment with her film assignments provided Carole with an unending flow of nervous energy. Although she often spoke of her need for a full night's sleep, this could hardly have been the rule during a year when she made six films in ten months along with strenuous war activities and a scarcely diminished night life. Only the illnesses contracted during her travels abroad would dull the edge of Carole's remarkable vitality.

Carole's first wartime film, the Victor Mature–Rita Hayworth vehicle *My Gal Sal*, was in production from late December 1941 to the end of February 1942 under the direction of Irving Cummings, a co-creator along with Walter Lang of the Fox Technicolor musical formula, with four Grable productions to his credit. Carole's unfortunate casting in *Sal* as the itinerant showgirl Mae Collins, her last appearance as a (strawberry) blonde until *Four Jills in a Jeep* in 1944, was also her final role in a color film.

The original screenplay, written by novelist Theodore Dreiser about his songwriter brother Paul, who Americanized his name to Dresser, does not include Carole's (fictional) character, which was added to provide a focus of conflict. Carole, billed fourth after the two principals and John Sutton, who plays Sally's producer, plays only a preliminary part in the story. The songwriter, played by Victor Mature, abandons Carole/Mae for Rita/Sally just under thirty minutes into the film. Carole is on screen for a total of less than eight minutes within an eighteen-minute segment; her role in the plot is to rescue and nurse Mature back to health after she comes upon him tarred and feathered as punishment for his involuntary association with a confidence man. Although Carole is supposed to be an itinerant fairground performer, we never see her perform, nor do we even learn of what her performance consists.

As we suspect from its unbalanced chronology, Mae's role was more important, albeit still more unflattering, in earlier versions of the screenplay. She was originally destined to reappear as a ghost from the past in Dresser's life in New York after he had become a success and gotten involved with Sally Elliott. But with each revision of the script from June through December 1941, the pages devoted to Mae's reappearance diminish, until the shooting script, dated December 22, suppresses her return altogether. Instead, Mae's sordid role of New York rival to Sally is replaced by the more elegant rivalry of an Italian countess, played by Mona Maris.

Dropping a major character for good after half an hour is not the best screenwriting practice. The motivation appears to have been to avoid contaminating Rita/Sally in her starring role with a taint from her lover's past; if Rita is not forced to confront Carole at the start of the film, why introduce such unpleasantness at the end? But although the purpose of the change was surely not to humiliate Carole, she understandably experienced it in these terms.

Although the two women never face each other, Carole's costumes, hairdo, and makeup are gaudy and cheap, as if deliberately intended to set off Rita's elegant gowns and coiffure. In Carole's final scene with Mature, she begs him pathetically not to leave her to follow Sally to New York. Although he claims to hate Sally, who has humiliated him, his desires have clearly turned in her direction; yet instead of losing gracefully, Carole taunts him by claiming that now that he's spent his savings on a faux-elegant suit he doesn't have enough money for train fare from Buffalo to New York City. In the next shot, Dresser is in New York and Mae has been forgotten.

Insofar as the press paid attention to Carole at all, it found that she "is wasted on a part much too brief for her career at this point, but plays it like a trouper." Both Carole and her fans were upset over this role, in which she is marked for the first time in her career as the lesser of two beauties. The more perspicacious among Carole's admirers could see how destructive this configuration was to her career. Although it is doubtful whether Carole could have carried off the main role with the panache of Hayworth, whose larger body type, more flamboyant style, and superior dancing ability were more suited to its costumes and overall manner (Rita didn't sing, but Nan Wynn dubbed her voice effectively, as Ben Gage did Mature's), she should have made every effort to avoid this staging of her defeat. But as the sole breadwinner in the household she maintained with her mother, she was not wont to turn down roles; she did so for the first time only in 1945, when her Fox career was coming to a close. After *Sal*, Carole asked her fans to write Fox in protest, demanding better roles for her. A number of such letters were written, but the studios were rarely sensitive to such efforts.

While Mature is recovering from his tar and feathers, he expresses doubt whether he can be of use to the troupe. Carole's reply that if he can't perform, he can always pound stakes reminds us that in *Road Show* she made John Hubbard perform this task before there was a Hayworth to rival her. That this long-lost epoch had ended not much more than a year earlier pointed up what could now clearly be seen as the strategic error of signing with Fox.

A final irony sums up Carole's participation in *My Gal Sal*. When a few months later a screen magazine asked several stars to describe their "most thrilling love scene," Carole—or more likely, the Fox publicity department—chose as her most memorable screen kiss the one with Victor Mature in this film; Mature's choice was a kiss with Rita Hayworth in the very same film.

It Happened in Flatbush, filmed in March 1942, was Carole's third movie under Ray McCarey's direction. Carole is once more the leading lady, second billed to Lloyd Nolan. On March 12, just before the start of production, Carole was declared by her doctor to be "suffering from nervous exhaustion as a result of her intense activity recently in various defense projects" and ordered to rest for a few days—Carole's fourth illness in a little over a year.

In *Flatbush* Carole wears some nice outfits and a couple of lovely hats, but what most strikes the spectator is that for the first time since her Republic days, her hair is dark. Studio publicity claimed that she herself had requested this change back to (more or less) her natural hair color, and we might take it as a sacrifice for the war effort on a par with her substitution, along with many other stars, of leg paint for stockings. But even in the unlikely case that the change was made at Carole's own request, Zanuck would not have permitted it unless he found it useful to tone down her blonde glamour-girl appearance. In keeping with Carole's more subdued look, the film offers no close-ups, very few medium close-ups, and no attention-getting lighting effects. One of Carole's more perceptive admirers reproached her with sabotaging her blonde image, which had already undergone considerable modification through changes in hairstyle— notably the tight curls and reddening in *Sal*.

Flatbush, originally entitled *Them Lovely Bums*, was intended as a celebration of the Brooklyn Dodgers' 1941 pennant—their first since 1920—and it does its best to capture the atmosphere of Brooklyn fandom. However, since the Dodgers, after due deliberation, decided against allowing the use of their name, rather than being tagged with a fictitious one, the team is simply, if lamely, called "the Brooklyn team." Nolan plays Frank Maguire, a former star whose notorious error had cost Brooklyn the pennant eight years previously, but whom the elderly owner has lured back from the minors to manage a slumping team. But on the very day Maguire arrives on the job, the owner dies and the team passes to her principal heir, Kathryn Baker, played by Carole.

In an extension of her *Gentleman* role, Carole gives a decent account of herself as a New York sophisticate. By this time she had become familiar with the city, having even attended the World Series that concluded

Brooklyn's dramatic pennant-winning season with a loss to the Yankees. Carole's obvious function in *Flatbush* is to provide it with a modicum of female beauty; she is the only attractive woman in the film. Carole's showgirl exoticism has been transferred to that of the socialite, but in either case she is tagged as belonging to an alien world. *Topper Returns* was the last time Carole would inhabit the upper-class milieu, familiar to audiences of the 1930s, that had all but vanished from Hollywood films by 1942.

As the leading lady, Carole receives the usual compliments from Nolan, but with little romantic enthusiasm. Strictly speaking, she gets the guy in the end; before the big game that will decide the pennant, Nolan gets her to promise that she'll meet him at a Manhattan restaurant at eight. But the tepid relationship between the rich society lady and the Brooklyn-bred ballplayer is lacking not only in chemistry but in narrative plausibility. As often in male-oriented B pictures, a romance is tacked onto the main plot with little concern for any anomalies thus created. *Flatbush* would surely have been a more appealing film had Nolan's romantic interest been a Brooklyn sweetheart rather than a society lady. Fox's choice of the latter suggests that a decision had been made to play down the love interest in order to keep the focus on the baseball theme. Although her character is presented as originally unfamiliar with baseball, athletic Carole made a number of publicity shots for the film swinging a bat, both with and without Nolan.

To speed up the courtship, Carole admits, in a baseball metaphor that recalls references to her sexual availability in previous films, that she has been "throwing herself" at Nolan without being "caught." Whereas in *Gentleman* Romero made up for Carole's similar declaration by the enthusiasm of his own, Nolan does nothing to assuage her humiliation. And whereas Carole's warm personal relationship with Romero contributed to making them a persuasive couple on screen, she strikes no sparks with the stolid Nolan.

In the final shot, after Brooklyn's pennant-winning victory, the men lift Nolan on their shoulders; but he slips from their grasp, and Carole, who had been watching the game from the team dugout, is right there to hold him up. Not in the original screenplay, this bizarre incident, which lasts but a second, seems an afterthought intended to provide a perfunctory closure to the principals' easily forgotten romance.

Flatbush received generally good reviews; one called it a "box-office natural," "batting 1000 percent." Similarly, Carole "does well," "displays advanced poise," and "complements persuasively" Nolan's role.

During the filming of *Orchestra Wives*, which occupied Carole throughout April and May 1942, she filed an action at Los Angeles Superior Court to change her legal name from Frances Lillian Hunt to Carole Landis; the decree was granted on April 22. Perhaps it was the contrast between Carole's celibacy and her domestic status in this movie that inspired her to purge her personal identity of the Wheelers and Hunts of the past.

Carole is billed fifth, below the title in *Wives*, which centers on the romance between George Montgomery, a trumpet player in Glenn Miller/Gene Morrison's band, and Ann Rutherford/Connie Ward, a small-town Illinois girl he meets on tour. Complementing Rutherford's ingénue, the second female lead, Lynn Bari, who never looked better, plays a sexy band singer (her voice is dubbed by Pat Friday) who out of jealousy attempts to exploit an old love affair with Montgomery. The situation is complicated by the gossip and machinations of the wives who travel with the band and give the film its title.

The screenplay, snappily turned into film by veteran Archie Mayo, serves as the pretext for a good deal of Glenn Miller music. *Wives* was only Miller's second film, following the 1941 Sonja Henie vehicle *Sun Valley Serenade*; sadly, it would prove to be his last. Miller's plane mysteriously disappeared over the English Channel in December 1944.

Carole's Natalie is the dominant personality and the cattiest of the three "orchestra wives"—the other two are played by second-string Fox ladies Virginia Gilmore (Carole/Natalie's chief rival) and Mary Beth Hughes. Aside from trading insults and even coming to blows, rivals Carole and Gilmore attempt to score points against each other by misusing highfalutin terms such as *ingénue* and *savoir-faire*. Just as several films morph Carole's desirability into a lack of resistance to men, in *Orchestra Wives* her well-attested propensity for witty wisecracks is travestied in the not quite compatible traits of cattiness and pretentiousness.

The wives' quarrels, catalyzed by Rutherford's gossip revelations, temporarily break up the band. Finally, Ann and unmarried Cesar Romero trick all the band members into coming together in one place. Carole is bought off by a diamond necklace and Gilmore with a mink coat (both charged to the surprised Miller), and the two forgive what we imagine to be their husbands' reciprocal infidelities—which the film, under strict orders from the Production Code Office not to be "sex-suggestive," does not invite us to imagine.

Thus, the band comes back together—minus Bari, whose devious attempt to persuade Rutherford of her husband's infidelity had nearly destroyed their marriage. Happily, another singer is available, a real one this time, in Betty Hutton's sister Marion, who delightfully puts over a couple of songs. The band's reconciliation, ending with a lengthy concert sequence in which the Rutherford-Montgomery couple, too, are finally reconciled, is not a mere artificial plot mechanism. As in many musicals, the harmony of the finale emerges from a ritual of discord and reunion that reminds us of the eternal function of art.

Yet even in reconciliation, Carole/Natalie remains less than likeable. She is the only one of the wives who speaks both of and to her husband in a tone of contempt, the only one who seems to enjoy not merely spreading gossip but inflicting discomfort. Rutherford is sweet; Bari is sexy; all Carole can be in this film is bitchy. There is nothing remotely resembling a glamour shot, and Carole's unspectacular outfits seem designed to show off Bari's quite attractive figure at the expense of her own.

Coming after *Gentleman* and *Flatbush*, *Orchestra Wives* is the last of three consecutive black-and-white films in which Carole plays "respectable" women. Whereas in both preceding films an upper-class background is contrasted with the less distinguished origin of the male lead, in *Wives* an undercurrent of frustrated ambition is Carole/Natalie's only mark of exceptional status. By an unintended irony, at the very time when Carole was devoting nearly every waking moment outside the studio—and occasional nightclub—to studying, patrolling, and entertaining the troops, she is given the role of a frustrated narcissist.

Reviews of *Wives* and of Carole's "catty" performance were favorable, if perfunctory; the film's real star was the Glenn Miller band. This remains all the more the case today; the 2005 DVD release was a gift to music lovers far more than to film buffs.

A recent article on *Wives* contains a revelatory account by Lynn Bari of an altercation between her and Carole on the set. Apparently, Carole "got out of line" by twice snapping her fingers at Bari when she felt that Bari was too slow with her comebacks in a comic scene. When an enraged Bari told Carole, "Don't you ever do that again!" Bari said, "[Carole] looked at me as if I had hit her. . . . she must have known what was going on because we got along fine after that. I think that in spite of her veneer, underneath Carole was quite emotional—things really got to her. Well, they must have, if she took her own life." Bari's word for Carole was "brittle."

This little incident tells us a lot about Carole. She acted impulsively and inconsiderately, and when Bari called her on it, she backed down—no doubt hurt by Bari's angry reaction and unable to defend her behavior. Carole had learned to get ahead in the world by confidently brazening her way through, yet she never ceased to suffer at the first sign of rejection. In most of her dealings with others, Carole was generous to a fault, but the overall paradox is the same: whether offering love, friendship, or aggression, Carole would imprudently thrust herself forward, leaving herself open for a painful blow.

Whereas watching Carole in any of her films through *I Wake Up Screaming* provides a revelation of beauty, the films of 1942 are increasingly unmemorable. She has been forced into the narrative mold of the B picture, where the form's typically superficial treatment of character became a means of hiding her light under a bushel. The only compensation for her secondary role in *Orchestra Wives* is that, marginally more than her previous few films, it gives Carole a chance to demonstrate her acting skills, albeit in a direction that detracts from the glamorous image established in her earlier roles. As one of her fans pointed out to her, effective acting in this part only dealt one more blow to her screen image. Yet the publicity press book for the film tells us that "Carole found it one of the most delightful [roles] she's ever enacted." And this might actually be true; acting is acting, after all.

There is a story connected with *Orchestra Wives* that shows what kind of stuff Carole was made of. The climactic concert celebrating the band's reunion is highlighted by the spectacular performance of "I Got a Gal in Kalamazoo" by Fayard and Harold Nicholas, an African American song-and-dance team famous for their acrobatics. In this sequence, one of the brothers runs up a wall, does a back-flip, and goes on dancing. Fayard Nicholas, who had recently done a commentary track with Ann Rutherford for the DVD release of *Wives*, was kind enough to speak with me in June 2005 (he died in January 2006 at the age of ninety-one). When I asked him for his recollections of Carole Landis, he related the following incident. Nicholas was stationed at Camp Van Dorn in Mississippi when Carole came to perform there on June 18, 1943. As soon as Carole, who "didn't have a prejudiced bone in her body," learned that he was there, she went over to the Negro quarters of the segregated base and brought him on stage to perform with her. A photograph showing Carole and Fayard in uniform clasping hands on stage appeared in the "Pictures to the Editors" column in *Life* on September 6, with a comment by the amateur photographer that despite "some race riot trouble" in the area—a reference to the controversial story of a massacre of black soldiers at the camp, which, while probably exaggerated, almost certainly reflected some real violence perpetrated against them—"[a] picture like this seems to show that white and colored people can get along all right, even in the deep South."

Manila Calling, produced between mid-June and the end of July, offers Carole her most appealing role of 1942 in a film where a female would normally be out of place. A reviewer remarked that Carole's great strength in *Manila* is that she doesn't get in the way of the action of this "man's film," a tribute to her unpretentiousness as well as to her acting ability. The male lead, originally slated for Pat O'Brien, went to Lloyd Nolan. *Manila* was the best of five Nolan films directed by the otherwise unremarkable Herbert Leeds, all in 1942; in 1946 Leeds would direct Carole's final Fox film, *It Shouldn't Happen to a Dog*. Like the better-known 1943 *Bataan* (in which Nolan once more plays a "soldier with a past"), *Manila*, made well before the United States had turned the tide in the Pacific, is a statement of defiance that shows the characters triumphing in defeat simply by refusing to give up.

Manila tells the story of a communications platoon that has escaped into the Philippine jungle after the Japanese took over their radio station. After recapturing a plantation from the Japanese, the platoon once again sets up their station at the behest of their leader (played by young Cornel Wilde) in order to counteract Japanese propaganda broadcasts. Lloyd Nolan's Lucky, the second in command, at first opposes this tactic, hoping to fight his way through the jungle to the coast, but he soon comes around.

Shortly after the platoon has taken over the plantation, Ralston (Lester Matthews), a neighboring plantation owner driven out by the Japanese, arrives with Carole in the role of Edna or "Eddie." Eddie is presumably Ralston's mistress (despite Production Code admonitions to the contrary) and is counting on marrying him on the sanguine assumption that his wealth will survive the Japanese invasion. As it turns out, Ralston attempts to betray the group to the Japanese, kills a soldier who discovers his treachery, and is shot as a traitor.

A former big-city telephone operator in the United States, Eddie took a similar job in Manila before becoming a dancer in a bar; her only explanation for these unusual career moves is that she "got tired of saying hello to the wrong people." She arrives in the camp, as movie heroines virtually never do, with a visible smudge on her face, a transparent metaphor of her moral state, which stays on for several minutes before she locates a mirror to wipe it off. But as we learn toward the end of the film from the dying

James Gleason, the "colorful" Irishman common in war films, like Edna, Lucky, too, is fleeing his past, one whose shame is much more specifically defined. Just as in *Flatbush* Nolan had lost a pennant for Brooklyn with a bonehead play, in *Manila* he was betrayed by a woman in Lisbon in 1931 into abandoning his post and letting the troops under his command be massacred in a riot instigated by the Germans, who wanted to take over the American "concession." (The historical reference is to the Lisbon riots of April–May 1931; the film doesn't attempt to explain this aggressive action by the German military two years before the Nazis came to power.) As a consequence, Lucky is hostile to all women, and he at first treats Carole with contempt, as do a few of the other men. But Carole gains the respect of all by tending to the wounded and generally making herself useful; we even briefly see her shooting from a window at some attacking Japanese.

Japanese ground and air power kill off the Americans and their Filipino allies one by one, until, in the last ten minutes of the film, Nolan finally begins to broadcast his message of freedom, "Manila calling!" Meanwhile, as a last chance for safety, a downed Japanese plane has been repaired by an aviator, who takes off with the wounded Wilde and, supposedly, Carole. But just as Nolan begins his broadcast, Carole returns to the radio room, telling Nolan that her "lonely, shipwrecked" feeling has vanished and that she wouldn't want to be anywhere else; he smiles and says he feels the same way. This brief, understated love scene is far more believable and affecting than anything in *Flatbush*. Nolan's unromantic persona is effective in the role of a hard-bitten soldier, and Carole successfully conveys world-weariness without cynicism.

Carole's supporting role in the couple's defiant patriotism within a soon-to-be-obliterated sanctuary makes her presence in this "man's film" strangely appropriate, as well as biographically prophetic of her tours to both theaters of war. Despite the obvious difference between a Hollywood movie star and a Manila B-girl, Edna's redemption through wartime self-sacrifice captures a significant truth about Carole herself. This little "B+" film hardly stands out among the war films of the time, yet it gives Carole her best and most appealing role of the year, one in which she was praised along with Nolan and Gleason as "unusually good." And framed by unglamorous surroundings and plain clothing, Carole's beauty is more in evidence here than in any other film of 1942.

The Powers Girl, for which Carole was loaned out to United Artists from late August to early October 1942, was Carole's last film before her departure on the Four Jills tour. It was made, with the approval of the Powers agency, under the direction of Norman Z. McLeod, one of the major comedy directors of the 1930s at Paramount, with the Marx Brothers' *Monkey Business* and *Horse Feathers* and the first two Topper films to his credit. Carole looked forward to playing this title role, originally destined for Joan Bennett (whom one source credits for persuading producer Charles Rogers to accept Carole in her place), and she is not known to have complained of it, although it was morally and even physically the most unflattering role of her career.

Anne Shirley is Ellen, a small-town schoolteacher who is dismissed when a photograph, taken by freelancer Jerry (George Murphy), of her being carried (involuntarily) across the street in a rainstorm in the arms of the town drunk appears on the cover of a New York magazine. Ellen comes to New York, where her sister Kay, played by Carole, has lived for several years, modeling cheap dresses in a bargain basement. Carole's dream has always been to become a Powers model and to be "somebody"; in her character's one authentic moment, she gives voice to the soul-destroying frustration of having worked so hard, so long, for so little fulfillment.

Ellen renounces suing Jerry's magazine for publishing her picture without permission in exchange for Jerry's promise to get Kay an interview with Powers, played by Alan Mowbray. As soon as Mowbray sees Carole, struck by her beautiful figure, he offers her a place in his training program. Carole is a great success, and in a spectacular sequence, accompanied by several real Powers models introduced by name, she is crowned "The Powers Girl of 1943" and set on the path to professional success. The film contains a "documentary" sequence that shows Carole along with four-teen real Powers models going through what we are led to assume are accurately portrayed training routines: descending a staircase carrying a tray, bending down to pick up an object from the floor and raising it over-head in a single motion, having their hair styled, and so on. Carole's choice as number one model is without irony; her triumph feels like an apotheosis.

Yet even in purely physical terms, Carole is not shown to her best advantage in this film. Once she becomes a model, she wears far too much makeup, especially lipstick, and an unattractive rolled hairdo not unlike the one worn by Lily Tomlin's telephone lady on *Saturday Night Live*. She is constantly photographed in profile, often in low-angle shots, and her face wears an irritating expression of self-regard consonant with her character's personality. As for the contrast with her sister, although Carole is the "glamorous" one, when George Murphy sees Anne in New York after spending some time with Carole, he tells her (in Carole's presence) that she is the prettier of the two. *The Powers Girl*, which of all her films most overtly puts Carole's beauty at the center of the plot, not only makes her an extremely unsympathetic figure but seems intent on caricaturing her attractiveness. The only aspect of Carole's physical presence that can't be tampered with is her figure; we understand why her body would convince Powers to admit her to his training program, but her face and charm are not allowed to attract us.

The Powers Girl returns to the root of the showgirl motif first explored in *I Wake Up Screaming*, the beautiful girl in a dead-end job who gets a chance to make her beauty her fortune; a 1943 news service article noted the sim-ilarity to Carole's own career. But the story that *Screaming* told as tragedy is repeated in *Powers* as farce. In both, success through beauty is presented as possible only at the expense of others, but the expiation that costs Vicki her life is extracted from Kay through denigration and humiliation.

Following her Powers apotheosis, Carole's screen presence is increas-ingly marginalized; there is no question here of anyone putting flowers before her portrait. Nearly every character finds a way to insult her. A friend tells Anne that she's the kind of girl men look up to, whereas Carole is the kind they look up. Nor is she even accorded the sinister dignity of the femme fatale. Seeing that Ellen is in love with Jerry, she perversely goes after him herself, keeping him out after the award ceremony instead of returning home to a surprise party she knows Ellen has prepared for her. Yet her effort to seduce Jerry succeeds momentarily only by default; Anne is clearly his true love. Carole's success in the professional world, however merited, is balanced by humiliation in the personal world—a humiliation that cannot, however, be dwelt on, lest it generate sympathy for her. The resentment of beauty that was realized in the symbolic, sacrificial murder in *I Wake Up Screaming* is realized now simply as resentment.

At the end, when Anne and Murphy marry hastily before he goes off to war, Carole is not even invited to the wedding. This film, which depicts Carole as indifferent to the war effort, was her last before her ground-breaking four-month USO trip to Bermuda, Ireland, England, and North Africa.

In this as in nearly all her films, contrary to the legend that she couldn't act, Carole was praised for her acting; even an unenthusiastic review of the film says that "in less sympathetic characterization [than Shirley, whose acting also came in for praise], Carole Landis nevertheless is well cast and her work is effective to a marked degree." But whether they praised or panned the film, the critics were opaque to the resentment motif, always a touchy subject when evaluating popular culture.

The final irony is that it was the image of Carole, the third-billed eponymous heroine, that dominated the advertising for the film, which in England was renamed *Hello, Beautiful*. One wonders how many spectators imagined that a film with this title would be so ugly, or noticed the ugliness when they saw it.

CHAPTER 7

The Gift of Beauty: Carole at War (1942–1944)

As Carole tells us in the opening pages of *Four Jills in a Jeep*, she had wanted to entertain Allied troops overseas even before Pearl Harbor. Since she was working on *The Powers Girl* in August 1942, she could not be part of the first group sent abroad, which included Al Jolson and Merle Oberon. Apparently, this first team made too many demands on its hosts and did not leave a positive impression; although Carole's book avoids criticism, columnists were less reticent. In contrast, "The Four Jills"—the film title was invented by the Fox publicity department while the ladies were still abroad and borrowed by Carole for her book—never gave themselves airs; the only thing they made a fuss about was getting as many opportunities as possible to visit the troops. Far more rough and ready than their predecessors, they were also far more successful. In 1943, *Time* called their four-month trip, including nearly two months in North Africa, where they more than once came under shelling and bombardments, "easily the biggest war-front enter-tainment hit of World War II." The Jills were the only all-female group to entertain soldiers overseas throughout the entire war.

The other three participants, Kay Francis, Martha Raye, and Mitzi Mayfair, had little to keep them in Hollywood. Kay Francis had been Warner Brothers' top leading lady—and the best-paid actress in Hollywood—as late as 1938. In part for that very reason, she fell afoul of Jack Warner and was replaced as queen of the lot by Bette Davis. Kay left Warners that year and in the early 1940s attempted a comeback, working mostly at Universal. On returning from the trip, Kay would not work again in Hollywood until 1945, when she would co-produce three *noir*-ish films for low-budget Monogram Pictures. Martha Raye had not made a movie in 1942. And although Mitzi Mayfair had considerable Broadway dancing experience, her Hollywood credentials consisted of a few Vitaphone shorts and a bit in the prologue of *Paramount on Parade* in the early 1930s. However unsatis-fying her recent roles may have been, Carole was the only one of the four with a really active film career and whose departure could reasonably be called a sacrifice—not that she saw it in those terms. As we have seen, since Pearl Harbor, the movie business took a back seat to the war effort. This long-awaited trip abroad was the natural continuation of the dozens of sorties Carole had been making to military bases near home or across the country whenever she had a few hours or days away from the studio.

The Jills left Los Angeles on about October 25, bound for New York and Bermuda, went on to Ireland via the Azores and Lisbon, and thence to England, reaching London in early November. They worked six days a week, often giving several shows a day, and socialized with young air offi-cers on their days off and during their free time—which created some ten-sions with the higher brass. Carole roomed with Mitzi, and Kay with Martha. Carole's memoir describes the paucity of creature comforts, notably the rigors of poorly heated rooms that sometimes forced the girls to cuddle up together for warmth. Unfortunately, she tells us almost nothing about the Jills' performances. The only one described in any detail is the command performance before the Queen, and even then the emphasis is more on Carole's stage fright and the girls' crash course in court etiquette than on the performance itself. The general formula they followed was that Kay served as MC, Martha sang and did stand-up comedy, Mitzi danced, and Carole did her "sigh" and sang, alone or with the others. None of these shows appear to have been recorded. According to Frank Rosato, Carole wanted an American band to play at the USO shows and obtained permission for his 156th Infantry National Guard Band to be transferred to London for that purpose.

All the Jills were laid up with health problems at one time or other during the trip. Carole had her appendix removed in England in December; in January, on the flight to Africa, she displayed symptoms of an intestinal infection. During the months spent in Morocco, Algeria, and Tunisia, the girls wore woolen underwear and witnessed bombardments at close range. In contravention of orders to stay in the safe zones to the rear of the fighting, they obtained special permission from Eisenhower himself to visit troops in the desert near the front, with Jimmy Doolittle supplying the air transportation. Life was rough in these battle zones, and the girls were all the more appreciated by boys who hadn't seen a Western woman since leaving home.

If Carole's book fails to describe her performances in detail, it is no doubt because despite her enthusiasm for entertaining the troops, her performances were not the trip's most absorbing experience. Unexpectedly, although in retrospect almost predictably, the tour became nearly from the start an occasion for romance.

Air Force captain and future major Thomas Cherry Wallace of Pasadena, California (originally from small-town Oakdale, Pennsylvania), had begun flying in the Eagle Squadron, composed of Americans who traveled to England to join the Royal Air Force before the United States entered the war. Carole's previous husband, Willis Hunt Jr., had gone abroad with the stated intention of joining this very squadron, but had he actually done so, so odd a coincidence could scarcely have passed unnoticed. Carole met Tommy in London on November 13, 1942, scarcely a week into the tour. In her book and magazine articles, including those written after their separation, Carole always spoke of the relationship as love at first sight; as she describes it, on seeing Tommy her heart went *"boom-boom-crash!"*

It has been said that Carole was always a sucker for a good-looking guy, and Wallace was handsome and dashing in his flyer's uniform, as well as a homeboy from respectable Pasadena, the other side of the Southern California tracks from San Bernardino. In the days before meeting Wallace, Carole and Mitzi had frequented a couple of American airmen who were taking advantage of a wartime flyer's brief life expectancy to bend the rules about staying on base between missions. But it was not in Carole's nature to endure a situation of privileged status. Although she surely did not plan such things consciously, her only way of maintaining a reciprocal relationship in the face of her own desirability was to desire as well, as if she were in competition with her admirer to admire him first.

As Carole describes her first exchange with Tommy, her service lighter had lost its "wings," and Tommy offered her his own lighter, proud to be exchanging it for that of a celebrity. Each gained from this exchange a token of the prestige of the other; at the same time, Carole's behavior was explicitly designed to allay Wallace's cynicism at dealing with a "snooty movie actress." Thus, when she was obliged to break her first date with him after being corralled by officers of higher rank, she was particularly anxious to forestall any possible impression of snobbery. The affair may have begun with *boom-boom-crash!* but it was reinforced or "crystallized" by her near-panic at the potential intrusion of asymmetry into a desperately needed haven of reciprocity. While she was singing and joking with the boys in this newly demanding but emotionally limited context, her new love added an element of vulnerability to her life that compensated for the one-to-many configuration of her performances.

Carole was aware that the sacrifices she was making were negligible beside those of the airmen she was entertaining. In an article written after her trip, she tells of a letter she received from the mother of a boy who was killed in action. The mother spoke of a letter from her son "written on the night of the day you girls were at his station. He said how swell you were to him, how many laughs you gave him, how good he felt because you had been there. A few days later I was notified by the War Department that he was gone. 'Killed In Action.' . . . I want you to know that you made his last hours happy ones and that, for me, the pain is a little easier to bear because I think he must have gone out with a smile on his face." On returning from England, Carole claims to have made 162 calls to the loved ones of the boys she met overseas, proud to have become through her marriage one of the loved ones herself.

Marriage was the only way to dissolve permanently the asymmetry of Carole's budding relationship with Tommy. It took him only a few weeks to persuade her to marry him, and after her recovery from appendicitis in late December, the couple raced around London obtaining authorizations and dispensations, including the Catholic Church's permission for Carole to have a church wedding, her previous marriages having been exclusively civil. They had hoped for a holiday wedding on January 1 but had to settle for the fifth, the day before Carole and the other Jills were to leave for North Africa.

The marriage took place at the Church of Our Lady of the Assumption and St. Gregory in the City of Westminster, Fathers Waterkeyn and Peter Harris presiding. Army Colonel Schullinger, the surgeon who had removed Carole's appendix, gave Carole away, Mitzi and Kay served as witnesses, and Mitzi also accompanied Carole down the aisle as her maid of honor. After the wedding night, Carole took the train to her embarkation point. As luck would have it, the flight to Africa was delayed for a day, and Tommy was able to join Carole for a few additional hours before departure. The couple's real honeymoon took place after Carole's return from North Africa: a few days in a boardinghouse near Tommy's airfield in England.

Carole's return to Hollywood on March 8, 1943, via Brazil and New York, was greeted with considerable fanfare; her tour and her marriage had captured Hollywood's imagination. Articles appeared in movie magazines with such titles as "I'm Glad I'm a Fighting Man's Sweetheart," "The Courage of Carole Landis," "All That a Woman Loves: Carole Landis' Wartime Romance," "Carole Landis, Fighting War Bride," "My Wartime Honeymoon," "A Heroine Comes Home!" "Carole Landis: Movie Star Finds Happiness in War Marriage," "Carole Landis' War Diary."

Carole's increased prestige may have played a part in her selection in mid-March to the New York Fashion Academy list of the year's fourteen best-dressed women in the highly competitive screen category. In an interview, Carole kidded that she was glad the academy hadn't seen her in Tunisia in her long underwear. As proof that the award was no fluke, Carole returned to the list in 1945, this time representing the stage, thanks to her starring role in the Broadway musical *A Lady Says Yes*. Carole was also chosen as Best Dressed Woman of the Month by *Motion Picture* magazine in September 1943 and May 1944. She had modeled clothes since soon after coming to Hollywood, and even when her Hollywood career slowed down, she continued to appear in movie magazine fashion sequences.

A number of articles described Carole's war-widow existence in her beach house in Santa Monica, where she and her mother continued to entertain groups of GIs, giving them dinner and putting them up for the night. Carole was portrayed in *Look* on June 29, 1943, as "[hanging] her happiness on letters from her husband"; the spread shows Carole writing a letter to Tommy decorated with little romantic drawings of herself and her "heart." Just another publicity stunt, Hedda would later say, but in Carole's case there was no inherent insincerity in exposing details of her private life to the press. Carole's problem was not insincerity; it was that in the absence of her husband, her private life really could not be distinguished from a movie-magazine fantasy. Carole's self-confidence and charisma made it easy to communicate her experiences to others. Had she lived longer, she might have found a way to create a space of intimacy closed off from the world, if only to shield others in her private life from the Hollywood publicity in which she herself saw nothing problematic.

Carole's emotional attachment to Tommy gave her no reason to rein in her patriotic activity. She became a regular at the Hollywood Canteen, which Bette Davis and John Garfield had founded in October 1942 as a West Coast version of New York's highly successful Stage Door Canteen. In June, she went on a three-week tour of the southern states, during which occurred the incident with Fayard Nicholas described in the preceding chapter; this was followed by a trip to northern California. On July 15, Carole not only christened a Liberty Ship at the California Shipbuilding docks in Wilmington but gave bond talks to all three shifts. After leaving for New York in mid-July to meet Tommy—whose arrival was delayed until the last days of August—Carole spoke at bond rallies in New York, played the Adams Theater in Newark, and on September 8 sang at the Harvest Moon Ball in Madison Square Garden while Tommy slept. On January 4, 1944, back in New York after filming *Four Jills in a Jeep*, Carole made a memorable appearance at a bond rally in the financial district:

> Former Governor Alfred E. Smith's three-day campaign to enlist the 20,000 [war-bond] salesmen moved yesterday into the financial district, where Carole Landis, movie star, addressed a crowd of several hundred who braved cold rain to hear and see her.
>
> "You can't stop a war for the weather. The boys over there don't," said Miss Landis. . . .
>
> "If every person in Manhattan could spend one hour at the scene of actual fighting, Al Smith would have 20,000 bond salesmen applying every hour," she said. Before passing out the pledge cards, Miss Landis, standing under a dripping umbrella, sang the "Oklahoma" hit, "Oh, What a Beautiful Morning."

Meanwhile, Carole's career in Hollywood proceeded with little advantage from the deluge of favorable publicity. Now, if ever, was the time for Carole to hold out for a starring role in an A picture that would move her career to a higher level. But Carole had earned no money overseas, and her mother's riveter salary at North American Aviation—a job Clara was to perform for over a year with only two days' absence for illness—could not meet the family's expenses. Carole's "trouper" attitude that made her take whatever was handed to her without regard to career strategy, coupled with Zanuck's evident disinclination to give her a leading role in an A film, made Carole's position at Fox on return to Hollywood less auspicious still than on her departure, when she was at least in constant demand for B pictures.

It was reported that rather than await a starring role designed for her, on returning from abroad Carole asked for the first available assignment. As a result, she found herself in *Wintertime*, a run-of-the-mill skating musical, Sonja Henie's last Fox film. Originally planned for color, *Wintertime* was shot in black and white over a four-month period, from March to July 1943. It involved background shooting in Quebec and Sun Valley, Idaho, and appears to have been delayed when a photographer fell ill and Sonja's original skating partner was drafted. *Wintertime* was the only musical directed to completion by John Brahm, who had been dismissed from *Orchestra Wives* the year before. Brahm is best remembered for *The Lodger* (1944) and *Hangover Square* (1945), two atmospheric dramas starring Laird Cregar in his final roles, and for his Chandler adaptation *The Brasher Doubloon* (1947); in the 1950s he became a prolific television director.

If Carole's role in *The Powers Girl* had been hateful, her fourth-billed *Wintertime* role of Flossie Fouchère, the band singer who sings a half-length song before star Henie arrives, is comically pathetic. Perhaps coincidentally, it was at the moment of Carole's greatest public prestige that she attained this nadir of narrative status; her three remaining films at Fox would give her higher billing and treat her screen persona with more respect.

The complex plot of *Wintertime* involves Carole only peripherally and need not be summarized in great detail. While Henie/Nora, a Norwegian ice skater, is working through her love affair with Cornel Wilde/Freddy Austin, the handsome co-owner of a rundown Quebec hotel at which she and her wealthy father (played by veteran Hungarian character actor S. Z. "Cuddles" Sakall) have been tricked into staying, the hotel owners work on Sakall to get him to invest his money in the place. But the Nazis have invaded Norway and all bank deposits are frozen. Nora can earn the money by starring in an ice show in New York, but she cannot enter the United States unless she marries an American citizen. For a moment Carole's singing partner Cesar Romero/Brad Barton thinks he is the one, but Henie eventually returns to Wilde and all ends well.

While Romero, with whom Carole sings "I Like It Here" in the opening sequence, keeps trying to exercise his imagined powers of seduction on Henie, Carole is constantly throwing herself at him. When Cesar offers to go tobogganing with her, Carole once more instantaneously switches from suspicion to grateful acceptance—only to be dumped unceremoniously when he gets a chance to take Henie instead. She succeeds in snagging him at the end only by bopping him on the head with a brick and carrying him off in the sled in which he was waiting to elope with Henie; we assume he will settle for Carole in her place.

In the course of the film, Carole/Flossie directs a couple of pitiable allusions to her "theatrical career" at the producer who will sponsor Henie's shows in New York, to which his sole response is a cutting exit line. In her most sympathetic moment, Carole gives Henie, jealous of Wilde's attentions to a pretty journalist, a few words of wisdom concerning love; but, all in all, Carole isn't really a sidekick, merely a bit of comic relief.

Henie being the glamour girl in this picture, Carole scarcely gets even a medium shot after the opening sequence. Yet the comic duo of Cesar and Carole, in their fourth and last film pairing, adds an endearing spark to the film. Reviews were tepid overall, but Carole received a few compliments for the opening duet with Cesar and was said to "click" as his pursuer.

Of all the Hollywood performers of her generation, Carole was probably the most drawn to autobiographical writing; none of the hundreds of other USO wartime travelers thought to turn their experiences into a book-length memoir. Carole began writing *Four Jills in a Jeep* shortly after her return in March 1943 and worked on it through the summer in her Santa Monica beach house while waiting for Tommy to come home on leave—their meeting in New York, where Carole had flown in anticipation on about July 22, would not take place until September. The book begins as a dutiful response to an aviation officer's pre-trip gift of a blank military diary bearing the title "My Life in the Service" and whose prefatory remarks read: "Your experiences in the armed forces of your country are your part of living history. Keep a diary! . . . This book, conscientiously kept, may prove to be the living record of your destiny five hundred years from now" (viii). Carole ends her own preface with this: "Oh, unknown historian five hundred years from now! Here is 'the living record' of five wonderful months of my destiny."

Four Jills in a Jeep tells of more than Carole's wartime romance, but had it not been for this romance it would doubtless never have been written. The whirlwind courtship, wedding, and concluding brief honeymoon provide the narrative's structure and focus. But Carole's love story does more than furnish *Four Jills in a Jeep* with a diegetic framework; it makes the book her personal *In Search of Lost Time*, a modest, flippant, ghost-(re)written tale of her love story as summing up the tour and, indeed, her entire life.

The little volume, which began in anticipation of an act of public service, then turned via the "diary" toward personal experience as the stuff of history, ends with a one-page coda dedicated to the love that Carole hoped would give her existence its definitive meaning. She begins it, poignantly, with the phrase, "This story will have nothing but happy endings," then turns discreetly to the couple's brief honeymoon on Carole's return from Africa, in a little inn in the British countryside. Their room had two beds, one tall and one short, and when the proprietress came to do their room, she was taken aback to observe that the couple had used only one of them. Her reaction supplies the book with its final words: " 'My goodness!' she said. 'But then, you arc young people' " (180). This remembrance of young love concludes Carole's most sustained attempt to give her life the significance of a well-constructed narrative.

Although Carole liked to take full credit for the book, despite her well-earned reputation for wit and a way with words, even a well-read high-school dropout is unlikely to craft such a sentence as, "She was a stout, dumpy, gray-haired, apple-cheeked little character out of Dickens" (180). And sure enough, the *New York Times* reported on December 10, 1943, that writer and publishing executive "Edwin Seaver, who in addition to his Book-of-the Month club activities is at present compiling a 300,000-word anthology of new American writing, . . . has found time to 'ghost-write' Carole Landis' story of her overseas adventures, *Four Jills in a Jeep*."

This would seem to settle the matter, save for a conversation between Carole and Broadway columnist Earl Wilson, which is also of interest as a portrait of Carole's public personality (although we should take the quotation marks with a grain of salt):

I interrogated [Carole] about a series of articles she'd allegedly written called "Four Jills In a Jeep." The *Saturday Evening Post* ran the series, which was the tale of her USO adventures, but, as always happens, a rumor of the very nastiest kind floated around to the effect that Miss Landis had no more written it than Doc Cook had discovered the North Pole. Always enjoying asking a glamour doll an embarrassing question, I said to Miss Landis, "As one writer to another, did you write about that or did some-body ghost it? There's a rumor around that it was ghosted."

"That's a lot of phony baloney," retorted Miss Landis, showing, what shall we say, her il-literary side.

"The studio gave me two ghost writers but they stunk it all up," continued the author. . . . "I finally decided to talk it to a stenotypist. Naturally with some scotch and soda under my belt. Yes, it was very droll. I'd go out to the kitchen and sneak a drink, and come back again with a lot of new inspirations. I had too many swear words, like hell, damn, and Christ in it. Edwin Seaver, the writer, whom I know, went over it, and he said, 'I think this part stinks,' or 'I think this part is strictly from Dixie,' and I cut a lot out. But I sweated it out and wrote it, let's face it."

Since Wilson refers to the abridged *Saturday Evening Post* series, which ran from December 18, 1943, through January 15, 1944, rather than the book version that appeared in March, we can place this conversation during Carole's trip to New York in January 1944. Even if we may be fairly certain that Carole is understating Seaver's role, the fact that she freely offers his name gives us some assurance of her veracity. It is certainly possible that when Carole traveled to New York in July to rejoin her husband, she brought a draft of the manuscript for Seaver to look over, and she may have continued to work on it while he touched up her sentences and advised her on which parts "stank."

A corroborating piece of evidence is the text of an interview with film journalist Marjorie Adams of the *Boston Globe* found in Carole's personal collection. The text bears no date, but Carole's references to her future work on Broadway in *A Lady Says Yes*, which opened in Philadelphia on December 4 and on Broadway on January 10, 1945, allows us to date it during the last months of 1944. With respect to *Four Jills*, Carole says, "First I tried a couple of 'ghost writers' who did their own version of my experiences, and which were untrue and had little to do with my personality. . . . Then I tried to type the stuff myself—and got nowhere. But when I obtained a typist, and talked my stuff to her, things worked out beautifully. It is true I'd have to have a couple of friends along, so I could talk without having the embarrassment of looking at a cold and uncompromising typewriter." Here the presence of friends has replaced the need for alcohol, and Seaver (one of the "friends"?) goes unmentioned; but the stories are broadly compatible, and highly professional Adams is a more solid guarantee of Carole's veracity than sensationalistic Wilson.

Cohering only weakly when its romantic story line is unavailable, Carole's book is full of little anecdotes: Carole trying to meet the baggage weight requirement before leaving for Bermuda; the girls averting a fight

Carole Landis publicity portrait, 1940.

A 1944 photograph, signed by U.S. Marines. Courtesy of Walter Ross.

A wartime pinup, from *Soldier* (8 June 1946).

The birth certificate of Frances Lillian Ridste (later known as Carole Landis), born on 2 January 1919.

Carole as a hula dancer, c. 1936. Courtesy of Walter Ross.

Carole starting out in Hollywood, c. 1938. Courtesy of Gwen Serna.

Carole with fiancé Busby Berkeley, 1938. Courtesy of Walter Ross.

Carole with John Wayne, in *Three Texas Steers* (1939), her first leading role. Courtesy of Walter Ross.

From left to right: Carole, her brother Lawrence, his wife Helen, unidentified crew member, and Carole's mother Clara, on the set of *One Million B.C.* (1940). Courtesy of Lyn and Henry Saye.

Carole as Loana in *One Million B.C.* (1940). Courtesy of Gwen Serna.

Carole with husband Willis Hunt on July 5, 1940, shortly after their wedding.

Carole with Joan Blondell in *Topper Returns* (1940).

Carole on the town with Gene Markey, 1941.

Lobby card from *Moon over Miami* (1941).

Carole at Twentieth Century-Fox
studios with Robert Cummings
and Charlotte Greenwood, 1941.
Courtesy of Gwen Serna.

Carole with admirers, in *I Wake Up Screaming* (1941). Courtesy of Gwen Serna.

Classic sweater girl pinup, 1941.

Singing for the boys in *Cadet Girl* (1941).

Carole with U.S. troops at Fort Ord, June 1941.

Carole with Cesar Romero,
collecting relief food, 1942.
Courtesy of Gwen Serna.

Carole with Lloyd Nolan in
It Happened in Flatbush (1942).
Courtesy of Gwen Serna.

Carole with monkey, in
Manila Calling (1942).
Courtesy of Gwen Serna.

Carole visiting the wounded in England, 1942.
Courtesy of Gwen Serna.

Carole with husband Capt. Thomas Wallace,
January 5, 1943.

Carole with tap dancer Fayard Nicholas
in Mississippi, June 1943.

Carole on the air with Robert Young, 1943. Courtesy of Gwen Serna.

Carole's best-known ad, for Chesterfield cigarettes, 1944.

The four Jills, from left to right: Mitzi Mayfair, Kay Francis, Carole, and Martha Raye, in a publicity photo for *Four Jills in a Jeep* (1944). Courtesy of Gwen Serna.

Carole with Jimmy Starr, 1944. Courtesy of
Gwen Serna.

Carole on tour in the South Pacific. From
left to right: Carole, unidentified officer,
June Bruner, Jack Benny, Martha Tilton,
and Larry Adler, 1944. Courtesy of Gwen
Serna.

Carole singing on stage in her butterfly dress,
1944. Courtesy of Gwen Serna.

Carole with fiancé Horace Schmidlapp at El Morocco, 1945.

Carole with Rex Harrison in London, c. 1947.

Carole with Ruth Nixon in *Noose* (1948). Courtesy of Gwen Serna.

Star Record imprinted with
Carole's autograph. July 2, 1948.

over their attentions between American and Canadian soldiers; the airmen burning the names of bombarded French and German cities into the ceiling; Mitzi forgetting her pants just before the command performance; the girls watching German bombs and bombers fall from the sky over Algiers. There is also the oft-repeated tale of the soldier at a North African show who, when at the conclusion of her performance Carole opens her arms to the audience, calls from the rear, "I can't stand it!"

Four Jills is also the source of a wartime anecdote commonly told of Carole. When the Jills are having their routines okayed for the command performance, Martha proposes what she calls "Kay's Lana Turner story": "There was a little English sailor who cut in on Lana Turner at a dance and asked her what kind of dress she was wearing. 'Oh, it's just a dress,' she said. 'I know,' he said, 'but what do you call that neckline?' She said, 'It's a V neckline.' He said, 'Sure, I know, V for victory,' and she said, 'Yes, but the bundles aren't for Britain.'" But just as hapless Marie Antoinette became the butt of the story told, well before the Revolution, in Rousseau's *Confessions* of a nameless princess who responded to the crowd's complaints of lack of bread with "*Qu'ils mangent de la brioche!*" or "Let them eat cake!" so, beginning with an Earl Wilson column on July 8, 1948, Carole became the heroine of this one, which her book tells at third hand about someone else—and which most likely took place only in a jokester's imagination.

A final point about Carole's book is worth making; although the truth is available in such reliable sources as the American Film Institute catalog, capsule accounts of Carole's career often state erroneously that the Fox film *Four Jills in a Jeep*, which began production in October 1943, was based on Carole's book. In fact, not only was the title itself created by the studio and borrowed by Carole, but the screenplay of the film was written by a team of Fox writers, including Fred Niblo and Froma Sand, on consultation with Mitzi Mayfair (whose contribution was already anticipated in February 1943) and Kay Francis, but not Carole. Although it deals with the same overall series of events, its choice of which of these to recount is very different from Carole's, and there is scarcely a trace in the film of the many hardships occasioned by the cold and lack of amenities that Carole lightheartedly describes in her book.

After appearing in a photo-illustrated and abridged form in the *Saturday Evening Post*, *Four Jills in a Jeep* was published by Random House in March 1944; it sold briskly. A Tower Books edition appeared later in the year that included photographs from the film, which had also come out in March in a coordinated release. Lucy Greenbaum, reviewing the book for the *New York Times* on June 4, 1944, is sympathetic to the descriptions of the Jills' interactions with the fighting men, noting that "the book brings the reader up close to the soldiers"; but, missing Carole's main point, Greenbaum says not a word about her love story.

When Fox finally got around to making a picture about the Four Jills, it would be a mishmash of canned musical material and facile comedy that would do nothing for the reputations of the women whose courage it was presumably designed to commemorate. Filming took place between mid-October and early December 1943; on the fourteenth, the director, William Seiter, threw an end-of-production party for the cast. Seiter, who directed a total of 132 movies in a career that began in 1915, was a prolific maker of comedies, including *Miami* precursor *Three Blind Mice* (1938) and the Ava Gardner vehicle *One Touch of Venus* (1948); his musical credits included the Astaire-Hayworth *You Were Never Lovelier* (1942). But one can hardly blame a studio-era director for the material the producer imposes on him.

Four Jills has a great deal of difficulty keeping focus on its principals, whose names—Carole is second billed after Kay—don't even appear above the title. Although the film was originally conceived as a musical vehicle for the Jills, their roles were pared in the course of production so that Fox could promote those it considered its more bankable performers. Nearly half the ninety minutes is taken up by musical performances, mostly by performers unconnected with the tour. The videotape is often sold as "starring" Betty Grable, who opens the film in close-up under full-bore lighting singing "Cuddle up a Little Closer." Grable is the only performer in the opening sequence, a *Command Performance* broadcast emceed by Kay Francis that begins after the other Jills have left the stage. Comparable techniques of enhancement are used in another *Command Performance* insert halfway through the film that features Alice Faye singing her wartime favorite, "You'll Never Know," Carmen Miranda in a costume number, and some terrible jokes from George Jessel.

The Jills display their talents in only one sequence, a luxurious show for servicemen in London that is staged more like a Hollywood musical than a USO performance. During this scene, again emceed by Francis, Martha Raye performs "Mr. Paganini" and Mitzi Mayfair dances both solo and with a female ensemble. An additional segment had Carole singing the catchy if unmelodic "You Don't Miss a Trick" in her sheer white "whisper dress" while weaving around a chorus of a half-dozen soldiers. This would have been Carole's most glamorous moment in the film, but it was cut from the final version, as were several other musical numbers performed by the Jills: "The Old Army Game" and "A Wing and a Prayer," sung by Raye with backup from Carole and Mitzi, and Raye leading an audience in "Silent Night." Carole's one remaining song occurs at the very end of the film and lasts only half as long as Grable's. Yet there are three songs from crooner Dick Haymes, and even Phil Silvers, the girls' (fictional) wise-cracking jeep driver, is featured in a clarinet sequence that seems modeled on Jack Benny's familiar violin shtick. On express orders from Zanuck, the film also supplies romances for the other three Jills to prevent Carole's—the only one with a basis in fact— from standing out; it only stops short of presenting other marriages.

The film gives very little of the flavor of the tour. Even the scenes that have some resemblance to reality are largely spoiled by flippant comedy and lack of development; we seem to be rushing through the narrative sequences to get to the music. The resulting film is neither documentary nor fiction, neither musical nor comedy nor drama, and certainly not a credible synthesis of these genres.

The critics savaged the film. Most, like the reviewer for the *Los Angeles Times*, whose article was titled "*Four Jills* Tumbles Down Hill," panned it as unworthy of its protagonists, but the dean of the East Coast film reviewers, the *New York Times'* Bosley Crowther, calling the film "Four Pills in a Peep," reproached the four women with coming home to boast about their actions and came close to denouncing the tour itself as no more than a publicity stunt:

> . . . merely a mediocre hodge-podge of undistinguished song and dance, coupled with some nauseating nonsense about the girls' incidental heart affairs. The entertaining they do appears mainly of a personal and self-indulgent sort. The principal intention of this picture seems to be a glorification of the dames.
>
> We don't mean to question the motives of these four ladies—or of any of the Hollywood folks—when they take time out from their labors to go on a USO tour. No doubt they are fired with generous spirit and a real desire to entertain the boys. But it does cause a fellow to wonder, when they hop right home, as some of them do, and make a moving picture all about it to tell the folks what a wonderful thing they've done.

This unfair and tasteless criticism is a not atypical example of East Coast journalism's contemptuous hostility to Hollywood in the days before transcontinental travel became commonplace. The Jills were in no way to blame for the studio's attempt to cash in on their achievement, not to speak of its own poor taste in loading the film with footage of stars who had never gone abroad. Carole, whose book shared the title of the film and was inevitably described as its originator, undoubtedly suffered the most of the four from this unfair criticism.

Even aside from the extraneous material and bad reviews, *Four Jills* was not a very good publicity vehicle for Carole. Despite her return to blonde hair, unflattering lighting and makeup combine to diminish her attractiveness. When Carole finally sings "Crazy Me" in North Africa just before the film ends, she is garishly lit from above by the soldiers' flashlights, the stage lights having been killed by a blackout—as if even flashlights would be allowed during a blackout. The scene's saving grace is that, in the words of hostile reviewer Crowther, it is the only such sequence in the movie "which rings remotely true." *Four Jills* marked the beginning of Carole's estrangement from Fox that would lead to her departure two years later. Only two more Fox films figure among the eight Carole would make during the remainder of her career.

Along with Fox's commercial feature, the army intended to produce for its own use a short film reproducing one of the Jills' performances. Although this film does not appear to have been completed, there exists a delightful clip of the three younger ladies (without Kay) singing and dancing the "SNAFU" song on stage; it is perhaps the most charming of Carole's filmed performances. The song plays on the "mystery" of the not-so-mysterious obscene meaning of the classic World War II acronym ("Situation Normal, All Fouled Up"). The girls' routine displays the energy, warmth, and humor with which the three worked together. They dance wildly, deliberately bump into each other, and the two others pull Carole back when she gets too much into her "sexy" dance routine. It is reflective of Fox's lack of spontaneity that this little number is far more entertaining than any of the musical sequences in *Four Jills*.

In December 1943, Carole moved from her Santa Monica beach house, where she had kept a vigil for Tommy, to the Sunset Towers apartments just above the Sunset Strip. This move back to the madding crowd of Hollywood—and to the same complex as her ex-husband Willis Hunt, with whom (and his new wife) she dined on January 14, 1944—emblematized, if not the end of her marriage, at least the end of the illusion that it could fill her life.

In January 1944, Carole made a couple of pilots as the hostess of a GI talent show for CBS radio called *Recreation Hall*. CBS wanted Carole to do the series, but Fox, although willing to lend Carole out for films, was unwilling to accommodate the broadcaster's terms. After an exchange of correspondence, the project was dropped in early April. A day or two later, on April 11, Carole appeared on *Duffy's Tavern*, where she briefly but effectively conveyed, in the face of Archie/Ed Gardner's uneasily dismissive humor, the wartime message that women can do any job that men can do and, in particular, that *she* could do anything *he* could do.

Secret Command, originally entitled *Pilebuck*, based on a series on stateside sabotage published in the *Saturday Evening Post*, was in production from January 17 to March 8, 1944. It was the first and only achievement of Terneen Productions, a company set up by Pat O'Brien and Phil Ryan, whose name combines those of two of Pat's children, Terence and Mavourneen; the distributor was Columbia Pictures. O'Brien, in praise of whose generosity and good character Carole published an article in the November 1944 *Movieland* entitled "My Pal Pat," saw Carole as a friend rather than a pin-up. Having befriended her back in her Warner days (she liked to recall her one line in his 1938 *Women are Like That*), as producer and lead actor in *Secret Command* he gave her a unique opportunity to display emotion on screen. As a noteworthy sign of respect for Carole's character, for the first time since her days with Roach she is allowed a transition between refusal and acceptance of male advances. On Pat's first kiss, she slaps him; on the second, she rushes to her room and slams the door; the third seals their intention to marry.

Along with Pat, Edward Sutherland, the British-born veteran who also directed Carole's (and Pat's) next film, *Having Wonderful Crime*, deserves a good part of the credit for this respectful treatment. Sutherland, said to be the one director who could get along with W. C. Fields, had both the personal distinction of having been married for two years to the legendary Louise Brooks and the professional distinction of guiding two of Carole's most effective performances. Less than four years later, Sutherland and Pat O'Brien would be among Carole's pallbearers.

The action of *Secret Command* takes place in a shipyard where Pat has been sent as an undercover federal agent to ferret out a Nazi sabotage ring. Carole, also a government agent, plays his "cover" wife; the family is rounded out with two orphaned children from Europe, whose accents are explained as the result of being brought up abroad. The espionage aspect of the film is treated rather casually; that Pat's former girlfriend, played by Ruth Warrick, is able to trick Pat and Carole into giving different answers to the simple question of where they were married (Pat says London; Carole says Paris) suggests that these secret agents (or the screenwriters who created them) were not very well prepared for their mission. Carole's emotional reaction to being forced to kill a Nazi spy who was attempting to abduct her is one of the film's finer touches; she gives a convincing picture of someone eager to do her job, yet not a hardened professional.

The conclusion of this film has a special poignancy. By the end of their mission, both Carole and Pat have become attached to the children, and the couple intend to adopt them in the context of their forthcoming marriage, prolonging in reality the family set up for purposes of deception. This is the closest Carole would come to having children on the screen.

No doubt Carole is a bit too glamorous for her role of housewife, but her beauty is neither foregrounded as in *Miami* or *Dance Hall* nor sabotaged as in *The Powers Girl* or *Wintertime*. Although she is still a bit drawn and underweight, she looks considerably better here than in *Four Jills*, and she is shot in a far more flattering manner, including a few well-chosen close-ups at emotional moments. The film garnered her first-rate reviews; the *Los Angeles Examiner* called her a "natural in the assignment," and *The Hollywood Reporter* had good reason to call her performance "in many respects . . . the best of her career."

Although it was made at a different studio, *Having Wonderful Crime*, in which Carole gives her most delightful performance, was in several respects a follow-up to *Secret Command*. It was shot between April and June 1944 (but released only in April 1945); production included a location trip to Northern California in May when Carole, taking time to entertain the boys at Camp Hunter Liggett, once more fell ill with the "flu" and collapsed on the set. Pat O'Brien had been scheduled to star in *Having Wonderful Crime* at RKO in late 1943 with Richard Wallace as director. But after working with Eddie Sutherland at Columbia in *Secret Command*, Pat appears to have

persuaded RKO to use him instead of Wallace; Sutherland was not attached
to any studio and worked at RKO as well as Warner Brothers, Universal, and
Paramount. As for Carole, Fox had no assignments for her and was quite
willing to lend her out once more.

Crime is nominally based on a novel of the same name by Craig Rice
(aka Georgianna Craig), a quasi-celebrity comic mystery writer, but only
the characters are borrowed from the novel, which has a entirely different,
gruesome plot about a body separated from its head. Helene Justus, Carole's
character, is part of a non-romantic triangle with her just-married husband, Jake, played by George Murphy, and lawyer Michael Malone, played
by O'Brien, whose legal cases the meddlesome Justus couple is always trying
to "solve." The film opens in Malone's office with Carole nervously holding a gun on a shady suspect. In the book, Helene is described by her husband as "the most beautiful blonde I ever saw"; for the first time since *Cadet
Girl* in 1941, Carole is made up and costumed, lighted and photographed
in such a way as to emphasize rather than diminish her beauty. Nothing
is left of her tired, drawn look in *Four Jills*, and Carole has clearly put back
a few pounds even since *Secret Command* just two months earlier. Having
aged a few years since achieving stardom in 1940 and '41, what Carole
has lost in youthful éclat she has gained in womanly presence. All in all,
Carole was never lovelier than in this film, whose attractive costumes
provided the material for several of her most widely distributed series of
photographs.

The comic heroine of *Having Wonderful Crime* is neither the hard-edged
Carole of her previous comic lead in *Road Show* nor the quasi-ingénue of
Topper Returns. Carole plays a ditzy dame whose subtle but significant difference from the heroines of screwball comedy proper is that her narcis-
sism is serene rather than obsessive. This trait is manifested with panache
near the beginning of the film when Carole, flanked by her two male side-
kicks, enters a theater wearing a large hat. On taking her seat, she immediately asks the woman in front of her to remove her much smaller hat,
while blithely keeping hers on to the discomfiture of those behind her. What

makes this scene comic instead of irritating is Carole's utter unawareness that she is violating the golden rule; she is not so much thoughtless or indifferent as sublimely oblivious.

It is not worthwhile to summarize the confusing plot of this murder-comedy in great detail. A stage magician disappears and is later murdered. His male and female assistants, who are in love, are suspected, but in the end we discover that the real villain is the manager of the resort hotel where all the principals are staying. The resort is owned by two elderly sisters, and the manager had been offered $10,000 by one of the sisters to recover a $50,000 check written by the other to pay for the magician's entertainment, a fee that in 1944 must have appeared wildly excessive. Preparing his final triumph, the manager locks Pat in the magician's trunk and throws it in the lake, then ties up George and Carole in the cabin of his boat, into which he pipes the motor exhaust in order to fake a double suicide. But magicians' trunks have false bottoms; Pat escapes and frees his friends, and the villain is brought to justice.

The subtext of the adventure (the need to dissimulate this subtext was the subject of a lengthy correspondence with the Production Code Office) is that George and Carole are newlyweds who are never alone long enough to consummate their marriage—the obvious explanation for the tears we see Carole shed one night. Since the trio seems to have been together for a while, one wonders what relationship Jake and Helene, whose teamwork with the reluctant O'Brien/Malone is revealed in the opening sequence as all too well known to the police, were supposed to have had the day before the action started.

The critics weren't particularly kind to this silly comedy, but Carole, billed third, got the best reviews and deserved them. Even more than *Turnabout*, this film offers her the opportunity to display both her considerable talent for verbal and physical comedy and the natural charisma of her personality, for once allowed to be not merely beautiful but sweet. Carole is able to say all kinds of silly things without ever being either a "dumb blonde" or "poor little me"; the complicity she creates with her audience makes us aware that she is playing a role and having fun with it. Carole's personal brand of screwball is a unique and wonderful comic mode that could certainly have been pursued successfully in other films with better screenplays and production values.

Perhaps because Carole didn't write a book about it, and because, coming later in the war, it was no longer a novelty and received far less media coverage, we know a good deal less about the circumstances of her trip to the South Pacific from July through September 1944 than about the Four Jills excursion. Jack Benny was the leader of the team, which included, along with Carole, harmonica player Larry Adler, singer Martha Tilton, and pianist June Bruner. The itinerary of this, as of all wartime USO tours, was not released to the public, but a map in Carole's family collection gives the dates below, to which I have added in brackets what additional information on her itinerary I possess. From what we know of the events of the tour, including Carole's illness that kept her in the hospital for several days after August 8, this itinerary seems to have been composed before and modified after her return: the item that shows her in a "Major care center" from August 9 through 22 can hardly have referred to a thirteen-day visit to a single hospital, nor been anticipated before her departure.

The original itinerary ends on September 8, but Benny's troupe must have stayed on in Hawaii at least through September 14. For on the fifteenth, *Tarzan* author Edgar Rice Burroughs, who was living in Honolulu, writes to his stepdaughter Caryl Lee that "Jack Benny was just here with his troupe. I gave a luncheon for him at the Outrigger Canoe Club. . . . The girls couldn't come. But I met Carole Landis the next day (that was yesterday). Jack invited me and some of my friends who were at the luncheon to come to his show at one of the recreation camps. I rode to and from it with Carole. She is very pretty and very sweet." In a similarly worded letter the next day to his daughter-in-law Jane Ralston Burroughs, he adds after the last quoted sentence the parenthesis "(Oh, to be seventy again!)" This last remark is no doubt ironic since Burroughs, born on September 1, 1875, had just turned sixty-nine.

Carole's South Pacific Itinerary

7/9 Honolulu

7/10 Fiji

7/11 New Caledonia

7/12 Brisbane

7/13–8/6 Colonel Metcalf, Brisbane

[7/14 Troupe lands in Port Moresby, New Guinea]

[7/24 Troupe still/again in New Guinea, in Lae (Fleming)]

[7/27 or 28 Troupe arrives in Cape Gloucester, New Britain]

[During this three-week period, Carole seems to have spent at least a week in the New Guinea area; the letter to Tommy reproduced below was begun July 28 in New Britain, an island just off New Guinea, and on August 3 she continues the letter from New Guinea itself.]

[8/1 Troupe performs for 90th Bombardment Group at Nadzab, New Guinea (Fleming)]

[8/3 Still in New Guinea, leaving for the Solomons. Carole must have become ill at about this time.]

8/7 Port Moresby, New Guinea [10 added in pencil, 7 crossed out]

8/8 Guadalcanal

[8/9 Carole returned to Australian hotel after near-pneumonia in New Guinea]

8/9–22 Major care center, Noumea

8/23 Travel

8/24 Tarawa

8/25–30 Marshall Islands

[8/28 Carole visits 25th evacuation hospital, Espiritu Santo, New Hebrides]

[8/29 Troupe on radio broadcast from New Caledonia]

8/31 Canton, Phoenix Islands

9/1–8 [–15?] Honolulu

From eye-witness reports, a few film clips—there is even a partly filmed performance that contributes to the meager footage of Carole in color—and a great many photographs in the press and in private collections, we can get a pretty good idea of these shows and of Carole's part in them. Jack Benny would tell a few jokes and pretend to play his violin; Martha Tilton would sing, accompanied by June Bruner on the piano; Larry Adler played his harmonica. Then Carole would come on, sing a little and joke with the boys. Since there was no Mitzi Mayfair in this group, Carole was by default the dancer, but she didn't dance solo; she invited the more daring of the GIs on stage to jitterbug with her. There is a photo from the tour of Carole dancing on stage with a soldier, her short skirt spinning around her thighs.

In addition to photographing her performances, a number of soldier-shutterbugs took snapshots of Carole in New Guinea with a Papuan native to whom she offered a cigarette. One of these pictures found its way to *Newsweek* accompanied by a letter from an "Incensed Territorian" complaining that Carole was encouraging "coons" to make advances to white women. If in this case Carole's sole offense was a lack of racial prejudice, a more incriminating case was sparked by an interview with Earl Wilson after returning home. Carole managed to offend two continents with one blow when she denounced an American star, unnamed but easily identified as Paulette Goddard, for wearing "immodest, revealing" clothes on tour. Carole said that the GIs "want sweet, representative American girls," whom she proceeded to contrast with the Australian women "they have to beat . . . off with clubs." A letter to *Newsweek* countered ironically with a provocative tour photo of Carole herself.

Indeed, Carole wore some of her sexiest outfits—and posed for some of her sexiest photographs—on her South Pacific tour. This little incident points up the ambiguity of her attitude toward sexual provocation. We can imagine this woman who eschewed dirty jokes and dirty words being perfectly sincere in condemning Goddard's costumes as immodestly provocative while judging her own "see level" décolletés as a natural display of her attributes. No doubt the cynical Wilson provoked fast-talking Carole into this tactless outburst. In an encounter the following year in New York,

Goddard confronted Carole and "the gals wound up the best of friends," a dénouement much like that of Carole's run-in with Lynn Bari described in the previous chapter.

It was during her South Pacific trip that Carole contracted an illness that some have called malaria but that appears to have been a malignant form of amoebic dysentery that bothered her for the rest of her life, leading to hospital stays in October 1946 and again in April 1948. Carole also fell ill with "near-pneumonia" in New Guinea and had to be hospitalized, eventually being flown back to Australia for treatment.

Carole's stay in the New Guinea field hospital was marked by an incident that reached the columns of the *New York Times*. On hearing of Carole's illness, a soldier on a jungle base eighteen miles from the hospital hacked his way into the jungle to pick a bouquet, then walked the entire distance in the heat to present his thoughtful tribute. Nothing more is known about the original source of this anecdote.

In November 1944, *Photoplay* published a letter from a woman relaying a message from her brother in another Pacific field hospital. The members of the Benny troupe visited the hospital on Saturday, but only Carole came back on Sunday to finish the job, staying until 6 p.m. in order to speak with every soldier, "joking and doing all that she could, which was a great deal, to cheer up the blind, the limbless and the sick."

It was also during her South Pacific trip that Carole and Tommy exchanged vows of eternal love for the last time. A single exchange of letters between the couple—which crossed in the mail—has been preserved in the family collection. These are the only letters exchanged between the two that I know to be in existence. Since Wallace's estate cannot be traced, only Carole's letter can be reproduced here. The fading ink on her last page makes her closing salutation illegible:

Friday, July 28, 1944
New Britain
Dearest baby—

We got here yesterday and we're really sweating it out! Had a lot of fun yesterday with two native boys—I gave them each a mirror and a Kress special ring—and what laughs watching them looking at themselves and jabbering over the rings. They go crazy for peroxide to bleach their hair and one of them made me understand he wanted me to give him my hair.

I'm having my second session of GI's. Murder!!

Sweetheart—the fellows of 143rd Field Artillery [sic] (if that's spelled right) gave us the most beautiful ash tray—it's made from a jap shell—and 50 caliber bullets—and it has a P. 38 on top—it's really beautiful.

Gosh, I'm missing you so terribly, dearest—I'm counting the minutes until I'll be with you again—I wish I were in your arms right now—and how I miss my letters from my everything in the world—Another six weeks and we'll be together—What heaven that will be. I sure hope everything is going well with you, precious—and every night I pray the transfer will go through and that you'll be home in our little home when I get back—

Aug 3—New Guinea again—Here I am again trying to get a letter completed—We have about 20 min. before our next appointment—We're really in a choice spot now—It rains but all the time and it's so damp everything mildews—This will probably be our last spot in New Guinea—from here we'll go to the Solomons—Darling, it seems like years since I've been gone. I was reading the beautiful note you had in the flowers—and I sure got a lump in my throat—just about 4 + ½ weeks and I'll be with you, precious—and what a day that will be—I'm fine— terribly busy of course, but everything in song swell—Angel, I've been thinking of you every moment, and every night I get so miserably lonesome for my everything—I love you so completely, and I'm only living for the day when we'll be together permanently—What a glorious life we'll have then—Over here we have to take pills called Atabrine every day to ward off malaria—It turns your skin yellow after a while and I think I'm getting it a bit now—I brought this ink with me and I think it has the New Guinea rot—

Dearest darling it's time to go again—remember how terribly much I love you that you are my whole life and I could never, ever live without you,

Be a good baby and I'll be with you every day and every night—

I love you, I worship you, I adore you—I idolize you—I cherish every blessed moment we've known together—I shall always be completely your—

Carole

y[ou k?]ing you

Tommy's letter, more banal and less engaging, as befits someone awaiting orders in New York rather than touring the Pacific, tells of his hope to be transferred to Santa Ana to be near Carole. Tommy, too, indulges in formulaic expressions of ardor: "I love you, I worship you, I adore you and I miss you so very very much."

Absent from both letters is any sign of a marriage in trouble. It seems hard to believe that the couple exchanging such passionate declarations was on the verge of a final breakup. No doubt the constant recourse to formulas on both sides betrays an attempt to recover lost passion from the words that once expressed it.

As early as January 1944, rumors had begun to appear in the gossip columns that all was not well between Carole and Tommy. The husband's resentment of his wife's fame and of the milieu to which she was bound must have become visible during the couple's stay in New York in December and January—interrupted by a lightning USO trip to England with George Raft during the first week of January that began the day after Carole's "You can't stop a war for the weather" speech.

After the separation became public, Carole described her marital problems at length in a January 1945 *Photoplay* article entitled "Don't Marry a Stranger." Carole tells us that on their 1943–44 trip to New York, Tommy insisted on lodging at a midtown hotel, away from the fancier uptown hotel frequented by entertainment personalities, where Carole felt she had to stay to fulfill her obligations to her public role. They visited each other in their respective hotels, but these experiences only fueled Tommy's complaint: "I've had enough of being the guy Carole Landis married."

The couple had two apparent reconciliations after this: in March 1944, when Tommy came to California and Carole made home-cooked dinners in an effort at domesticity, afterward realizing its artificiality; and during the South Pacific trip, when they exchanged the letters mentioned above and doubtless others in the same vein—Carole refers in her article to the flowers from Tommy that she mentions in her letter. But on her return from the trip, they had a "last quarrel. . . . When it was over there was no going back, no trying again." Like Willis Hunt before him, Wallace felt out of place in the milieu that was the source of Carole's professional identity—and her income. On October 1, back from a stateside army camp tour begun a couple of weeks after returning from the Pacific, Carole announced to the press that her marriage had dissolved; in July 1945 she would go to Las Vegas for a divorce.

Clearly, Carole and Tommy loved each other. Although Walt Ross, Carole's sister Dorothy's eldest son, was only four years old when the marriage broke up, he could sense their feeling for each other and retains warm memories of Wallace and his relationship with Carole. But the couple had too little in common; the fact of being from the same geographic area, which created a bond when they were abroad, could not suffice to connect them once they returned home; and even before the war ended, Tommy's heroic military role was not enough to put him on an equal footing with the celebrities of the entertainment world. Just as in her previous marriage to Willis Hunt, who at least was socially connected to the Hollywood scene, Carole found herself unable to reconcile career and marriage. Her desire to give herself to others as a celebrity could not be reconciled with her desire, equally real but not equally realizable, to maintain a stable domestic life independent of Hollywood. If Carole never lived with any of her other husbands for more than a month or two at a time, her time with Wallace was measured in days. In "Don't Marry a Stranger,"

Carole gives as the fundamental reason for the breakup that she and Tommy really didn't know each other; theirs was a wartime marriage, inspired like many others by the need to grasp at life while under the threat of imminent death, a love that had had no time to mature.

Were there other reasons for the breakup? Neither movie magazines nor legal documents—Carole's suit alleges the usual "extreme mental cruelty"—can give an accurate picture of a relationship. What might have been the effect on Wallace of suspicions of infidelity, rumors of San Francisco, stories of past relationships with figures more prestigious than himself? For a respectable husband in 1944, the past loves and sexual experiences of one's wife were a serious matter, one unlikely to come up in a wartime London pub but one that would almost certainly emerge when Wallace was introduced to the Hollywood milieu.

Once again Carole was the victim of her incurable romanticism, of her conviction that when something feels right one should not question the feeling's authenticity. It would be wrong to see this attitude simply as one of self-indulgence. It was founded on Carole's faith in her intuitive grasp of reality—the very faith that gives her beauty its special quality of openness and generosity. But as cynical Hedda Hopper put it, "beauty attracts but does not hold"; a relationship founded on the instinctive attraction that beauty inspires is not likely to endure.

CHAPTER 8

Regrouping (1945—1946)

Having made public the impending dissolution of her marriage, and with no immediate engagements in Hollywood, Carole returned in early October 1944 to New York, which would remain her base of operations until May of the following year, when she would travel briefly to Hollywood, then go on to Reno and, finally, Las Vegas for her third divorce.

Instead of seeking film work, Carole accepted a role in a new Broadway musical, a Shubert production originally entitled *A Lady of ?* but renamed *A Lady Says Yes* when it hit Broadway. The stage had never ceased to tempt Carole since her abortive attempt at a theatrical career with *Once upon a Night* in 1938; this time, as an established film star, she would receive top billing. The show's book was written by a dentist, Dr. Maxwell Maltz, with music by Arthur Gershwin, the late George's younger brother; the action takes place both in the present and in several dream sequences, including one in China, triggered by the ether given a naval lieutenant undergoing a nose job. The major sequence is set in Renaissance Florence, with Carole playing the role of Ghisella.

After a couple of minor delays for late arrivals of scenery and costumes, the play opened (as *A Lady of ?*) at the Forrest Theater in Philadelphia on Saturday, December 9; on January 10, 1945, it had its Broadway premiere at the Broadhurst Theater. Even before the show reached New York, Carole was reported to be dissatisfied with her role and with the overall mediocrity of the production. Reviews ranged from so-so to abominable. Carole was praised for her physical beauty but for little else; her physique, seconded by that of former stripper Christine Ayres, was said to be attracting more spectators than either the story or the music. The *New York Times* review of the Broadway opening called Carole "more a visitor from Hollywood making a personal appearance than an actress trying to put over a musical comedy." The *Wall Street Journal* was more categorical: "Miss Carole Landis, a tall and beautiful cinema lady making her stage debut, did not have either the material or the talent to do a good job."

With regard to the musical itself, the *Times* review took the near-irresistible tack of saying "no" to *A Lady Says Yes*: "The new musical is at best second-rate. It is handicapped by a book which well might drive a saint to drink, and it has a score which but for one number is mediocre. . . . [T]he players for the most part seem lifeless. . . . As a musical it lacks the necessary sparkle, freshness and gaiety; it drones along over one joke and that not a good one." The *Journal* reviewer said "no" yet more emphatically, calling the book "abysmal," the dancing "mediocre," and the play as a whole "one of those cynical productions which assumes the very worst of its audiences." Walter Winchell put it succinctly: "The only good lines in it are those Mother Nature gave Carole Landis." An interesting exception was a reviewer in the neighborhood paper *Brooklyn Heights Press*, who put into words the sentiments of Carole's admirers both then and now: "Well we say 'No' to the Critics' 'No' and if it's a show Carole is in . . . we are going to say that's all we want to know. . . . [I]t's enough just to see Carole in person."

The one party who received decent reviews was second-billed comic Sue Ryan, whom the *Wall Street Journal* review called "a vociferous but accomplished product of the rough and tumble school of comedy." Carole was reported "lunching with [Ryan] almost daily" to show she wasn't "peeved" with Ryan's better notices. The show finally closed after a modestly respectable eighty-seven performances on March 25. At the time, Carole had been out with laryngitis for a few days and was being replaced by Christine Ayres. Although Carole expressed her willingness to continue to May 1, the expiration date of her contract, it is a reasonable assumption that the smaller audiences during her absence sparked the decision to close the play.

During this period, Carole found time between stage performances to make a film for the Signal Corps and to write a humorous two-page preface to Corporal Vic Herman's *Winnie the Wac* drawings.

Jacqueline Susann, later to set publishing records with her luridly readable novels *Valley of the Dolls* (1966), *The Love Machine* (1969), and *Once Is Not Enough* (1973), was billed sixth in *A Lady Says Yes*, her sixth and penultimate Broadway role. Jacqueline, Carole's near-contemporary, was born on August 20, 1918, in Philadelphia, where she won a beauty contest as a teenager; she would turn to writing in the early 1950s. Credited with many affairs with persons of both sexes, Susann reportedly told her biographer Barbara Seaman that Carole "fell in love" with her and that they engaged in a lesbian relationship; Susann particularly recalled an occasion when they "stroked and kissed each other's breasts." Just as with every other detail of Carole's real or fancied sexual life, this relationship has been extrapolated into an entire life of Sapphism.

Given what we know of Carole's unpuritanical attitude toward sexuality, we have little reason to doubt Seaman's secondhand words, but even taking them literally makes it difficult to draw conclusions about the precise nature of the relationship; for all we know, these caresses may have been as far as it went. If Jennifer North, the character largely based on Carole in *Valley of the Dolls*, has "the only truly satisfying love of her life with a woman," this goes far beyond the plausible limits of Carole's "bisexuality" into the realm of Susann's wish-fulfillment. But whatever the extent of the intimacy, the relationship does not seem to have outlasted the play. According to Seaman, it was, in fact, Susann who introduced Carole to her fourth husband, W. Horace Schmidlapp, the scion of a wealthy Cincinnati distilling and banking family, who was involved in theatrical production and who had apparently been attracted to Carole for a long time. Weeks before the show closed in late March, Carole and Schmidlapp had already been noted by Louella Parsons as a "new romance," and by March 28 they were already said to "have marriage on their minds."

The only other indication we have of contact between Carole and Jacqueline is a call Seaman claims Carole made on V-J (Victory over Japan) Day, August 15, 1945, expressing her fear, now that the days of touring army camps and hawking war bonds were over, that "she was getting too old for the sexpot roles but that no one would give her a chance to act." There is nothing further, not even a note from Jacqueline at Carole's funeral less than three years later.

In *Valley of the Dolls*, a number of Jennifer North's attributes are inspired by Carole, whose name is also mentioned in the book as an exemplar of beauty. Susann's description of Jennifer's first appearance is perhaps the most insightful portrait anywhere of Carole's public persona—a well-observed, affectionate tribute by an intimate friend to her unselfconscious beauty and openness to others:

> Her white dress, shimmering with crystal beads, was cut low enough to prove the authenticity of her remarkable cleavage. Her long hair was almost white in its blondeness. But it was her face that held Anne's attention, a face so naturally beautiful that it came as a startling contrast to the theatrical beauty of her hair and figure. It was a perfect face with a fine square jaw, high cheekbones and intelligent brow. The eyes seemed warm and friendly, and the short, straight nose belonged to a beautiful child, as did the even white teeth and little-girl dimples. It was an innocent face, a face that looked at everything with breathless excitement and trusting enthusiasm, seemingly unaware of the commotion the body was causing. A face that glowed with genuine interest in each person who demanded attention, rewarding each with a warm smile. The body and its

accouterments continued to pose and undulate for the staring crowd and flashing cameras, but the face ignored the furor and greeted people with the intimacy of meeting a few new friends at a gathering.

Elsewhere Susann calls Jennifer "about the most beautiful girl in the world." In the novel, Jennifer commits suicide on discovering she has breast cancer, a curious fictional conflation of Carole's suicide with her concern that her bosom would not age well. Nonetheless, Jennifer North had other sources, and many aspects of her career, which includes an aborted pregnancy and work in European soft-porn films, have little or no resemblance to Carole's.

Following the closing of *A Lady*, Carole remained based in New York but made plans for a tour singing at the St. Charles in New Orleans from April 12 through the eighteenth and at the Oriental in Chicago from April 20 through the twenty-sixth. In mid-May, she returned to Hollywood, but only briefly. Anxious to spend the six weeks in Nevada required to establish residence and divorce Wallace, leaving her free to marry Schmidlapp, Carole refused the female lead in the B mystery *The Spider*, scheduled to start production in June. Then, according to Louella Parsons, she took the ill-advised step of turning down the starring role in the musical *Doll Face*. However, Carole's legal file, which mentions *The Spider*, indicates a leave of absence from May 28 through July 22, but contains no evidence that she turned down *Doll Face*, which would normally have led to a reprimand or a suspension. As it happened, *Doll Face* went into production only in early August, after Carole had returned from her leave. Although Louella appears to be reporting a *fait accompli*, it is also possible that this was just one more of the over three dozen films that movie columnists erroneously assigned to Carole as far back as her Roach days.

Doll Face, eventually released in December, was a screen adaptation of a popular Broadway play, *The Naked Genius*, which had starred Joan Blondell. It was co-written by literate burlesque queen Louise Hovick, better known as Gypsy Rose Lee; and, indeed, "literature" is at the center of the plot: the heroine, Mary Elizabeth "Doll Face" Carroll, is a burlesque performer who uses a ghost-written autobiography to help her make it on respectable Broadway. The movie role went to Vivian Blaine.

Coming near the end of her Fox career, Carole's presumed turndown of *Doll Face* was symmetrical with her fateful rejection of a chance at Doña Sol at its beginning. In contrast with the highly publicized *Blood and Sand*, this black-and-white musical, despite its box-office success (eleventh on Fox's 1946 list with $2.5 million domestic gross), was a B+ at best, but it would have capitalized on Carole's recent Broadway experience and had the potential of putting her on track for future high-profile starring roles.

Yet to compare the two reported refusals is to reveal how much had changed in the four-year interval. Carole's earlier decision came at a time when she was in increasing demand and was motivated by genuine career considerations, however poorly assessed. In mid-1945, Carole had not made a Fox movie in over a year, yet she apparently turned down an attractive role for purely personal reasons. Having patriotically focused her energy on the war at the expense of her film career, with the coming of peace Carole seemed to have trouble recovering the energy and ambition that had marked her early years in Hollywood.

In early June, Carole traveled to Reno, but quickly changed her mind and moved to Las Vegas, which was just beginning to replace Reno as Nevada's divorce and gambling capital. During her six-week stay, which ended on July 19 with a divorce decree, she took time to entertain the troops at the Las Vegas Army Air Field.

Near the end of July, Carole returned briefly to Hollywood, where it was reported that she intended to marry Schmidlapp in "two weeks." She was then sent East by Fox's publicity department. On August 1, Carole was in Columbus, Ohio, for the premiere of *Captain Eddie*, a Fox film honoring a local hero, World War I ace Eddie Rickenbacker; also present, along with Rickenbacker himself, were Lloyd Nolan and Richard Conte, who acted in the film, and Ohio native child-star Peggy Ann Garner. The festivities included an Army Air Forces Day ceremony at nearby Lockbourne Air Force Base, celebrating the U.S. Air Force's thirty-eighth anniversary. On August 14, Carole was once again with Rickenbacker, rolling out the first postwar civilian Ford at a new plant in Edgewater, New Jersey. She subsequently attended the premiere of *State Fair* in Des Moines on August 29 with the film's singing costar Dick Haymes, receiving an Iowa pig from the governor as a publicity stunt.

Meanwhile, Carole and Horace were reported to be arguing over the latter's desire that Carole live in New York and abandon her Hollywood career. Walter Winchell reported as early as August 2, when Carole was in Columbus, that the Landis-Schmidlapp "merger" was expected to be "mutually canceled." Carole later explained to a columnist that she had broken the engagement because "[Horace] wanted me to give up my work and stay in New York." Yet after telling reporters in mid-August that her engagement to Horace had been called off "by common consent," Carole continued to be seen with him in various nightspots, while also dating "young Buffalo moneybags" Courtney Kane. At loose ends, Carole was reported by Dorothy Kilgallen on August 28 to be considering an offer of an extended South American tour. Finally, she was cast in a Fox movie, *Behind Green Lights*, which went into production in mid-September, following which she was loaned to Arnold Pressburger for *A Scandal in Paris*; work on these two films kept her in Hollywood through the end of November.

In what appeared to signal a decision to marry Schmidlapp and move East, perhaps even abandon her film career, Carole gave up the Sunset Plaza apartment she had moved to in late 1943 and put her household goods up for auction from September 3 through 6 with the firm of Lewis Hart and Marvin Newman. As a place to live in the meantime, she rented violinist Jan Rubini's house at 621 North Hillcrest Road in Beverly Hills, which would serve her more as a pied à terre than a home through February 1946. Yet Carole continued to be seen with other beaux; in September, she was courted both by Jay Gould and, most assiduously, by

Kimberly-Clark (Kleenex) heir Commander James Kimberly, whom she saw regularly for about six weeks between mid-September and late October. After a rumor-monger announced on the radio that Kimberly had given Carole a car, he revealed that he was "happily married" and had never given Carole "any expensive gifts." Such goings-on cannot have done wonders for Carole's reputation.

Carole's Hollywood night life went on unabated at least through mid-November. She threw a number of parties in her new—and more spacious—home: an intimate housewarming on October 10 with distinguished guests including Sonja Henie, Otto Preminger, the Edward Sutherlands, and a group of Carole's "writing friends"; another in mid-October at which men reportedly—and intentionally—outnumbered women four to one; and "a whingding of a party" on October 23 or 24 for the nineteenth birthday of young socialite Buff Cobb, Kentucky humorist Irvin S. Cobb's granddaughter, who, coincidentally, would play a bit part the following year as the king's wife in Rex Harrison's first Hollywood movie, *Anna and the King of Siam*.

In a career dominated by B films, *Behind Green Lights* (originally *Precinct 33*) is probably the most mediocre of Carole's feature roles. The director was Otto Brower, who had worked at various studios in the early 1930s, predominantly on Westerns, and was used at Fox mostly as a second unit director; in *Moon over Miami*, Brower took a crew to Florida for background location shots. *Lights* was Brower's last directing job; the following year, after directing the second unit in the cult classic *Duel in the Sun*, he died of a heart attack at the age of fifty-one.

Production began on September 13 and lasted approximately a month. Although Carole was first billed for the first time since *Cadet Girl*, it seems unlikely that she worked more than a few days on this film; unfortunately, the production files of her Fox films are unavailable. Carole is on screen for a total of eleven minutes out of sixty-four, appearing only at the beginning and end; during the heart of the story she is absent from the screen for over forty consecutive minutes. No doubt the fact that male lead William Gargan was not a Fox regular explains Carole's first billing, which demonstrates at the very least that Zanuck thought her name at the top of the marquee would attract customers. Nor was this a flash in the pan; in contrast to 1941 and '42, when Carole made nine films for Fox but had top billing only for the two B musicals *Dance Hall* and *Cadet Girl*, Carole made only three films for Fox between 1944 and 1946, but was second billed to Kay Francis in *Jills* and first billed in her final two. Although these films remained solidly in the B category, they presented Carole as glamorous and put her character in a positive light.

Not only does *Lights* have little of Carole in it, but what we see is not very impressive; it is probably her least effective acting job. Perhaps because she has so few lines to speak, she shows little interest in speaking them convincingly. This is almost certainly the film Carole referred to in a late confessional article as an assignment she disliked and "merely walked through."

The "green lights" in the title are those of a police station, one constantly overflowing with reporters. The opening scene, the only one in which Carole, as Janet Bradley, contributes to the action, shows her entering a blackmailer's apartment. She tells him she has been unable to come up with the twenty thousand dollars he is demanding for some incriminating documents. Contrary to logic and prudence, he gives Carole a glass of whiskey while holding in his hand the small envelope containing the documents, threatening to release them if she doesn't pay up. With a presence of mind born of despair, Carole throws her drink in the villain's face, snatches his gun—conveniently exposed in a shoulder holster—and takes off with the incriminating envelope.

Later in the evening, however, the blackmailer is murdered, and a search of his apartment turns up an appointment book with Janet's visit neatly recorded. Thus, Carole/Janet, now revealed to be the daughter of the classic "reform" mayoral candidate with the usual powerful enemies, is called to the police station. When the lieutenant (Gargan) threatens to book her, jeopardizing her father's chances in next week's election, she agrees to remain in custody to give the cops time to exonerate her. And so Carole spends two-thirds of the film off screen in the waiting room of the police station.

After the usual false leads, the poisoner turns out to be a crooked police doctor who was being blackmailed for previous crimes. Carole is released, leaving her father's reputation untarnished. Since she's spent the night at the station house, she accepts Gargan's friendly offer to take her to breakfast; the last shot shows them driving off in a police car. In contrast with the abrupt turns from coldness to receptivity that had characterized Carole's interactions with Romero and Nolan, her friendly acceptance of Gargan's shy request suggests that Fox had reevaluated postwar Carole's more mature persona from "available" to "respectable." As another sign of filmic prestige, she is rewarded with one of the few close-ups of her Fox career.

In a humorous article, a (female) interviewer notes with some dismay that while working on the picture, the "very buxom" actress is wearing "a business suit that covers up all of Carole's curves!" Avoiding any overt display of desirability—an element that would be openly exploited in Carole's next film, *A Scandal in Paris*—*Lights* uses her name and brief presence as a mere connotation of glamour. As one reviewer remarked, the film seems to be punishing her as not a criminal but a school child by keeping her locked up in the waiting room all night. The most favorable description of her role was "decorative"; one reviewer thought that, given that "nothing much develops" in the main plot, Carole was just as well off in her waiting room. Yet *Behind Green Lights* seems to have attained minor cult status; it is the only one of Carole's films listed in Doug McClelland's *The Golden Age of "B" Movies*, where the author remarks, apropos of Carole's "junior leaguer" role, that despite the curve-disguising clothing, "she was still unmistakably someone more likely to have passed through Earl Carroll's portals than Vassar's."

Running between coasts seems to have taken a toll on Carole's health, which would never be the same after her South Pacific trip. In late

September, after she finished *Behind Green Lights*, it was reported that doctors wanted Carole to put back some weight after falling from 124 down to an alarming 106 pounds.

Even before production wrapped up on *Behind Green Lights*, Carole began work on *A Scandal in Paris*, a far more interesting and demanding assignment for which she had been contracted, with Fox's permission, as early as September 20. *Scandal* was produced by Arnold Pressburger for United Artists and directed by German-born Douglas Sirk, né Detlev Sierck. *Scandal* was only Sirk's third American film, following a dozen made in Germany as late as 1939. Like his first two Hollywood efforts, *Hitler's Hangman* (about the assassination of Reinhard Heydrich) and *Summer Storm* (a Chekhov adaptation), *Scandal* betrays its European roots. Sirk would acclimate himself by directing a series of lighthearted all-American comedies in 1951 through '53 before achieving recognition as the master of the 1950s "woman's picture" with such films as *All I Desire* (1953), *Magnificent Obsession* (1954), and *Written on the Wind* (1956).

    Scandal was loosely inspired by the memoirs of François Vidocq (1775–1857), who after a career of crime became so successful a police informer that in 1811 he was made the first chief of the Paris *Sûreté*, or plainclothes police; he is often considered the father of modern police procedure. Connoisseurs of French literature will recognize him as the chief inspiration, including his homosexual tendencies, for Honoré de Balzac's arch-criminal Vautrin, who appears notably in *Le père Goriot* (1835) and *Splendeurs et misères des courtisanes* (1847). Much like Jean Renoir's *Diary of a Chambermaid*, produced a few months earlier for the same distributor, Sirk's film hovers uncomfortably between drama and farce. These European characters created in Hollywood exile are no longer at home in their own world but not yet believable inhabitants of ours.

    Vidocq, played by George Sanders, accompanied by his sidekick Emile, played by Akim Tamiroff, escapes from jail at the start of the film thanks to a file in a cake. (How far back does this corny trick go?) An artistic priest has the pair pose for a painting as St. George and the Dragon, respectively. But unsaintly Sanders steals the priest's horse and the pair take to the road, which brings them to Marseilles, where Sanders encounters Carole/Loretta performing in a cabaret.

Carole's performance, wearing a black bodysuit, wig, and neck ruff, is spectacular albeit, like all her film singing performances, quite brief. It begins with her celebrated "silhouette dance" behind a circular paper screen, which she then sets on fire. She steps through the singed gap to entice her masculine audience, all the while singing the "Flame Song," which contains the "scandalous" words, "I've got a flame that's too hot to handle." This sequence got Carole a good deal of publicity, including a spread in *Life*.

Circulating among the crowd, Carole is intrigued by Sanders's seeming indifference. After the show, Sanders meets her in her dressing room, where she has him place a ruby-encrusted garter around her thigh. No doubt at the behest of the producer, Carole gave this movie sequence some advance publicity by sending out garters to (male) guests, who were invited to come on the set to attach them. Sanders entices Carole into a cab, where he steals the garter during an ostensibly passionate embrace; but to her future husband, elderly Parisian police chief Richet (Gene Lockhart), she describes the thief as old and bald.

The middle of the film is taken up with the tepid romance between Sanders and his nominal costar, Swedish import Signe Hasso, daughter of the minister of the interior. After Sanders returns some jewels that had been stolen by Tamiroff and his criminal family, the minister makes Sanders chief of police of Paris in place of the incompetent Lockhart. Sanders is still unreformed, however, and has only returned the jewels as a means to gain access to the vast wealth of the Bank of France.

On coming to the capital, Sanders runs into Carole, now Lockhart's shrewish, spendthrift wife, who still obsessively seeks the thief of her garter. Sanders gallantly buys her a couple of hats and even pays her debt at the milliners' shop. No more intimate details of their relationship could be given in an era when, as a critic pointed out mockingly, even the

Carole-Lockhart married couple had to be shown in twin beds—separated by a considerable distance. Insanely jealous, Lockhart follows Carole to the milliners' upstairs room, where she is trying on a new dress behind a screen, as if reprising her famous dance. Lockhart pulls a gun and, while debating whether to shoot himself or her lover, accidentally fires and hits Carole, killing her instantly. For Sanders, the sight of his mistress's body provides the final impetus to reform. To the dismay of Tamiroff and his clan, he shuts down the bank-robbing plans. Before marrying Hasso, Sanders gets to play a real-life Saint George to Tamiroff's dragon, transfixing him with a spear when Tamiroff attempts to avenge what he understandably sees as Sanders's betrayal.

Carole considered the role of Loretta "the best part [she] ever had," and on a number of counts *Scandal* is, indeed, her most impressive film. Although Carole may have done her best work for Sutherland, Sirk was the most distinguished director with whom she worked; Edward Dmytryk, her other first-line director, was at the beginning of his career when he made *Mystery Sea Raider* in his characteristically energetic style. *Scandal* was shot in black and white, but it deserved to be in color; it has a spaciousness and ambition that contrasts with the perfunctory plotting and characterization of most of Carole's films.

It is also in this film that Carole's sexiness is presented most emphatically; her elaborate costumes are more revealing than any others she would wear on screen. But as previously noted, Carole lacks the resentful edge of the femme fatale; Loretta's wickedness never goes beyond petulance. However unpleasant she is to Lockhart, one never feels she gets a kick out of humiliating him; she would simply rather he not be there at all. Absent this sadistic nuance, Loretta is one-dimensional, and although Carole is on the screen for over twice as long in this third-billed role as in her preceding first-billed outing, her function in the plot remains ultimately episodic; she is the "bad girl" in contrast with Hasso's "good girl." We see little here of the charm and charisma so delightfully displayed in *Having Wonderful Crime*.

During the production of *A Scandal in Paris*, on the evening of November 14, lawyer Charles Gramlich of Marietta, Ohio, a former resident of a mental institution, accosted Carole in her dressing room and ineffectually attempted to unzip the tights of her flame-dance costume. (In Carole's entire career only one other such incident made the news: she was the recipient of an obscene letter in 1940.) Carole screamed, and Sanders and a couple of gatekeepers expelled the assailant from the studio. It was only when Carole filed a complaint of "attempted rape" two days later that the police apprehended Gramlich, who once again found himself committed to a mental institution, this time in California. This incident, along with the garter party, figured prominently in the *Life* article; as befitting the name of the film, scandal was its chief publicity vehicle.

When *Scandal* was finally released in July 1946, the reviewers were generally appreciative of Carole's performance. If the *New York Times*, as was its wont, found nothing and no one to like in the film, *The Hollywood Reporter*, which had little praise for the other principals, thought that Carole was "a solid hit as Loretta" and "embellish[ed] a brief but memorable character with needed vitality"; other reviewers called her "exciting" and praised her "umph" and her success as an "ersatz Dietrich . . . gams and all."

Shortly after the Gramlich incident, which coincided with the end of the production of *Scandal*, Carole received an order to report to Fox on November 23 to begin wardrobe preparation for the role of Phyllis in the film noir *Somewhere in the Night*. This was the second directing effort of Joseph L. Mankiewicz, whose fame rests on a number of classic films, including *A Letter to Three Wives* (1949), *All about Eve* (1950), *Julius Caesar* (1953), *The Barefoot Contessa* (1954), and the over-the-top blockbuster *Cleopatra* (1963). The female lead was new discovery Nancy Guild ("rhymes with 'wild'"); Phyllis was the third-billed female role and seventh overall. Carole, who already had wedding plans afoot with Horace, replied to Fox's telegram that she was turning down the role "on the basis that it would be detrimental to my career." Indeed, it is hard to imagine that this "sexy" minor part—which eventually went to Margo Woode, who would appear briefly in Carole's last Fox film, *It Shouldn't Happen to a Dog*—would have done anything to enhance Carole's prestige. Nor did her refusal do her more harm than a brief contract suspension.

Instead of reporting to Fox, Carole flew to New York, where she and Horace would finally marry on December 8 in a private ceremony at his apartment at 22 East Forty-seventh Street—"the first bride in history to be wed in green satin." The couple seemed to have found a compromise; following their honeymoon, Schmidlapp remained in New York while Carole, after making one more film for Fox in early 1946, put her movie career on hold for an entire year.

Although the wedding must have been prepared by an intense exchange of communications, nothing transpired in the press. Less than two months previously, reporters were still talking about Carole's real or imagined romances with Gould and Kimberly ("a bonfire"), while the last reports of her relationship with Schmidlapp, which dated from mid-August, described their engagement as having been called off. Had Carole been able to keep the press off the scent, or was it simply that, prone to impulsive decisions, she was herself unaware of what the final outcome of Horace's courtship would be? We may surmise that by dint of persistent negotiation, Horace, smitten with his less enthusiastic bride, found the formula that would finally win her consent: Carole would be based in the East but fly out to Hollywood when necessary for work on a film. The newlyweds stayed in New York until mid-December and then were off to Cuba for a three-week honeymoon; Carole's family collection includes a few photographs of the happy couple wading in the surf, bicycling, and acting lovey-dovey.

On January 7, 1946, Carole, either still in Cuba or just back in New York, asked Fox through a representative if she could live in New York and come west only to make films. In lieu of this, Fox offered Carole six months' leave; she turned down that offer, no doubt because it would have extended her contract, and telegraphed Fox on the same day that she was "ready, willing, and able to render my services to you." Carole flew immediately to Los Angeles, and on January 14 she reported to the studio to begin wardrobe testing for *It Shouldn't Happen to a Dog*.

Carole's last Fox film, in production from January 22 to February 21, 1946, is another undistinguished concoction, one of the final efforts of Herbert Leeds, who had directed Carole in *Manila Calling*. Its convoluted plot features a scarcely believable romance between Carole and wry but unimposing Allyn Joslyn, whose role as a newspaper reporter complements his columnist in *I Wake Up Screaming*. Carole is first billed as a dog-handling policewoman, and although she is on screen for less than a third of this seventy-minute film, she is clearly intended to provide it with its chief element of glamour. There are a number of other attractive women in the film, notably Franchot Tone's wife, Jean Wallace, who does a fine job as a newspaper colleague who took over Joslyn's police beat during his war service, and Margo Woode, whose third billing is justified more by her role in the plot as a sought-after missing girlfriend than by her brief screen presence and few words of dialogue. There are also a few "sweater girls" in the newspaper office; Joslyn remarks that these female "copy boys" are a wonderful postwar innovation.

In the context of this focus on female attraction, Carole's glamour has shifted its emphasis from sex appeal to fashion. Although Carole's hairdos and costumes—including the constant wearing of fussy little hats, in contrast with the attractive larger ones of *Having Wonderful Crime* and *A Scandal in Paris*—corresponded to the 1946 norm of what a "best-dressed" woman would wear, her fashion-conscious appearance, implausible for a policewoman, seems less appealing today than Wallace's relaxed attire. From Fox's standpoint, this role was a modestly successful way of exploiting both *Scandal's succès de scandale* and Carole's self-reliant persona. It also exploits Carole's previously noted—and well-publicized—passion for dogs.

No self-respecting policewoman would have let herself be fooled by Joslyn's obvious machinations—visiting her apartment, he gets the dog to run away by tossing a ball out the window, and throughout the film pretends to be helping her find it—but this is not surprising in a B film. Yet although *Dog* evinces the usual unconcern for giving Carole's character a biography, like *Behind Green Lights*, it never treats her "availability" with the lack of respect it met with in *Flatbush* or *Wintertime*. In the final sequence, Joslyn proposes marriage to Carole in a phone booth, whereupon she declares her intention to retire from the police force for the pleasure of "policing" her new husband. The glamour of Carole's disreputable role in *Scandal* has, as if in a parody of Vidocq's, been transmuted into police work and thence into mature respectability; it can also be seen as a continuation of Carole's secret agent in *Secret Command* and a preparation for her crusading reporter in her final film, *Noose*. When a year later Carole would reappear on screen as George Brent's bossy wife in *Out of the Blue*, this "casting against type" was really just a continuation in an ironic vein of the "happy ending" of *Dog*.

Despite the unconvincing nature of Carole's policewoman's role, the most memorable moment of which is her immortal line, "Drop the roscoe [gun] or I'll fill you full of lead!" a spokeswoman for a policewomen's association expressed appreciation to Carole for contributing her glamour to the profession. The reviewers, for their part, were more interested in Carole herself than her role; one said that she "dresses and steps smartly but hasn't much to do," while another noted that she is "more often the movie queen than she is a policewoman," but adds that "no one who enjoys looking at this lovely, and that should include everyone who looks, will mind what she plays. The only complaint is that she isn't seen frequently enough." Ironically, the eight hundred thousand dollars earned by *Dog* made it the only one of Carole's starring efforts to make the studio's annual list of highest-grossing films, albeit at the very bottom. *Dog* would be Carole's final movie role as a blonde. As part of a strategy she hoped would eventually win her an Oscar, Carole abandoned blondeness for good in fall 1946, convinced that it was an obstacle to being considered for serious roles.

Although the question of whether Carole would sacrifice her career for Horace's sake, which had put the Schmidlapp-Landis marriage in jeopardy in the fall, appeared to have been definitively answered by Carole's repeated assertions that she would "go on with [her] career" by living in New York and commuting to Hollywood, there was talk of an alternative. As early as December 14, 1945, Louella Parsons claimed that Horace had told her he was giving up stage production and had invested heavily in a startup firm called Associated Filmmakers that was building a studio in Yonkers, just north of New York City, to produce both "commercial films" and "entertainment pictures." Elsewhere it was announced that the studio was expected to be ready for business in July; Carole was touted as hoping to star in her husband's productions. Unfortunately, it does not appear that this project ever got off the ground. Schmidlapp was aware of the emerging New York-centered television industry and hoped to produce films for that medium; it seems he was a couple of years too early.

Carole spent most of the year in the East, making personal appearances for the American Cancer Society—which gave her a plaque honoring her distinguished service on June 1—and attending other benefits, from the Greater New York Fund luncheon at the Hotel St. George in June to the United Jewish Appeal "Night of Stars" at the Madison Square Garden in November. Carole also participated in for-profit activities. She appeared at the Cleveland Sesquicentennial in June, where she also took in a boxing match; she christened a Douglas Skymaster in Newark in July, then later in the month went on stage for a week at the Earle Theater in Philadelphia. She made guest appearances on a number of New York-based radio shows. On April 26, Carole was reported by the *New York Times* as having attended the previous day's opening session of the United Nations Security Council at Hunter College, staying about an hour. Yet although Carole seemed to be adapting to the movieless life of the East Coast, by the end of 1946, Edith Gwynn's *Hollywood Reporter* column noted that she was seeking a publicity agent to help restart her film career.

As for remaining at Fox, however, the January rejection of Carole's request to live bicoastally was probably the last straw. It is likely that even before making *Dog* Carole had already decided to leave the studio and try her hand at freelancing, which was becoming increasingly common in the postwar era; Louella Parsons hadn't even expected Carole to return for *Dog*. Hence, despite some writers' reports to the contrary, there is no reason to assume that Fox took the initiative in terminating Carole's contract in October. Although Carole wasn't getting any major roles, it is not clear in what sense the parts she was getting, including the *Doll Face* lead she reportedly turned down in 1945, were any worse than those she had had in 1942. We have seen both that *Dog* was Fox's most financially successful film with Carole in a leading role and that since the war Carole was given higher billing and her screen persona treated with more respect than before. At the time of her separation from Fox, Carole was earning $1,350 per week, the fifth level of her seven-year salary scale; had she remained, her salary would have gone to $1,750.

In "Now It's for Keeps," a Gladys Hall article based on a May 1946 interview that appeared in the July *Silver Screen*, Carole enthusiastically describes her life with Horace during the first few months of their marriage, while she shuttled between Los Angeles and New York, as making her "happier than ever in [her] life." She told Hall, "This is it! He's my definition of an ideal husband. In Horace I've found a man instead of a boy." Carole extols the domestic pleasure of sending "her man" off to the office and even claims to be more jealous of him than he is of her—a remark that would take on ironic overtones less than a year later. The sense of financial security Horace provided made Carole feel "for the first time" like a woman instead of a man, a statement that should be interpreted as an affirmation of traditional gender roles rather than as the words of a gold-digger. Although Tommy Wallace was not wealthy, Willis Hunt had been quite well off, albeit considerably less so than Schmidlapp. But in 1940, whatever Carole thought about her husband's income, she did not conceive it as a possible substitute for her own earnings. At the time of her marriage to Hunt, Carole was on the way up and full of ambition; by 1945, Hollywood disappointments and the intervention of the war had taken the edge off her single-minded focus on her career.

There is no sign that Horace or his family ever treated Carole with anything other than respect. Although the family fortune had been made in business affairs far from Hollywood, that Horace's mother, and presumably the rest of the family, was fully accepting of the marriage is evident from the warm tone of her correspondence with Carole as late as October 1947, when Carole was in London, and from the touching telegram she sent Clara after Carole's death: "My heart aches for you and my boy I have always loved her." In February 1946, Carole told columnist Gene Handsaker, "I have the most divine mother-in-law in the world."

Yet as early as June 20, Carole was obliged to deny rumors of a "rift" with Horace. Perhaps Carole was bored now that the war was over and her film career had slowed down; personal appearance tours and benefits are meant to fit into a busy schedule, not to *be* that schedule. And even if we can assume that she and Horace had come to an agreement concerning her future film projects and the absences they would occasion, what we know of Carole suggests that she was too impulsive to maintain an emotional attachment under such conditions. Awaiting Tommy during the war was bowing to necessity, and even so it took its toll on the marriage, whereas this bicoastal arrangement was a matter of mutual convenience that led Carole to answer a columnist's query as to what was keeping her and Horace apart with one word, "Distance." This flippant reply may well have had an undertone of bitterness, directed less at her husband than at her once-more-demonstrated inability to combine career and marriage in a single life.

In October 1946, Carole was hospitalized for about ten days for treatment of an "acute abdominal condition," most likely a recurrence of the amoebic infection sustained during her Pacific trip, although E. J. Fleming speculates that the real cause was a suicide attempt, a subject that will be examined in some detail in the final chapter. What is certain is that these episodes had a depressing effect on Carole, who had surely not expected to encounter major health problems at so early an age.

In mid-November Carole returned to Hollywood to resume her film career as a freelancer. She spent the Christmas season in New York, co-hosting a dinner at the Waldorf honoring Joe Louis and doing her one turn as hostess on *Command Performance* the day after Christmas. Louella Parsons reported on December 28 that Carole was about to have the lead in an unnamed play to be produced by Horace, as well as to host her own radio show entitled *What's My Name?*—perhaps an ancestor of the long-running TV show *What's My Line?* on whose panel Carole-friendly columnist Dorothy Kilgallen served from 1950 through 1965; nothing came of either of these speculations. But in mid-January 1947 Carole was back in California meeting with her agent Arthur Lyon, and a month later she had signed a two-film contract with the short-lived Anglo-American "Poverty Row" studio, Eagle-Lion Films, with an option for eight other films. Carole was to receive for each film $2,083.33 per week for a minimum of six weeks (a total of $12,500); salary for the optioned films would have risen to a maximum of $40,000 each. The two films she was scheduled to make were *Out of the Blue*, which she completed in April 1947, and *The Amazing Mr. X*, which was made after her death with Lynn Bari in her place.

CHAPTER 9

Anglophilia
(1947—1948)

The year 1947 began with a curious incident that contributed to Carole's sense of being—as in the subtitle of the *Liberty* article that recounts it— "made and marred by publicity." On January 6, the national press published a list of the six "best undressed" women drawn up by lingerie model Joan Smith, who claimed to have posed for over five thousand underwear and swimsuit ads. These included Lana Turner, "prettiest in a slip," Rita Hayworth, "most languorous in a negligee," Jane Russell, "most gorgeous in a brassiere," and, finally, Carole Landis, "loveliest in a nightgown." But in the first version of the United Press release, this appeared as "*liveliest* in a nightgown." It was soon corrected, and as *Liberty* put it, "everyone, except Carole, had had a good chuckle."

Horace arrived in Los Angeles from New York on January 23; by the first days of February, Carole and Horace were in Palm Springs, and once more columnists were retailing rumors of a split. Yet the following week, after Horace had returned East, Carole was observed to be house-hunting; and toward the beginning of March, Horace paid seventy-eight thousand dollars for the house at 1465 Capri Drive, just north of Sunset Boulevard between Brentwood and Pacific Palisades, that would be Carole's last. In April, Hedda Hopper reported that the Schmidlapps were adding a nursery to the new home, and that if they didn't have a baby within the year, they would adopt. Another columnist claimed they were already adopting a child from an eastern orphanage.

Given the lack of results from earlier attempts at conception, Carole must have been aware that her chances of conceiving a child were problematic at best. It is not clear whether she knew for certain that this was an anatomical impossibility, or if, as is probable, she had been told the truth, whether she fully believed it. We do not know what made conception impossible for Carole, but the coroner's examination established this beyond doubt. One story is that she had endometriosis, an extension of uterine tissue outside the womb that makes menstruation painful and pregnancy difficult but not impossible; her sister Dorothy apparently suffered from this condition, which did not prevent her from bearing four children. However, according to Carole's niece Sharon Ross Powell, Carole's condition was not endometriosis but a congenital malformation (she was unable to be more specific) that was a residual effect of the influenza epidemic, which was just getting started at the time she was conceived on about April 1, 1918.

Perhaps Carole's often-expressed hope of having a child of her own dissuaded her from going through with adoption. Yet the fact that rumors of adoption surfaced in both this and her previous marriage strongly suggests that Carole's inability to bear children was a given of Hollywood gossip. At any rate, Carole did not inform Horace of her condition. Carole's family papers contain a letter dated February 8, 1947, that Horace sent her from New York—the only known extant correspondence between them—in which he expresses frustration at their inability to have a child and, fearing himself to be at fault, states his intention to have his fertility tested by a physician.

Out of the Blue, Carole's last American film, was in production between late February and early April 1947. The director was Leigh Jason, a former

UCLA instructor who had worked at various studios, largely in B come-dies, a genre in which he excelled; his 1940s work for Columbia produced such gems as *Three Girls about Town* and *Dangerous Blondes*. Carole was cast "against type"—although we have observed the continuity with the domes-tic conclusion of her previous film—in a secondary role where she felt she could display acting talent rather than glamour.

In this lively comedy in which Ann Dvorak's comic flair steals the show from romantic leads Turhan Bey and Virginia Mayo, Carole plays Mae, the shrewish wife of Arthur Earthleigh, played by George Brent. Brent and Bey are neighbors in terrace apartments, and the story begins with Bey's dog leaping the fence to bury a bone in Carole's zinnias. But the real plot revolves around what happens after Carole leaves for a Connecticut vaca-tion. Brent meets the uninhibited Dvorak/Olive in a bar and they strike up a conversation. He is fascinated by her and they end up spending the evening together in his apartment; although their behavior remains well within the limits of the Production Code, Dvorak's bohemian tipsiness gives Brent a vacation from his wife's henpecking. Dvorak also happens to be an interior decorator, and she profits from Carole's absence to rearrange her fussy décor, taking the antimacassars off the chairs and stowing the ubiquitous bric-a-brac.

The plot turns on the feeble conceit that when Dvorak drinks too much brandy, as occurs rather frequently, the alcohol activates a heart con-dition that makes her pass out and appear lifeless; we're not to worry about the likelihood that one day the catalepsy will become permanent. When Dvorak has an episode in Brent's apartment, to avoid scandal he surrepti-tiously lays her inert form in plain sight on Bey's balcony. This motivates a couple of nosy spinsters upstairs to call the homicide squad, thinking Bey must be the serial killer who has been haunting the neighborhood. The plot has several further convolutions in which Dvorak continually upstages everyone.

When Carole returns near the end of the film, she shows not the least jealousy of Dvorak, although she is quite ready to believe that dog-owner

Bey is a murderer. But the real serial killer is caught and Dvorak's "murder" is dismissed as the old ladies' fantasy. Bey and Mayo pair off, Dvorak goes back to her old haunts, and we are left with the Earthleighs. Brent had at first returned under his wife's thumb and put back all the antimacassars, but inspired by Dvorak, he finally rebels and dons the family pants. At the end of the film, having declared that he *likes* dogs, he acquires a puppy of his own, and instead of serving Carole breakfast as he did in the opening sequence, he has *her* serve *him*. As we might expect in this postwar comedy—written, incidentally, by a woman, Vera Caspary—Carole is more grateful than resentful of her newly subordinate role. Her happy domestication reflects the apparent reestablishment—in hindsight, quite short-lived—of traditional family relations after the disarray brought about by the war.

In terms of Carole's evolving screen persona, *Blue* begins where *Dog* ends, but the interest of the passage from romance to marriage is that it entails playing a character other than Carole's all-too-frequent worldly-wise glamour girl. Carole acquits herself of this least natural of her roles surprisingly well, to the general approval of reviewers. The film concentrates on Mayo as the ingénue and shows Dvorak in a provocative dance-hall photo; Carole's appearance is toned down by a generally severe wardrobe and coiffure as well as by her decidedly unsensual body language. Only in a brief sequence at the very end, when, without any slipup in her housewifely performance, Carole dons an attractive dress and is given a few solo shots on camera, do we realize what a beautiful woman she is.

Carole's social life during this period was marked by the usual sightings and public appearances; at Don Loper's "slipper party" for designer Seymour Troy in early April, she confiscated the watches of the male guests, then threw another party a week later at which they could retrieve them. As Kurt Kreuger pointed out, Carole stood out in a crowd in good measure because she made a deliberate effort to do so; her effort to restart her career led her to court the public eye more deliberately than since before the war. Her contract at Eagle-Lion still had another film to run, but except for speculations about Horace's projects, there was no word of other movie offers. On Memorial Day weekend in 1947, Carole traveled to Indianapolis as the first of thirteen movie stars selected to present the Borg-Warner trophy to the Indy 500 winner; photographs in the June 9 issue of *Life* show Carole exchanging a rather awkward kiss with wiry little Mauri Rose, who would again win the race the following year.

Perhaps as a spin-off from her attendance at Indy, Carole subsequently became associated with midget car racing in California. The papers reported that she had purchased from Johnny Balch a half-interest in a midget racing car, which Danny Oakes piloted to victory several times under her sponsorship, beginning with a race at Gilmore on June 26. Oakes himself claimed that Carole's association with the car was purely for publicity and that no money changed hands. Oakes also hinted that although Carole was not receptive to his own advances, this may not have been the case for all his racing colleagues. It was around this time that Jean Porter, by then Mrs. Edward Dmytryk, ran into Carole at the auto race track; as she put it, "Carole always had a man with her," and if she did on this occasion, it was certainly not her husband.

While the racing continued, a professional opportunity arose in early July, when Carole was mentioned for a lead role in Ross Hunter's tent theater production of *The Play's the Thing*. But by this time Carole had acquired a more serious preoccupation that would prevent this opportunity from materializing.

One gets the impression that in this period of her life Carole was restless and discontented. Her marriage could not yet be called a failure, but the "distance" that separated the couple was clearly a source of dissatisfaction and an encouragement to infidelity. In March 1947, Carole hired a private investigator to check on Horace's net worth and the truth of his representations to her of his personal income, which he had apparently drastically understated by concealing it in a trust, so that (in the words of Carole's friend and lawyer, Gregson Bautzer) she was contributing to the family joint account "approximately twice as much money" as Horace—"$45,000 to $22,000," to use the figures in the letter. As she later reportedly told her mother, "Marry a rich man—and then support yourself."

If pictures of Carole during the preceding year show her as a blonde wearing flashy clothes and just a bit too much lipstick, the dark-haired Carole of 1947 had a more mature beauty and, despite the loss of weight noted by Sidney Skolsky, a forthright seductiveness. A photograph in the July men's magazine *Esquire* shows Carole in a white fur stole over a black lace dishabille, a distant ancestor of Madonna's bustier. A photograph of Carole in this same outfit had appeared in the *New York Sunday News* on March 2, and still another version served as the final photo in the Westmores' beauty book. This is still the sweet and generous Carole celebrated by her fans, a number of whose letters to her survive from this period, yet there is something imperious in her stare. It was probably soon after this photograph was taken early in 1947 that she became involved with Rex Harrison.

Much of an unflattering nature has been written about Carole's affair with Harrison, and depending from which side it has been approached, about one or both of the principals. Most people who knew both thought Carole "got a raw deal." Cesar Romero did not hesitate to call Harrison a "pompous cad"; Kurt Kreuger, who worked with Rex in *Unfaithfully Yours*, found him incapable of talking about anything but "means of transportation." But whatever Rex's shortcomings, and however unhappy the affair's ultimate outcome, the evidence tells us not only that he inspired in Carole the great passion of her life, but that he treated her with respect and affection, and that it was with him rather than any of her four husbands that Carole experienced her most stable and long-lasting love relationship. This was no doubt the closest she came to being part of a genuine couple who found enjoyment in sharing their lives, intimate and professional, beyond sexual pleasure and the thrill of infatuation.

It is not certain exactly when the affair began. The story told by Rex himself is that they met at Palm Springs during the filming of *The Foxes of Harrow*, which took place between mid-April and July 18, 1947. It is difficult to imagine that Carole was absorbed in a love affair while shooting *Out of the Blue*, which lasted until early April 1947. Alexander Walker claims that Harrison situated their first meeting during the summer, which he may have done elsewhere, but not in his autobiography, and that Harrison "had secretly been meeting the twenty-eight-year-old actress at several quiet rendezvous outside Los Angeles," without, however, giving any date for the beginning of their liaison or, therefore, any reason to doubt Harrison's own account. Harrison was making *Anna and the King of Siam* at Fox in February and March 1946, at the same time that Carole was doing *It Shouldn't Happen to a Dog*, and it is possible that they met at that time, but highly unlikely that they began an affair so soon after Carole's marriage to Horace.

A party given by John Huston and Evelyn Keyes in July 1947 provides a latest date for the beginning of the affair. At the party, Betty Garrett clearly recalls an inebriated Rex dancing with Carole and "leaning all over her," while Lilli Palmer tapped her foot impatiently, waiting to leave. Keyes's own account, which almost certainly refers to the same incident (she discreetly mentions no names), is much more vivid: "We . . . had an altercation of two women, one the wife, the other the girlfriend, squabbling over the husband . . . all three of them stars. The girlfriend reached in and pulled the falsies out of the wife's dress." Under the circumstances, one can certainly imagine full-bosomed Carole demonstrating in this manner her advantage over her rival. Although such a display was both imprudent and gratuitously cruel, after a few drinks Rex and Carole might well have half-guiltily confessed their love in this manner. What is clear even from Garrett's milder account is that an intimate relationship was already well under way. The last event at which Carole and Horace had been reported together in Hollywood had been a supper party on or about June 14, just before Carole began befriending midget race drivers. Clearly, Rex was a more intriguing companion.

Rex Harrison was a versatile actor, especially gifted for light comedy, whose immortality rests largely on his unforgettable performance as Professor Higgins in both the stage and film versions of *My Fair Lady*. As Rex himself put it in his autobiography—where, unlike most of his biographers, he speaks of Carole with unfailing respect—both he and Carole were outsiders in Hollywood. He was a foreigner who had not been there long and had made little effort to ingratiate himself, and Carole, who for various reasons had never been a pillar of Hollywood society, since the war seemed increasingly indifferent to presenting an image of respectability; with her husband on the East Coast most of the time, this would have entailed spending her evenings in the tranquility of Capri Drive.

Harrison's biographers, convinced of their subject's immeasurably greater significance, emphasize Carole's naïve illusions about the relationship, which certainly existed, while playing down the factors other than sexual that made it work. Although Rex was no intellectual and tended to impress those who were as ignorant and even dull, he could be witty in the right circumstances; and however little he knew about other things, his knowledge of theater must have fascinated Carole, whose theatrical aspirations had hardly been satisfied by a few performances in 1938 and four months of *A Lady Says Yes*. Nor should the element of sexual attraction be neglected. Rex, although scarcely incarnating the virile ideal, had been known for good reason as "Sexy Rexy" well before coming to the United States. He was clearly attracted to female beauty, and the attraction was mutual; five of his six wives were strikingly attractive women, not to speak of his extramarital partners.

Alexander Walker mistakenly explains Carole's British films as made for Eagle-Lion, which made films only in the United States. This inaccuracy destroys the credibility of his claim that Carole went to England because she had no other offers and that Rex only subsequently arranged to go there himself, although he arrived first. Carole's British film contracts were made with British production companies unrelated to Eagle-Lion and negotiated for her by British agent Felix de Wolfe. The simplest and most parsimonious explanation for the trip is that she and Rex decided on it together. Aside from the increased opportunities it offered their liaison, Carole's attachment to England was undoubtedly increased by her love affair with an Englishman. For his part, Rex had a financial incentive to work in England. His new Fox film, *Escape*, was the first postwar American production in Britain under a tax agreement whereby British subjects filming at home would pay only British taxes rather than being subject to double taxation as they were in the United States. As a result of his American productions, Harrison had a major British tax debt and had previously been reluctant to return to Britain.

Little is known of the arrangements Carole and her agent made to obtain contracts for the two films she would make in London, but there is no sign that Rex had a part in either of these negotiations. Since her performances with the Four Jills, Carole had remained popular in Great Britain, as attested by the number of letters and photo requests from fans in her family collection; and despite her recent low level of film activity, Carole's Hollywood glamour made her a good box-office investment in the postwar era. On July 18, Louella Parsons announced that Carole was going to England for a personal appearance tour and that she would "talk over a picture offer." A month later, on August 20, Louella had the name of her film, *The Brass Monkey*, and its producer, Samuel Bronston. Louella also mentions that a film crew was to board Carole's ship in Dublin to shoot the opening shipboard sequence; this information, probably given her by Carole herself, indicates that the production had been planned in some detail before her departure.

That summer, most likely in mid-July, Carole and Horace hosted, under the probable sponsorship of Eagle-Lion, a "Christmas preview" party on Capri Drive that would be written up in the December 1947 *Screen Guide* under the title "Christmas at Carole's." Attendees included Franchot Tone and his wife, Jean Wallace; June Lockhart; and Betty Garrett and her husband, Larry Parks. The photographs show Carole in a Santa Claus beard distributing gifts to her guests; they are perhaps the last photos in which Carole and Horace appear together as a couple.

On August 4, Carole flew to New York. Before leaving for England, she had scheduled a week of personal appearances in Baltimore and another week in Boston. Carole was scheduled to sail for London on August 20, but the sailing was postponed by a three-day wildcat longshoremen's strike; the papers printed a photograph of Carole carrying her own luggage on board when she finally departed on the twenty-third. Horace was supposed to join Carole in London in early October, but his trip was postponed so that he could accompany pioneering African American choreographer Katherine Dunham to England. Harrison was already there; he had arrived on August 21, in preparation for filming *Escape*. This Joseph L. Mankiewicz film went into production in mid-September in Devon; the site outside London afforded the couple numerous trysting opportunities. Meanwhile, Lilli Palmer, who had accompanied Rex to England, was rumored to be returning to Los Angeles before him, although as it turned out the couple spent Christmas in Europe and returned together in January.

Brass Monkey was produced by Alliance Film Studios in their Twickenham facility between September and (probably early) December 1947. Its director, Thornton Freeland, was an American who since the 1930s had worked mostly in England for Fox and others. Carole's contract called for a salary of thirty thousand dollars over ten weeks of filming.

The main plot is a poor man's version of *The Maltese Falcon*. A brief voice-over prologue informs us about three "priceless" brass monkeys, Buddhist cult objects centuries old. The film proper opens on shipboard— the sequence shot on the *Mauretania*, on which Carole was traveling to England. Carole/Kay Sheldon is returning to Great Britain from an entertainment career in America. Carole's shady-looking fiancé Max is in possession of one of the three monkeys, which he intends to deliver to a sinister art dealer, a reduced-size version of Sydney Greenstreet played by Campbell Cotts, who arguably delivers the film's most vivid performance. But Carole gets hold of the monkey, pretending (as we later discover) to be ignorant of its priceless value, and apparently on a whim—but really to avoid detection—makes a friendly gift of it to the nominal star of the film, Canadian-turned-Englishman Carroll Levis. In real life, Levis was the host of a popular radio show featuring newly discovered talent; he appears in the film in this role, under his real name.

As a demonstration of the penury that reigned in Britain after the war, the original owner offers for the return of all three *priceless* monkeys the less than fabulous sum of sixty thousand pounds, which is nevertheless sufficient to motivate the murders of first Max and then the dealer. Suspicion first falls on Levis, who was known to have had a monkey in his possession, but then, more intensely, on the sinister art dealer's still more sinister associate—the Peter Lorre character in *Falcon*—played by a young Herbert Lom, who was to play many more sinister characters in his long career.

But as it turns out, it is Carole who is the guilty party, caught at the very end of the film when she inexplicably tries to run away from the studio broadcasting Levis's radio program. She is carrying the three monkeys—the one brought home by Max plus the two that had been in the art dealer's safe. Since Carole was not suspected, one imagines that had she not started running she would never have been apprehended; nor do we learn why she is carrying the precious monkeys around with her in the proximity of police officers. The guilty femme fatale is a final, unconvincing nod to *Falcon*'s Brigid O'Shaughnessy.

But by this time we no longer care. The main plot is all but lost sight of in the last third of the film, which is taken up by Levis's variety show, with a young Terry-Thomas as the star performer along with a pianist, an accordionist, a musical sawyer, Levis's scatterbrained assistant Avril Angers singing a rousing comic song, and a few other performers—including Carole herself, who sings (with a dubbed voice) "I Know Myself Too Well." By the time Carole is caught, we have lost interest in figuring out how she or anyone committed the murders and took the monkeys, all of which is perfunctorily explained at the end. How an apparently successful nightclub singer working in the United States was made aware of the value and location of the monkeys and how her greed brought her to kill two men in cold blood are questions simply left unexplored. In a strange piece of direction, after Carole is physically caught she futilely tries to run away from her captors not once but twice, in both cases being pinned to the floor.

Although second billed to Levis, Carole is the film's main attraction, but, in contrast to her role "against type" in *Out of the Blue*, more as a beauty than as an actress. Unlike in *Dog*, there are no other attractive women to draw away our attention; screwball Angers, the only other woman in a prominent role, is emphatically unglamorous. Although *Monkey* shows Carole's mature beauty to good advantage, there is something a trifle overripe in her glamour, standing out as a symbol of American prosperity against the drabness of her English surroundings.

No doubt as a result of Carole's suicide, the film's British release was delayed until early 1951, when it was recut and renamed *Lucky Mascot*; it was finally released in the United States on October 11, 1951. Consultation of the files of many newspapers has not unearthed a single American review of this film.

The highlight of Carole's fall season was the command performance in London on November 25 on the occasion of the marriage of Princess Elizabeth and Prince Philip, which had taken place five days earlier. A number of American film personalities crossed the Atlantic to attend the ceremony, including Loretta Young, Robert Montgomery, Bob Hope, Alexis Smith, and Craig Stevens; they were joined by a similar number of British stars, including David Niven, Margaret Lockwood, John Mills, Vivien Leigh, Sir Laurence Olivier, and, of course, Rex and Lilli. Carole, as a current London resident, was part of a reception committee for the new arrivals. There is a revealing photograph of a group of these stars in which Lilli Palmer can clearly be seen glaring at Carole, as well she might. The command performance included a premiere showing of *The Bishop's Wife* as well as a stage show in which Carole reprised her earlier command performance with the Four Jills in December 1942 by singing "White Christmas."

In a December 1947 letter to her fan club, Carole tells how thrilled she was that "Their Majesties" remembered the song. She writes of her nervousness before delivering her little speech and performance and of how British actors, including Rex, helped her steady her nerves. The letter also describes two trips to Paris. The more extensive one, which must have taken place in September or October, included dinners at the Eiffel Tower restaurant and Maxim's, tourist visits to the Louvre and Notre Dame, and an unsuccessful day at Longchamps racetrack. The second, briefer trip took place in November in order to purchase a gown for the command performance; Carole then returned to London, where she watched the wedding procession on November 20. Carole also states in the letter her intention to travel to Dublin for a charity benefit under the auspices of the Catholic Church, then to spend Christmas with the troops in occupied Germany; no mention is made of Christmas with Horace. This report, while displaying the unpretentious warmth and directness of Carole's rela-tionship with her fans, gives proof that, whatever the toll taken by her more intimate experiences, Carole's enthusiasm for the wonders of the world had scarcely changed since her schoolgirl days in San Bernardino.

Although Horace was supposed to arrive in England in October, the absence of any news of his presence there suggests that he did not make the trip at that time. When we do have news of his sailing, it is on December 16, supposedly in order to spend Christmas with his wife. Yet we have seen that Carole's plans did not mesh with this project; on January 8, 1948, Dorothy Kilgallen, who kept pretty close tabs on Carole, says that Horace was taking off only then for London "and a reunion with Carole Landis on the 16th [of January], after which the direction of their marital path should be decided." We may take Carole's statements to columnists that offer hope for the marriage as pro forma attempts at preserving privacy; there is no indication that the couple spent Christmas or any other time together.

Donald Bogle's biography of Dorothy Dandridge states, without giv-ing an exact date, that Carole joined Dorothy, the Nicholas brothers, and other family members in Paris, whereupon rotund playboy King Farouk, who already knew Carole, flew them all to Egypt. Fayard Nicholas, when I spoke with him in 2005, did not recall this story, which is not confirmed in any other publication. Hedda Hopper uncharitably adds a possible point of evidence in its favor: in her April 28, 1948, column, after praising Rita Hayworth for entertaining the troops in Germany, she remarks that "Carole Landis disappointed them twice and will never be forgiven." Given Carole's and Rita's respective levels of wartime service, this conclusion is certainly dubious, but if we assume that the double disappointment has a basis in fact, Bogle offers a possible account of what Carole did over the holiday. Nevertheless, a final piece of evidence tells against the Egyptian trip: Carole's answer to her fans' questions about foreign travel in the "Quizzing Carole" attachment to her December letter states, "I do mean to go one day to Egypt, India, China, Japan, and I hope to have visited Switzerland, Denmark, Belgium, Norway and Italy by the time you read this."

Whatever the truth of Bogle's story, Hedda's is disturbing enough. The idea of canceling a Christmas army tour for a jaunt, whether to Denmark or to Egypt or, more probably, for a tryst with Rex (Lilli, according to Louella, planned to spend Christmas away from Rex, in Switzerland), would have been unthinkable for Carole a couple of years earlier. Hedda's unflattering words should be understood in the light of Roy Moseley's statement that (quoting drama and later film producer Ross Hunter) Carole was "absolutely insane over [Rex]" (to which Hunter added "and he was wonderful to her"); in Moseley's own words, "Carole's obsession with Rex was extreme and she took numerous photographs of him. . . . These pictures were then put on display so that the house resembled a shrine to her lover" (*Rex Harrison*, 106)—a troubling inversion of Laird Cregar's shrine to Carole in *I Wake Up Screaming*.

These judgments all suggest that in the last year of her life Carole found it increasingly difficult to maintain her self-control. In this respect the Harrison affair was as much an effect as a cause; however attractive Rex was to Carole, his attractiveness would not have had such an unsettling effect on her had she not been in a state of emotional insecurity beyond anything she had previously experienced. Carole had been deeply hurt by Franchot Tone and undoubtedly experienced other failed love affairs between her separation from Hunt in late 1940 and her encounter with Wallace in November 1942, but she remained in command of her career throughout this period. And although her marriage to Wallace eventually broke up, none of the other attractions she may have felt at the time could be considered the chief cause of that breakup, as the Harrison affair was of her marriage to Horace.

To understand this spinning out of control is to begin to set the stage for Carole's ultimate decision to end her life. Carole's reported complaint to Jacqueline Susann on V-J Day had touched on a problem far graver than the end of her duties entertaining troops in wartime: the inevitability of growing old. A beautiful woman's fear of mortality is not simply the contemplation of her future death. Carole's words reported by Jean Porter were prophetic: she could not and would not get old. Turning thirty in an era when, as was the case at least through the 1960s ("don't trust anyone over thirty"), that age was considered the end of youth and the onset of middle age must have been an event Carole looked forward to with dread since adolescence, and now her thirtieth birthday was only a year away. Her overpowering attachment to Harrison, including her obsession with his image, was among other things a way of turning her eyes elsewhere.

As for what Carole would do after *Brass Monkey*, in her absence from Hollywood the columnists speculated more broadly than usual. Hedda claimed Carole would return "by Christmas" to begin a second film, *Beggar's Choice*, for Eagle-Lion, which was later spoken of for June Lockhart but never made; Harrison Carroll gave the same dates for *Out of the Red*, a planned follow-up to *Out of the Blue*, again featuring Ann Dvorak, that was not produced either. Sidney Skolsky claimed that Carole was thinking about doing *The Brass Monkey* as a Broadway play. But Louella Parsons, who had it straight from Carole herself, tells of her plans to work in *Noose* as early as November 12, well before Carole had finished *Brass Monkey*; Louella adds, perhaps ironically, that "Carole said she was very happy in London."

The principal attraction for Carole of doing a second British film was no doubt that Harrison was still in England; he would not leave (with Lilli) until mid-January, arriving in the United States on the twenty-third. But Carole had other reasons to enjoy England. Her second command perform-ance was a happy reminder of the warm feelings left behind by the wartime triumph of the Four Jills, and she must have enjoyed the buzz provoked by the star quality of a Hollywood actress in a country still digging out from the war. For Carole the continuation of wartime privations recalled her earlier trip and the sense of purpose she had had at the time; the long letter to her fan magazine describes the difficult economic conditions in detail, with obvious fascination. It seems clear that for Carole, Harrison's status on the English stage was not merely a potential source of career advantage but a link to a world where she felt accepted without reservations. Had Harrison stayed on in England, had Lilli been out of the way, Carole might never have returned to Hollywood. As it was, the day before her departure for the United States she told a movie journalist that she had seriously thought of purchasing an English country home and relocating there for good.

Carole's last film, *Noose*, shot in London during the first two months of 1948, was not released in the United States until July 1950, preceding the rarely shown *Brass Monkey* in American theaters by over a year. The story was taken from a play by Richard Llewellyn, best known for his novel *How Green Was My Valley*, the film version of which won Best Picture and Best Director Oscars for Zanuck and John Ford in 1942. This time, Carole's contract called for seven weeks at $3,500, for a total of $24,500.

Noose, directed by the transplanted Frenchman Edmond Gréville—best remembered in France for his sole acting credit as Albert Préjean's sidekick in René Clair's classic *Sous les toits de Paris* (1930)—is a generally well-made film, far superior to *Brass Monkey*. It not only has well-developed characters and a fairly credible story, but is creatively shot; the artistic, at times even arty camerawork is probably that of the film's second cinematographer, Otto Heller, who had begun his career in his native Czechoslovakia in 1920, and following the German annexation, worked in Holland and France before coming to Great Britain in 1942.

Noose tells the story, timely in postwar London, of the downfall of the racketeer Sugiani, who exploits England's postwar shortages by counterfeiting money and ration coupons and smuggling in goods for sale on the black market. Sugiani is forcefully and convincingly portrayed by Joseph Calleia, but the film's real show-stealer is Nigel Patrick as Sugiani's assistant, "Bar" Gorman; Patrick, the first actor to appear on screen, manages to make his role menacing, comic, and pathetic all at the same time.

The plot turns on the discovery in the Thames of the strangled body of a prostitute, Milly Sharp, who had been Calleia's girl. Milly's friend and successor, Annie Foss, played by a French actress under the name of Ruth Nixon, knows Calleia is responsible and fears becoming his next victim. Carole in the role of Linda Medbury, a fashion reporter who has emigrated from Chicago to impoverished postwar London for the sake of her British fiancé, finds Annie weeping hysterically in the ladies' room of a café and pries the story out of her. On learning of Calleia's dastardly deeds, Carole abandons her fashion work and begins a crusade to expose and destroy the gangster, who until now has averted any investigation of his activities by either the press or the authorities.

In contrast to the terrified Annie, who makes a genuine appeal to our emotions, Carole is irritatingly insouciant, even when threatened first by Patrick and subsequently by Calleia himself. Intent on conveying the moral outrage and determination that motivate her crusade, Carole less fails than refuses to portray any other emotion, oblivious to the consideration that to show her character struggling with the fear of provoking a powerful and unscrupulous criminal would have made her both more human and more credible. As it is, she treats Calleia with such arrogant scorn, constantly taunting him with the name "Milly Sharp," that she makes us sympathize with *him*.

It is not to exonerate Carole of this acting misjudgment to point out that it could not have been committed without the encouragement of the director. One gets the feeling that Carole was hired to embody a high-spirited American bull-in-a-china-shop whose single-minded disregard for anything but her own high purposes is meant to demonstrate Yankee panache in sober postwar Britain. As a result, if in *The Powers Girl* it is Carole's *role* that is unsympathetic, here what is off-putting is the smugness and moral arrogance of her screen *persona*. Nevertheless, the one available American review of *Noose* praises Carole's portrayal of "one of the smartest" of "smart newspaper girl heroines."

As in *Brass Monkey*, but more insistently so, Carole is made to incarnate feminine glamour. Carole's costumes and hairdos are fashionable enough, but her overall appearance lacks sparkle and she is shown from her entrance to the final sequence as losing her shoes and limping. As a figure of female desirability, she is upstaged by Brenda Hogan, nearly ten years her junior, who appears toward the end of the film in a snappy performance as a young gold-digger; even the French Ms. Nixon is more appealing than Carole. It is hard to believe that scarcely two years have passed since her sensual performance in *A Scandal in Paris*.

In the dénouement, Carole's fiancé, played by British B protagonist Derek Farr, having returned from wartime service at just the right moment, puts together a group of boxers and other "good" thugs as an army to combat Sugiani's henchmen, striking quickly before the latter can bring in reinforcements from other cities. Sugiani, seeking refuge in a church, is strangled by his own hit man. Their good work done, Carole and her beloved limp off into the night, an ironic end to the career of an actress who got her first big chance by running "like a deer" for D. W. Griffith.

To the gloomy final shot we may contrast this glimpse of the real Carole in her last film: "Her leading man in *Noose*, Derek Farr, remembered her with affection. 'I enjoyed working with her enormously. Everyone adored her in the unit—she was a real Hollywood pro.' "

After finishing *Noose* at the end of February, with Rex already back in Hollywood, Carole immediately booked passage home; she was in New York by March 4 and in Los Angeles by the ninth. Horace, too, was in New York during this period, but there is no indication they saw each other.

As might be expected, Carole's public statements on this subject cannot be taken at face value. On the ninth, she spoke through an agent of her hope for reconciliation and her desire to "make a go" of the marriage, a desire hardly compatible with her ongoing passion for Rex. Two days later, however, her agent reported that she had engaged an attorney "and will sue for divorce if a reconciliation seems impossible." Whereas Carole had rhapsodized a year earlier over the couple's shared domestic bliss, she now claimed that they had been separated "almost from the day of our marriage"; she blamed Horace for not returning her calls and for traveling to Paris and St. Moritz without her, claiming that Horace "was in Europe three months while she was in England making two movies and saw her only three days in that time."

The Landis-Harrison affair, although surely no secret to the cognoscenti, was not yet known to the general public. This would change abruptly a week after Carole's return to Hollywood. On March 16, in the lead item of his widely read column, Walter Winchell, after repeating Carole's confirmation of a rumored "split" from Horace that implied an impending divorce action, declared that "her next husband (if and when) will be Rex Harrison, the British star." Winchell even claimed that Lilli "knows all about the romance, which started only recently in London." Whatever Lilli knew—and she clearly knew everything, including that the affair had not begun in London—this knowledge was henceforth shared with the world.

Winchell had always been friendly to Carole and would compose a touching elegy after her death, when many of the columnists who had assiduously recorded her activities said not a word. He could not have failed to realize that his revelation was more than an ordinary piece of gossip. Perhaps in boldly bringing the affair out in the open and claiming that Lilli was aware and presumably accepting of it, Winchell's hidden intention was to help bring about what he announced as already the case. What is certain is that by making public an illicit romance, Winchell profoundly embarrassed the two principals and their spouses and almost certainly precipitated the divorce proceedings that Carole initiated against Schmidlapp on March 22, less than a week later.

The sudden publicity created an even greater crisis for Rex. According to Alexander Walker, it led him to acquire information from Zanuck and others about Carole's sex life that made him put the idea of marrying her out of his mind. Walker reports a conversation between Zanuck and Rex, presumably reported to him by Rex himself: "The hardest part of Zanuck's reprimand, where Rex was concerned, was his disclosure of Carole's lengthy history of promiscuousness. She was 'booked continuously,' she had had 'everyone on the lot,' he told his nervous leading man." It would be rash to dismiss these statements out of hand, although Zanuck was neither a disinterested observer of Carole's sex life nor a contemporary one (over two years had passed since Carole last worked at Fox), and moreover had a clear interest in preventing a scandal that would jeopardize his investment in Rex and Lilli.

Carole appears to have believed, or wanted to believe, Winchell's prognostication. Lloyd Shearer, editor of the syndicated newspaper weekly *Parade*, tells of a lunchtime conversation with Carole, almost certainly after her return to the United States in March, during which she struck him as "surprisingly gullible," spinning "impossible daydreams" of an idyllic future life with Rex. Shearer's words, although written after the fact, are one more confirmation that for Carole the affair with Rex corresponded to a loss of equilibrium, even a state of desperation.

During the last few months of her life Carole made plans to sell her house and drew up a divorce settlement with Schmidlapp that gave her custody of the house and its contents, minus the thirty thousand dollars that he had invested in the down payment; he would eventually refuse to honor this agreement because at the time of Carole's death it had not yet been signed by both parties. Despite being under a doctor's care for a recurrence of amoebic dysentery in late April, Carole continued to do her usual star turns, throwing out the first ball for the Western States Girls Softball League on April 30 and participating in a bond drive on May 3. According to

Louella, Edmond Gréville, who had just completed *Noose*, came to Hollywood in May "for the express purpose of signing Carole to a three picture deal." Carole also had a contract for her second Eagle-Lion film, *The Amazing Mr. X*, in which she was to play the starring role with Turhan Bey.

According to her secretary Nan Stuart, on Friday, July 2, Carole bought three hundred dollars' worth of new clothes; on the same day, she cut a brief 78 rpm disk for the fan-oriented "Star Records" series, describing two rather silly parlor games and ending with a request to her listener to "invite her back" in the near future. Carole had plans to go east right after July 4. Winchell noted in his July 14 column that the July 3 *New Yorker* listed Carole as appearing in *Laura* for the week of July 5–10 at the Carter Theater in Princeton, New Jersey, and a mailing card from the Lake Whalom Playhouse in Fitchburg, Massachusetts, advertises her in the same play for the week of August 9. And in an April 28 letter, Carole had stated in no uncertain terms that she was returning to England in the summer to act in another film. Nothing in Carole's behavior during this period suggests despondency or despair, let alone an intention to take her own life.

CHAPTER 10

The Good Die Young (1948)

If there is one area of Carole Landis's life that has been explored in detail, it is her suicide. In the months following the event, hints were dropped that some major revelation was in the offing, but nothing new was ever reported. Today the police files are gone or at any rate unavailable, and it seems unlikely that any new facts will emerge. But as in many so-called mysteries, despite some gaps in the evidence, there is not much doubt as to the basic facts of the case.

Rex and Carole had been together a great deal since he ended work on the ironically titled Preston Sturges comedy *Unfaithfully Yours* on April 20, 1948. Lilli Palmer, perhaps judging that leaving Rex alone with Carole would dull the excitement inherent in juggling two women, flew to New York in late May to stay with her sister. Possibly Carole interpreted this strategic retreat as a victory and was convinced that Rex would divorce Lilli to marry her. According to Alexander Walker, in order to smooth divorce proceedings, Carole had even taken the precaution of hiring a private detective to obtain evidence of Horace's "misconduct"—and, indeed, since Winchell's column and the divorce filing, gossip columnists had noted Horace's apparent interest in a number of other women. Carole "was very keen on a holiday in Lisbon" with Rex, but he feared that such a trip would stretch the limits of Lilli's tolerance and might precipitate an unwished-for divorce.

At this point, fate intervened in the form of an offer for Rex to perform in Maxwell Anderson's *Anne of the Thousand Days*, which would take him to Broadway and away from Hollywood and Carole. By Walker's estimation, Rex received the text in mid-June. Here is Rex's own account of what from the standpoint of the Harrison-Landis affair must be considered the proximate cause of Carole's suicide. We should note the clear indications of the relationship's intensity:

> [In the spring of 1948] Carole and I continued to meet, especially at weekends and in the evenings; when my film [*Unfaithfully Yours*] was finished, we were free to spend our days together on the beach and in her pool. Our feeling for each other showed no sign of abating. From time to time Carole seemed to withdraw from what was going on around her, as though temporarily she had gone elsewhere, except in the physical sense; but in a few minutes she would be herself again, and I attached little significance to these times.
>
> Just then I had a chance to do a play on Broadway, which thrilled me very much, for greatly as I had enjoyed working with Sturges, I was still restless for the theatre. When Leland Hayward offered me the part of Henry VIII in Maxwell Anderson's *Anne of the Thousand Days*, I saw it as a marvelous change of pace and a chance to get away from the lush life of Hollywood. [Rex would, indeed, play this role on Broadway in 1948–49; the play was subsequently made into a film in 1969.] . . . I read this play and loved it, and as I always like to have friends' opinions on plays that interest me, I told Carole of the offer and asked her to read the script and let me know what she thought of it.
>
> On the eve of July 4, the night before Leland was to take me down to Malibu Beach to meet Maxwell Anderson, I went up to Carole's for

supper. Carole said she thought it a fascinating play and a marvelous part. She seemed a little down, but I was so high myself on the idea of getting back into the theatre that I'm afraid I didn't notice the extent of her downness. I left quite early to go over to see Roland Culver, my old friend from the days of *French Without Tears* [the play that had made Rex's London reputation in 1936], who was working out there for Paramount. I had given him a copy of the play too and was anxious to know what he thought about it before I met the author. Roland and I had a long chat, and I shouldn't think I left there much before one o'clock. [In his deposition after the suicide, Rex gave the time as 1:30.] I went home and called Carole to say good night, and at the back of my mind I thought, Well, she sounds a little strange—but I made nothing very much of it.

On Sunday July 4, 1948, Carole had invited some friends for lunch and a pool party at her home on Capri Drive; the names of the attendees are not known. Later that evening, she had dinner, also in her home, with Rex; after the conversation he describes, he claimed at the coroner's inquest on July 8 that he left her, sober, between 9 and 9:30 p.m.; he also mentioned that he had discussed with Carole helping her to make another film in England, adding, "I have influence with producers there." The indication that Rex called Carole after returning home some time after 1:30 a.m. is not generally remarked upon in accounts of her suicide. If accurate, it means that Carole could not have taken the pills before that time; perhaps Rex's call precipitated her decision to do so. Carole was alone in the house; her regular maid, Susie Smith, had remained in New York on their return from England, no doubt because of Carole's delicate financial situation. (Curiously, Rex apparently used a variant of the maid's name, "Suzie," as a code for Carole when others were present.) Fannie May Bolden, who was temporarily filling the maid's position, did not stay overnight and in any case was off duty for the holiday.

Moseley quite plausibly suggests that apart from the pleasure of returning to the stage after nearly seven years, Rex's interest in getting away from "the lush life of Hollywood" reflected his need to have some time away from Carole to sort out his feelings about this intense but troubling relationship, while also reassuring Lilli that he was not abandoning his marriage. Walker goes farther, speculating that the July 4 conversation ended with Carole's refusal to accept Rex's departure, signaling from Rex's perspective "the end of the affair." All we may assume for certain is that there would have been a time of separation; Carole may well have feared, not without reason, that the spell of constant contact once broken, the relationship would never be the same.

Rex's statement that Carole "seemed a little down" without his quite realizing it, taken at face value, implies that she never gave voice to her disappointment. Rex may, of course, be dissimulating a violent quarrel; but given our knowledge of Carole's character, it seems more likely that she reacted with resignation. Carole was a "trouper," not one to seek to impose her will on someone who expressed a contrary desire of his own. She also had a fatalistic streak, seeing herself as an eternal fall guy in matters of love, even of simple friendship. We have witnessed this propensity in Carole's 1941 article "Glamour Girls Are Suckers" in the aftermath of her relationship with Franchot Tone, and it no doubt became more intense as she grew older and less sure of her future. Chicago journalist Michael Sheridan recalls a conversation with Carole, whom he calls "one of my closest and dearest friends," that took place "prior to the tragedy," that is, not long before it:

> Carole Landis was in a sad mood when she lunched with me in Beverly Hills. She was deeply shocked because she had befriended a young man in Philadelphia and, paying all his expenses, had brought him to Hollywood to work as her press agent. At the end of a few days, he had suddenly left without explanation, without even a murmur of thanks, and she had never heard from him again.
>
> "I should have been a clown," she said, ruefully, "I am always getting slapped. The slaps come from every direction, from the people I want to help, from those I want to love, from the big and little guys I'm sorry for."

If Carole had any character trait conducive to suicide, it was this tendency to take these "slaps" without retaliating. We may therefore assume that she did not quarrel with Rex that evening; a quarrel would likely have deflected onto him the violence she would soon turn upon herself.

Some time after Rex's call, Carole took a number of red tablets constituting a massive overdose of Seconal, a powerful barbiturate that Lupe Velez had already used to commit suicide in December 1944 and that would figure in a number of other high-profile deaths, including Charles Boyer's suicide in 1978, two days after the cancer death of his wife, and Dorothy Kilgallen's mysterious death in 1965. (Tennessee senator Estes Kefauver, later a Democratic vice-presidential candidate, suggested in 1949 that emetics be added to sedatives of this kind so that ingestion of a large dose would provoke vomiting; this suggestion had been generally implemented by the 1950s, although it was evidently not effective in every case.) The approximate time of Carole's death was given by Captain of Detectives Emmett Jones as 3 a.m.

According to a story faithfully repeated by everyone, including Rex, his biographers, and the press at the time these events were occurring, Lilli Palmer was in New York on the fourth and flew to Los Angeles only the following day, after Rex discovered Carole's body. Yet in her memoir, *The Million Dollar Mermaid*, published in 1999, over fifty years after the events, Esther Williams specifically recalls having spent the evening of July 4 at a barbecue given by Lilli in her Mandeville Canyon home, and that she stayed late chatting with Lilli while waiting for Rex, who never showed up (we recall that, according to his own story, he stayed at Culver's until about 1:30 a.m.). Williams insists on the strict enforcement of the cover-up she claims took place when Lilli arrived, supposedly from the airport, on the sixth. Williams's persuasive exposure of the studios' strenuous methods of averting scandal lends considerable credibility to her story, even in the absence of independent confirmation. Yet given that it was common knowledge that Lilli was in New York that spring, if we accept Williams's version of the events, the question arises as to exactly when and why Lilli *did* return to Hollywood. Unfortunately, confirmation of the details of Williams's book is not available.

Wherever Lilli was on the night of Carole's suicide, her autobiography tells of the following incident on the evening of July 6 that provides evidence of Carole's actions on that fatal night:

> A lawyer came to tell us that a Mrs. Haymes from New York was on the telephone. Rex went to take the call and was gone a long time. When he returned, he looked better. Mrs. Haymes, mother of the pop singer Dick Haymes, had been Carole's best friend. She wanted to tell him that Carole had made several suicide attempts before she ever met Rex. That is, she'd often taken an overdose of sleeping pills. Then she would call Mrs. Haymes, who would have time to summon a doctor with a stomach pump. The night before last, Mrs. Haymes had come home late and found a message that there had been a call from Los Angeles. But she hadn't called back, because it was so late.

Lilli's narrative leads us to assume that the Los Angeles call came from Carole, although she does not say explicitly that the number left in the message was hers. Lilli calls Carole's suicidal brinkmanship "going *va-banque* with life." It is not clear how many are "several" attempts, or whether it is reasonable to extrapolate from "several" to "often"; but even one or two would give credence to Lilli's analysis. Newspaper reports shortly after the event referred to two previous attempts, without giving specific dates or other details.

When Fannie May Bolden arrived for work on July 5, she tells us, perhaps in hindsight, "On my way up to the house I had an awful feeling. Something told me that something was wrong. . . . I went on in and the table was full of food and dishes from when they had dined that night of the fourth of July. I cleared up everything and went into the living room. All her cameras and diaries and portfolios were on the table and I dusted them all off." Rex called at about 11:30 and was told by Fannie May, as she had answered a previous caller, that Carole was still sleeping. Rex then had lunch as expected with producer Leland Hayward at Maxwell Anderson's house to discuss Anderson's new play. Rex called Carole again at about 3 p.m. and, becoming concerned that she was not yet up, came to the house, went upstairs, and found her body.

Despite the suspicions that inevitably arise in such cases, there is no reason to believe that Rex moved Carole's body or otherwise tampered with the evidence. Fannie May stated at the inquest that "[Rex] put his hand on her and he thought he felt life and asked me about a doctor." As Walker observes, this would certainly be grounds for condemning Rex's behavior in the following moments; instead of calling the police or an ambulance, he returned to his own home several minutes away at 1928 Mandeville Canyon to call his own doctor. But given that the time of Carole's death was estimated at 3 a.m., by the time Rex found her over twelve hours later it is certain that nothing could be done.

As seen in a widely distributed coroner's photograph taken later in the day, Carole, still wearing the outfit in which she had dined with Rex the night before—dirndl skirt, frilly white blouse, and gold sandals—was curled up on the floor on a plush gold rug near the doorway of her upstairs bathroom. Carole was described in the July 6 *Herald Examiner* as wearing a locket around her neck on a gold chain, although this may be an inaccurate description of Diana Lewis's small cross. Her head rested on a jewelry box, her hand held a rosary as well as an envelope from Horace's Carleton House address containing a single pill; it bore the handwritten words, "Red-quick-2 hrs., Yellow, about 5. Can take 2." Carole's hands were positioned under her body as if she had made a final effort to rise but no longer had the strength. Four empty sleeping tablet bottles were found nearby. Propped on a nearby dressing table was a suicide note addressed to her mother that has often been reproduced:

> Dearest mommie, I'm sorry, really sorry, to put you through this. But there is no way to avoid it.

I love you darling. You have been the most wonderful mom ever. And that applies to all our family. I love each and every one of them dearly.

Everything goes to you. Look in the files, and there is a will which decrees everything. [This will was not found.]

Good bye, my angel.

Pray for me.

Your baby.

The note is touching, but as might be expected under the circumstances, it fails to explain why the suicide could not be avoided. Carole's close friend Florence Wasson mentioned a second note handed her some time that afternoon by an unknown man, which she then handed back to him; of its contents, she recalled only instructions to take Carole's cat Miss C. (the correct name, although it is sometimes spelled Missy or Mitzi) to the veterinarian for a sore paw. Whether such a sore paw existed has been questioned; Carole's mother examined the cat and found nothing out of the ordinary. The second note was probably not left in the bathroom along with the note to Clara; perhaps it was written before Carole formulated her suicide plan and left downstairs as a routine communication between late-sleeping Carole and her maid.

Lilli Palmer recounts that just before Rex was to give evidence to the coroner on July 8, a policeman came to her door and offered her a note that he claimed had been found in Carole's clenched hand, asking five hundred dollars for it because "it contained something highly compromising." When Harrison's lawyers decided to pay him the money, the note they received was "a small piece of crumpled paper. . . . On it, a few almost illegible words: 'The cat has a sore paw. She must go to the vet.'" But Walker claims to have spoken to a former Los Angeles police officer who told him that he had seen the note and that it was in fact "a three-line lover's farewell to Rex Harrison. He has no idea what happened to it." If Palmer's story is true, save for the note's contents, it is all too clear what must have happened to it. But none of these statements has a clear ring of truth. All we can say is that under normal circumstances, Carole would have avoided compromising Rex by writing him a note that she had no assurance he would be first to find—yet the last moments of one's life are not normal circumstances.

Another account refers to a note to Rex left in a more plausible manner. Rex's old friend Roland Culver claimed in his 1979 autobiography that Carole had left two small cases full of letters and other personal materials with a note to Rex that night at the generally unused front gate of Culver's house at 750 Napoli Drive, Pacific Palisades; the cases had remained undetected until two friends came to visit later in the day. Culver claims that these materials were "miraculously" preserved from prying eyes when the press failed to come to his house to verify Rex's story. (Culver also backed up Lilli's story that she flew in after the suicide; is this something he would lie about thirty years later? Surely he would have known had she been in Los Angeles on July 4.) Culver confirmed his story to Moseley in a conversation "shortly before his death" in 1984.

Walker, without revealing a specific source, reduces these cases to "a package" that Carole deposited "in the mailbox at the Culvers' front gate and left Rex's portfolio beside it"; he adds that Leland Hayward brought these materials, discovered by Culver's wife, Nan, to Rex "under cover of darkness" and that Rex burned in his fireplace the letters and the "slower-burning photograph albums" containing the many photographs of Rex that Carole had taken and developed herself. On the basis of Culver's story, Walker claims that "Rex and his friends concluded" that since Carole knew that Rex was going to Culver's after he left her, she left the materials in order for him to discover them, not knowing that he would not use that gate—an interpretation that makes good sense, assuming that Walker had direct evidence that this "conclusion" was actually drawn by Rex and friends at the time. Walker goes overboard, however, in speculating that since Fannie May reported that Rex felt a sign of life, Carole had actually taken the Seconal late in the morning (despite Captain Jones's 3 a.m. death estimate) and left the cases in the expectation that the mail would be delivered as normal that Monday (instead of being cancelled because the fourth fell on a Sunday) and that Culver would go to the gate, find the cases, and perhaps prevent her death.

If Carole did leave the cases—and why would Culver have imagined such a story?—this would indicate at the very least that her suicide was rather less impulsive than it seemed and that it was, like her previous over-doses, a cry for help, this time addressed to Rex as well as Mrs. Haymes. Otherwise, the act of leaving the cases could have been intended as any-thing from a gesture of rejection to a thoughtful attempt to protect Rex from scandal, nor can we assume that Carole had a clear intention in her own mind. Napoli Drive was a little over a mile from her house, in the opposite direction from Rex's. Given Carole's normally unvengeful dis-position, it made sense for her to leave the cases at Culver's rather than at Rex's own home—all the more so if Lilli was really in town.

We recall that Fannie May, arriving on the morning of July 5, found "all [Carole's] diaries and portfolios" scattered on the dining-room table. Is this evidence that Carole had extracted the compromising parts to take to Rex? Was she going through these things in preparation for her suicide? Or were they simply props for Carole's conversation with Rex the night before? As for the note to Rex that Culver's autobiography claims was attached to one of the cases, this was apparently not confirmed in his conversation with Moseley, who, noting that Culver's story first appeared thirty years after the event, calls this reference a "curious, inexplicable statement."

The coroner's examination showed that Carole had a blood alcohol content of 0.12, close to the level associated with drunkenness; presumably, she had either continued to drink after Rex left or had taken alcohol along with the pills. Another revelation of the coroner's report was that Carole was unable to bear children because of a "peculiar natural condition"; no anatomical details were divulged.

Rex's detailed interrogation at the coroner's "informal inquest" on July 8, which is, along with Fannie May's testimony, the source of most of our information about the circumstances of the suicide, received a great deal of publicity. A reporter mentions the controlling presence at the hearing, along with Rex's lawyer, of a "man from Twentieth Century-Fox studios." Rex understandably did not reveal that he and Carole were engaged in a love affair. Although his testimony left open many questions that still remain unanswered, we have no reason to doubt its accuracy in general terms.

Following the coroner's hearing, the police case was closed. Carole's handwritten note to her mother in conjunction with the absence of any sign of foul play gave seemingly indisputable proof that her death was by her own hand. There is no plausible alternative; the idea that Rex somehow got Carole to write the suicide note and take the Seconal is preposterous. And from everything we know of her, Carole was the last person who would have threatened Rex with blackmail or given him any other motive for murdering her. On the contrary, Carole's death brought great embarrassment to Rex and his family.

Carole's sister, Dorothy, the strongest figure in the family, made the funeral arrangements. On July 8 Carole was taken to the Wilshire Funeral Home in Santa Monica and decked out in the blue "butterfly" dress she loved; the *Los Angeles Times* reported a hundred visitors. A plot was obtained and the funeral ceremony set for Saturday, July 10, in the Church of the Recessional at Forest Lawn Cemetery in Glendale.

Carole's funeral attracted a large contingent from Hollywood, a number of family and friends, and a huge crowd of fans, who could not all fit in the church. Rex and Lilli attended, Lilli wearing blue rather than black, which a friend had told her was the appropriate color for the funeral of one's husband's mistress. Schmidlapp, estranged from Carole for several months and having already moved on to other romances, attended in bewilderment.

Since Carole's death was a suicide, her funeral service could not be conducted by a Catholic priest. Bishop Fred L. Pyman of the Evangelical Orthodox Church delivered a seven-minute funeral eulogy, broadcast over a loudspeaker to the crowd outside, that began with a quote from *As You*

Like It: "All the world's a stage and all the men and women merely players. But life is merely a dress rehearsal for what is to come afterward. If we do not play our parts right, we will have a chance to play them over again. . . . She was a regular trouper who never overplayed her lines. You never had to call on her twice; in spite of heartache and illness, she went through with her work. I don't think Almighty God will judge her too harshly."

Carole's pallbearers were actors Pat O'Brien, Cesar Romero, and Willard Parker; Bill Nye, Carole's former makeup man at Fox; golf pro Lou Wasson, husband of Carole's friend and former stand-in, Florence Wasson; and the sixth, missing from some accounts, director Eddie Sutherland, who replaced Dick Haymes, delayed by bad weather in Chicago. News accounts tell of the crowd's unruliness and its despoiling the fresh grave of flowers; a more charitable description might be that people took home souvenirs of the funeral out of affection for the deceased.

Condolence flowers, letters, and telegrams were received from numerous Hollywood personalities, including Carole's former boss Darryl Zanuck, former "Jill" Martha Raye, Carmen Miranda, and David Niven; Willis Hunt and his new wife sent flowers, and the mothers of both Tommy Wallace and Horace Schmidlapp wrote very warmly to Clara. In the late fall of 1948, Carole's fan club published a final, memorial issue of her fan magazine, *The Caroler*, containing letters from Olivia de Havilland and Cesar Romero, as well as many touching tributes from fans in whose affection Carole was more a personal friend than a movie star. The common theme of these tributes was that Carole's greatest beauty was that of her soul, not her body.

Carole's grave at Forest Lawn, just off the curb on a hill in the Everlasting Love section, lot 814, space 8, is covered with a brass plate bearing a lovely inscription formulated by Dorothy: "To our beloved Carole, whose love, graciousness and kindness touched us all—who will always be with us in the beauties of this earth until we meet again."

In the following months, articles appeared in a few movie magazines and in such publications as *True Confessions* telling the story of Carole's life and attempting to explain her suicide. Although a few columnists included touching tributes, most of the writers and periodicals that had followed Carole's career made no mention of the suicide. Walter Winchell on Friday, July 9, under the pen name "Your Girl Friday," wrote: "Can't get that photo of Carole Landis crumpled up on the floor out of my mind. She was so full of pep, laughing, yelling, 'Hi!' and being All Girl All The Time. All the time, that is, except when the heart can't stand the pain, anymore." Winchell also included in his July 15 column a letter from Commander Bonney Powell, who described Carole's performance on Guadalcanal in 1944: "Never have I seen a more compassionate, inspiring and under-standing person." Winchell himself concluded, "The Landis tragedy proves that the greatest dramas in Hollywood are not filmed—they're lived."

News items appeared quoting Carole's purported reaction to Lupe Velez's suicide, by identical means, in December 1944: "I know just how she felt. I've often thought of suicide. You fight just so long, and then what have you got to face? You begin to worry about being washed up. You get bitter and disillusioned. You fear the future because there is only one path for you—that's down." This story may well be true, but it would have been more credible had it appeared before Carole's own suicide.

A great deal was also written about the Harrisons. Lilli gained public sympathy for standing by her husband, and one movie writer even sug-gested that Harrison's box-office value had benefited from the notoriety generated by the scandal. The Harrisons nevertheless left Hollywood, first for Paris and then, encountering serious fiscal problems, for New York, where Rex eventually won a Tony for the role of Henry VIII that he had discussed with Carole that Independence Day. He appeared on some tele-vision shows and finally returned to Hollywood in 1952 for *The Four Poster*, a low-budget picture at Columbia in which he and Lilli played the leading roles, the marriage bed acting, so to speak, as a counterweight to *Unfaithfully Yours*. But their marriage had suffered a fatal blow. Rex divorced Lilli in February 1957 in order to marry the terminally ill Kay Kendall, who would die of leukemia two years later. He somehow thought that Lilli would remarry him after Kay's death, but that was not to be. Rex went on to marry three more times; his fourth wife, actress Rachel Roberts, also committed suicide. Rex Harrison died in 1990 at the age of eighty-two.

The hours preceding the suicide on the morning of July 4–5, 1948, have been discussed on many occasions and in great detail in the hope of finding some specific clue to Carole's motivation. We have no need to quarrel with Rex's account that he left Carole sober but "down" after hearing of his Broadway plans. The burden of the various analyses from Rex's side of the equation is that Carole's relationship with Rex was a desperate passion that she perceived as her last chance to set aright both her personal and professional life, so that the prospect of a lengthy separation, even if it did not signal an explicit break, was sufficient to push her over the edge.

One point that has tended to be forgotten, although it is insisted upon by Carole's anonymous "lifelong friend" in her November *True Confessions* article, is that for Carole this adulterous relationship was a source of considerable guilt and anxiety. With all her sexual experience, Carole had a strong moral sense. Although she hoped to regularize the situation by marriage, which explains her readiness for a new divorce, she was no doubt aware in the back of her mind that Rex would be unlikely to divorce Lilli to marry her. At the same time, as even Walker acknowledges, there is no evidence that Rex intended to end his relationship with Carole; it may even be that Carole herself wanted to do so. There was as much despair for her in imagining that the relationship would continue as in accepting that it would end.

There is direct evidence of Carole's anguished emotional state. Her family collection contains•an undated poem in typescript with corrections added by hand entitled "Through the Looking Glass Window," evidently addressed to Rex, in which Carole reveals the intensity of her guilty passion and her knowledge of its destructiveness. The handwritten portions are less regular and appear more agitated than Carole's writing on a draft letter to Horace's lawyer dating from March or April 1948. The poem expresses her despair and inability to continue the relationship and asks her lover to free her from it and the pain of the desire he inspires in her; at the same time she speaks of the joy of their love, the gentleness of her lover, and the intensity of her desire. Carole has at last found the one she has sought, but he is not free, so they can only steal moments together. The poem ends by affirming that the couple will be punished in Hell for their love.

Carole's personality lent itself to sharp emotional ups and downs; today we might even call her "bipolar." She had learned from earliest childhood to put a smiling face on things, not to reveal her depressive side to anyone other than family and intimate friends. Carole's behavior was often described as "uninhibited," but her wildness was strictly contained. She could hike up her skirt to show Earl Wilson her slightly bowed legs and display her bosom in low-cut dresses, and on occasion she could have a bit too much to drink, but there is no record of incidents of public disorder, crashing cars, and the like that had to be hushed up by "fixers." As a number of post mortems pointed out, Carole's sometimes boisterous gaiety was often a way of disguising her moments of depression.

I insist on this for two reasons, one general and one specific. In the first place, unless one is terminally ill, irremediably disgraced, or otherwise facing "a fate worse than death," there is never a *reason* for suicide. We all have our problems, and few even of those in the most horrible difficulties do away with themselves. Suicide can seldom be predicted; it can only be explained after the fact. The second, more specific reason is that if there *is* a factor that is a good predictor of suicide, it is neither a specific misfortune nor even a degree of misfortune; it is *depression*. When someone gives up on life, the "cause" is to be found more in that person's depressive pre-disposition than in the circumstances of his or her life that triggered this predisposition. Fox actress Martha Stewart, who worked in *Doll Face* and took over the second female lead she claims was originally meant for Carole in the 1947 musical *I Wonder Who's Kissing Her Now*, told me that Carole was in a depressed state when Stewart spoke to just a few days before her suicide; Stewart told her not to be upset over Rex.

This being said, it is important for an understanding of Carole's life to be able to *situate* her suicide, both in relation to the specific circumstances that preceded it and to her life and career. Some writers have alleged Carole's financial difficulties as a contributing cause. These difficulties were real; at her death, Carole left over $51,000 in obligations, including unpaid bills of $6,500 from Maximilian Furs, $2,771 from Don Loper's apparel company, $2,025 to a jewelry firm, $1,896 from Elizabeth Arden for cosmetics, as well as payments to her attorney; the total could not have been covered without the sale of her home. Yet these debts did not prevent her from making a $300 clothing purchase two days before her death. Nor did Carole lack for sources of income, including another film under contract with Eagle-Lion (for which she had received an advance of $7,500) and the possibility of several others, as well as probable offers from England; she was scheduled to perform at the Princeton Drama Festival and at least two other venues in July and August. Carole's divorce agreement with Schmidlapp would have given her the proceeds of the sale of their home, which came to $66,000 in March 1949—and which would probably have been higher absent the scandal that became attached to the property.

A sinister variant on the financial theme, which appeared in Florabel Muir's post-mortem article, "What's Behind the Carole Landis Tragedy?" is that Carole's financial difficulties were due to large sums she was paying a blackmailer not to reveal the nature of her activities in her early days in San Francisco. Considering that Jimmy Starr's account alone would have sufficed to destroy Carole's reputation, this story is far from implausible. Blackmail would certainly have added to Carole's stress. Yet it is curious that the facts supposedly being covered up were never revealed after Carole's death.

Crawford Dixon's explanation that Carole was "jaded" and that, once she realized the impossibility of Rex "belonging to her," she lost hope of ever finding a stable love relationship is probably closer to the mark. What was despairing about the love affair was not that Rex wanted to leave but that the situation could not be stabilized; there was nothing to hope for and no end in sight. If Rex went to New York, Carole would be once again in limbo as she had been in 1943 and '44, except that the new "Tommy" was married to someone else. One imagines that had Rex simply decided to drop Carole it would have been a source of pain and humiliation, but also of relief.

An all-too-obvious contributing cause of Carole's suicide was her frequent use of, and partial dependency on, barbiturates to put her to sleep. Biographer Frank Smoot mentions a prescription for fifty Seconal tablets written on October 26, 1946, a few days after Carole's release from the hospital after an attack of amoebic dysentery. Carole herself suggests a complementary dependency on what we call "uppers": "Mitzi was feeling so tired I gave her a Benzedrine pill. Back home my doctor had given me some of these pills and I always carried them around with me in a little bottle, in case of emergency." The suicide attempts Lilli Palmer describes as preludes to the final one could only have been brought off by someone all too much at ease, like many Hollywood personalities then and now, with powerful medications—the "dolls" of Jacqueline Susann's Carole-inspired novel. Carole's personal physician, Dr. Maynard D. Brandsma, claimed never to have prescribed sleeping pills, but there was no lack of other sources.

In my judgment, the most prominent background factor in Carole's suicide, which made it increasingly likely that a passing setback would trigger a depressive impulse to end it all, was that mentioned in the previous chapter: her dread of aging. With the first days of July, Carole had entered the second half of her thirtieth year. Her remark to Jean Porter that she shouldn't grow old was now about to be tested in practice.

No doubt there is more to live for than physical beauty, even for a woman as beautiful as Carole. But like a number of her contemporaries whose deaths were fully or partially self-inflicted—among many others, Marie "The Body" McDonald, who took an overdose at forty-two; Maria Montez, one of the truly beautiful women of Hollywood, found dead in her bath at the age of thirty-four (some say thirty-nine); or Carole's lovely African American friend Dorothy Dandridge, a barbiturate suicide at forty-one—Carole's fundamental way of relating to others of either sex was mediated by her beauty.

Carole enjoyed the assurance of knowing that the mere sight of her gave pleasure. Carole's attractiveness also gave her power over men—which she was generous enough in most circumstances to exploit only for benign purposes. The prospect of losing the instrument of both the power and the gift must have been very painful. Whatever other hopes Carole might have nourished, including the possibility of a career in the nascent medium of television, the age of thirty probably seemed to her a full measure of the fatigue of life, giving her decision to leave it before the fatal date something like an objective justification. Carole's beauty was living and dynamic, and an examination of her later photographs, particularly in her last few months, suggests that it had, indeed, lost something of its freshness. No doubt Carole would have remained a beautiful woman for decades; but she could not hope to retain indefinitely the synthesis of beauty and desirability that made her unique.

Carole had often expressed the desire to "have a very wonderful marriage and children whom I may love and make a fuss over long after the movies are gone." Had she remained with Horace and adopted a child or two, she could have had such things; but for Carole this image, modeled on Dorothy's happy family life, was never a real alternative. Perhaps in her last months she fantasized that with Rex, a man of theater and cinema with whom she could share her career as well as her private life, things would be different; but however intense the relationship became, it was never the equivalent of marriage. To the extent that the prospect of coming separation raised in her conversation with Rex on the fatal evening brought this reality home to her, it can rightly be called the "sudden great shock" that her attorney Jerry Giesler judged to be the precipitating factor, the Aristotelian efficient cause, of Carole's suicide.

Carole left little to her heirs. Shortly after her death, her estate was estimated at a mere $20,000. Horace, as was his right, was unwilling to honor the unfinalized divorce agreement. On November 9, he filed a claim on Carole's estate for 50 percent of community property plus $35,000 he claimed he had contributed to the purchase of the house on Capri Drive, alleging that Carole had reimbursed only $12,000 of his contribution. On January 21, 1950, nearly a year after the house was sold, the *Los Angeles Times* reported that Horace's claim was finally settled for $15,000. After a few more years of playboy life, Horace remarried and settled down; he died in Florida in 1987.

From March 21 to 23, 1949, Carole's possessions were sold at auction at the Lewis H. Hart Gallery; the estate included furniture, furs, jewelry, and flatware valued by some accounts at over $100,000. Yet the *Los Angeles Times* reported on March 24 that Carole's grand piano went for $1,750, her Chinese Chippendale bedroom set for $925, and her silver flatware for $700; the total proceeds were a mere $16,910. When the moneys from the sale of the house ($67,500) and other items (including $50 for her Great Dane) were all added up, the total came to nearly $85,000, leaving some $34,000 after deducting Carole's $51,000 in debts. After Schmidlapp took his $15,000 settlement for the house in January 1950, Carole's final inheritance came to about $19,000—and millions of memories.

Given the overall mediocrity of the films in which she appeared and the malaise left by her suicide, it is understandable that for several decades after her death Carole all but dropped out of sight. She scarcely figures in the books devoted to either the studios where she worked (Republic is an exception) or the screen beauties of her era. Even accounts of Hollywood's contribution to the war effort barely mention her. In the popular mind, if Carole was remembered at all, it was for her suicide. Beyond that, references to her in mass-circulation film literature and reference works often took their cue from Sperling's "studio hooker" story of her trysts with Zanuck, no doubt borrowed at secondhand from Kenneth Anger's dismissive account in *Hollywood Babylon II*. Nor did Carole benefit from the wave of feminist film criticism that began in the 1970s. Although one might have expected the "studio hooker" line to be a red flag for critics of Hollywood "patriarchy," Carole goes unmentioned in both Molly Haskell's widely read *From Reverence to Rape* and Marjorie Rosen's *Popcorn Venus*.

Today, there has been a modest renewal of interest in Carole. No doubt it would be going too far to call it a revival, but two recent books, E. J. Fleming's and the present work, as well as a sympathetic chapter in another (*Hollywood Blondes*, by Liz Nocera and Michelle Vogel), along with several active Web sites and online newsgroups, give evidence that Carole speaks to us today as she could not while the circumstances of her suicide and the chaos of her personal life cast their shadows over her memory.

The harmonious and self-confident femininity of the 1940s stands out between the contrived artiness of the '30s and the gaudiness and banality of the '50s. It embodied civilization's fundamental affirmation of life amidst war and massacre and showed the Allied forces "what they were fighting for" in defending it. No one better than Carole incarnates this privileged era. There is scarcely a trace in her films of sexual exhibitionism; her famous sigh was the limit of her public sensuality. Carole was not a seductress because for her the possibility of her own response was a necessary condition of provoking the other's desire. Nor does Carole ever allow the other's gaze to become a token of superiority; she is always a subject, never an object. Hence, it is no surprise that the majority of Carole's most devoted fans have been and still are women.

To retain our dignity before someone whose beauty is so uncompromisingly sexual grants us a moment of freedom from the tension between "disinterested" appreciation and desire. For the person of either gender who contemplates Carole at the height of her beauty, the erotic ceases for a moment to be transgressive; carnal knowledge no longer banishes us from Eden. Of all the beautiful women of the age of glamour, none more than Carole allows us to experience beauty as truth, as human generosity made visible. That is why I am certain that she will not be forgotten and that the years will only add to the wonder the traces of her presence inspire.

NOTES

Introduction

"one or two sympathetic biographical essays": Notably, Kirk Crivello's chapter in *Fallen Angels* (Secaucus, N.J.: Citadel Press, 1988), which expands on an article in the November 1973 *Film Fan Monthly*, and John Austin's chapter in *Hollywood's Babylon Women* (New York: SPI Books, 1994). When I began my research, Frank Smoot's Web site at www.carolelandis.net contained a lengthy biography of Carole, as well as some bibliographical data; it has since been taken down. Subsequently, E. J. Fleming's *Carole Landis: A Tragic Life in Hollywood* was published by McFarland in the spring of 2005.

"studio hooker": Leonard Mosley, *Zanuck: The Rise and Fall of Hollywood's Last Tycoon* (New York: Little Brown, 1984): 243.

"prostituted herself": Mart Martin, *Did She or Didn't She?* (Secaucus, N.J.: Citadel Press, 1996), 101: "She kept prostituting herself in Hollywood—frequently making her sexual favors available to high studio execs at both Warner Bros, and 20th Century-Fox, in hopes of obtaining larger and better roles." Martin's book is a compendium on movie stars' sex lives.

"brassiere-worship": "Casualty in Hollywood," Time, July 19, 1948. The text of this obituary article begins, "Like millions of other American girls, Frances Lillian Mary Ridste had a voracious hunger for happiness. Like millions of others she was certain she knew the definition of that sad and elusive word. It meant being rich and famous. It meant having a big car and fine clothes. It meant having a shapely body, unashamedly shown. It meant being madly in love with a handsome man. It meant applause.

By dint of this wild thinking, and because she lived in what may become known as the era of American brassiere-worship, Frances Lillian Mary Ridste became a motion-picture star. . . . But Carole Landis was still Frances Lillian Mary Ridste, a lovely torso, not an actress."

"Walter Winchell's remark": In his column of July 12, 1948.

"artist James Montgomery Flagg": The quote is from the text accompanying Flagg's November 7, 1941, silhouette drawing of Carole in the *Los Angeles Evening Herald Examiner*, entitled "Carole Landis, Silhouette Girl."

"Many of their letters": A collection of Carole's letters that recently sold, one or two at a time on eBay, illustrates Carole's assiduity as a correspondent. These thirty-five letters, including a few that Carole's secretary wrote when Carole was on tour, cover the years 1941–1947; their content makes clear that when they began, Carole's correspondent could not have been past her early teens, nor does her name figure among the officers of Carole's various fan clubs. The letters give evidence that Carole's policy was to answer promptly every single letter she received. In the posthumous edition of *The Caroler*, one correspondent mentions having received "over 100 letters and cards" from Carole.

"excess of beauty became a theme of her films": The closest comparison that comes to mind is with the equally intelligent, very differently beautiful Louise Brooks, whose role in the little-known French film *Prix de beauté* (Genina, 1930) bears comparison with Carole's in *I Wake Up Screaming*. But Brooks's career problems in Hollywood stemmed from her rebellious personality rather than her beauty per se.

Chapter 1. Beginnings (1919–1945)

Most of what we know about Carole's childhood comes from three articles published after her suicide in July 1948: Clara Ridste Landis, "The True Story of Carole Landis," *True Story*, October 1948; D[orothy] Ross, "The True Story of My Sister," *Photoplay*, November 1948; A lifelong friend, "The Truth about Carole Landis," *True Confessions*, November 1948. Additional material is found in "I Am Carole Landis," *Life Story*, August 1943, a first-person, although obviously ghost-aided, account. A letter from Dorothy Ross in Carole's Special Collections file at the AMPAS Herrick Library contains a few additional details (including a suggestion for the identity of the "lifelong friend"). The childhood reminiscences scattered throughout Carole's various interviews and publicity bios are almost always focused on a few emblematic incidents.

"Carole's mother was born": Census data for 1900 to 1930 are taken from the ancestry.com Web site, birth and other data from copies of birth certificates and other official documents.

"Fairchild, a small village": The quoted passage is from "A small-town midwest beauty," a biographical sketch of Carole on Frank Smoot's now defunct www.carolelandis.net Web site. Smoot is a resident of Eau Claire, Wisconsin, and can be relied on for his knowledge of the region, although his account of Carole's life contains many inaccuracies.

"To judge from the letters she wrote later": Thanks to Carole's second cousin Diane Madir for supplying me with copies of some of Clara's letters as well as the snowmobile photo.

"but because there were so many other Andersens": Diane Madir also gave me a copy of a fragmentary genealogy prepared by Clara in 1973 that contains this information.

"If we credit the story": This was told to me by Dorothy's daughter Sharon, who cited complications resulting from the pandemic as the cause for Carole's inability to bear children.

"on January 2, 1919": This is the date and time on the birth certificate. E. J. Fleming's speculation that Carole was really born a month or two later is based on Clara's declaring Frances as "11/12" months old to the census taker on January 28, 1920. In the absence of any obvious motive for falsifying Frances's date of birth, it is absurd to attribute more credibility to an unverified statement by Clara than to an official birth certificate dated in three places.

"Clara and the children returned to Denton": Clara's account speaks of the trip to Denton, although she diplomatically fails to mention her divorce and remarriage to Fenner. Copies of the marriage license and divorce decrees were obtained from the Fergus County courthouse at Lewistown, Montana.

"rejoined Ridste in San Diego": Curiously, Clara does not mention the detour to San Diego. At the time of her divorce from Fenner, in late March and early April 1921, the court decree states that Clara was residing "temporarily" in San Diego "by reason of necessity." Dorothy mentions vague early memories of San Diego. Clara says that she moved to San Bernardino when Carole was "just three," that is, early in 1922.

"a job, not a reconciliation": "I Am Carole Landis," *Life Story*, August 1943.

"Carole attended Jefferson Grade School": This information is from Kirk Crivello's *Fallen Angels* chapter on Carole, p. 86; Crivello gives no source for this information, which is plausible given the proximity of the schools to her home. Unfortunately, the San Bernardino School District refuses to release Carole's school records for reasons of "privacy."

"The unhappiest event": The most thorough account of this incident is in the *San Bernardino Sun*, July 17 and 18, 1925; the description of Lewis's wound is confirmed by his death certificate.

"performance of the bouncy 'That's My Weakness Now' ": Aside from Clara's article, the story is found in "Love Would Come First!" *Movies*, January 1944; a June 1944 Fox publicity bio; "Make Up Your Mind: Carole Landis' Real-Life Movie," *Screen Guide*, October 1944; "Movie Star and Millionaire," *Movie Show*, September 1946; and in many other publications.

"a patsy for a handsome male": Quoted from Carole's former publicity agent and near-fiancé Kenny Morgan in Elgar Brown's postmortem biography in the *Chicago Herald-American*, July 8–14, 1948.

"The two beauty contests": Sources aside from Clara's article are "It's Out-Landis!—Intimate Close-Up of That Gentlemen-Preferred Blonde," *Modern Screen*, October 1941; "If I Were Victor Mature," *Silver Screen*, July 1942; "Carole Landis: Movie Star Finds Happiness in War Marriage," *Look*, June 29, 1943; "Love Would Come First! Carole Landis on Marriage and Career," *Movies*, January 1944; January and June 1944 Fox publicity bios; "Movie Star and Millionaire," *Movie Show*, September 1946.

"she never seeks to invade our world": My thanks to Kathlene Avakian for this formulation.

"In a letter to Carole's fan club": In Carole's file at the Herrick Library. Since Dorothy mentions only herself and a friend as spectators of Carole's "grace and beauty," it seems probable that there was no third party present other than Carole herself.

"the names of a tableful of people": The November 6, 1945, *Los Angeles Times* column, "Farmers Market with Mrs. Fred Beck," recounts an incident at the market where Carole, introduced to "nine low characters" at a table, heard all their names once, then repeated them, getting only one wrong.

"her teachers called her a 'bad girl' ": Quoted in Elgar Brown's *Herald-American* bio.

"She was a smart girl with a wonderful memory": This quote and the following is from Carole's "lifelong friend," whose list of Carole's occupations is suspiciously similar to that given by Carole herself in "I Am Carole Landis," *Life Story*, August 1943, where she tells of her difficulty in making change.

"The one academic achievement Carole claimed": Vera Cecil, "Screen Beauty: Carole Landis Tells Intimate Details of Her Life," *Police Gazette*, December 1944; also the source of the "old jalopy."

"she claimed to have broken both her nose": The source for this is Sidney Skolsky's "Tintype" of Carole, several versions of which appeared in his daily column through 1945; the first came out on March 18, 1941. Skolsky also describes Carole's "jalopy" more precisely as "a runabout with one smashed fender, a light out, and ragged upholstery."

"A fellow (female) high-schooler described her as 'boy-crazy' ": Charlotte Vaughn, quoted in Smoot's Web bio.

"She would develop crushes on older boys": Carole describes one such infatuation in Cyril Vandour's "Carole Landis: Love Is What You Make It," *Movies*, July 1941, where, after getting her "prince charming" to ask her on a date, she discovered he was "so boring!"

"what she most demanded of men": In "What Carole Landis Demands of Men!" with Gladys Hall, *Screenland*, October 1941. This important article is analyzed in chapter 5.

"a capsule description of Carole by Phil Silvers": Phil Silvers with Robert Saffron, *This Laugh Is on Me: The Phil Silvers Story* (Englewood Cliffs, N.J.: Prentice-Hall, 1973), 122.

"a nice-looking boy of 19": "I Am Carole Landis," *Life Story*, August 1943.

"another was to get out of school": Judith Banner, "Lucky Landis," *Hollywood*, May 1941: "So intensely did she dislike school (except for English, gym and sewing) she ran away to Yuma and got married when she was 15 because she thought a married woman would be exempt." This is the only place where Carole tells us she liked English!

"having obtained her father's permission": This information is provided by Carole's "lifelong friend" in her November 1948 *True Confessions* article, along with Irving's aqueduct-digging job and Carole's inability to cook.

"someone who always believed in romantic love": In Cyril Vandour's "Carole Landis: Love Is What You Make It," *Movies*, July 1941, Carole calls herself "an incorrigible romantic and optimist." In her contribution to the multi-star article "You Love Him If . . ." in the November 1943 *Photoplay*, she claims, "In my opinion real love has nothing to do with friendship or respect. . . . Real love is love at first sight."

"diaries, sadly forever lost": Two movie magazine articles purportedly contain extracts from Carole's diary: "Dear Diary" (*Modern Screen*, April 1942) and "My Dog Is Dead" (*Motion Picture*, April 1944); the introduction to *Four Jills in a Jeep* refers to a service diary given her by a British wing commander just before her departure for England in October 1942.

Chapter 2. In Northern California (1935–1937)

"the financing of her departure": This tale, with the iconic figure of $16.82, is told in a number of autobiographical articles, many of which have already been mentioned; Kyle Crichton, "Determined Lady," *Colliers*, May 10, 1941; Dudley Early's biographical piece in the January 2, 1942, *Family Circle*; "Carole Landis: Movie Star Finds Happiness in War Marriage," *Look*, June 29, 1943; Elizabeth Wilson's "Landis without Leopard Skins," *Liberty*, July 19, 1947; and several others as well as a number of Fox publicity bios.

"the most reliable account": In Carole's mother's heavily ghosted article, "The True Story of Carole Landis," in the October 1948 *True Story*, Clara quotes the following conversation: " 'I have a hundred dollars,' [Carole] told me. She had saved it from her earnings at the café. 'I won't go to Hollywood first. That's too tough for a beginner. I'll start with San Francisco. The bus ticket is nearly seventeen dollars. That will leave me almost eighty-five dollars to live on until I get a job.' " The "nearly seventeen" is a good sign that the $16.82 figure was one Carole remembered from her trip and repeated as a guarantee of authenticity to her interviewers. In "I Am Carole Landis" in the August 1943 *Life Story*, Carole speaks of having saved up $26; the $47 figure is from the otherwise highly inaccurate portrayal of Carole's life in "Suicide of a Sex Symbol," *Headlines*, November 1972.

"in any newspaper": this refers to newspapers whose archives are available on line, including the *New York Times* and the *Los Angeles Times*, small-town papers indexed by ancestry.com, as well as many others, including the *Fresno Bee* and the *Oakland Tribune*—which has extensive San Francisco coverage—but no San Francisco paper, at newpaperarchive.com.

" 'favorite name' ": Sidney Skolsky in his "Tintype of Carole Landis" on March 18, 1941 (repeated with changes on March 10, 1942, July 22, 1943, and November 23, 1945; Skolsky got the most out of his copy), asserts, "Carole was always her favorite name." Skolsky also mentions finding "Landis" as one of two hundred names selected from a telephone book. Judith Banner's profile, "Lucky Landis," in *Hollywood*, May 1941, states, "She took the name Carole because she liked it, and thumbed through a San Francisco telephone book for the Landis part." But in James Reid's "No Advice to the Lovelorn" in the March 1941 *Silver Screen,* Carole says "she picked 'Landis' out of a newspaper headline," and Frank Smoot identified it as the name of the baseball commissioner.

"never gave this story credence": The quote is from Elgar Brown's five-part *Chicago Herald* series on Carole, July 8–14, 1948.

"including the St. Francis Hotel": In James Reid's "No Advice to the Lovelorn," we learn that Carole "didn't know anyone in San Francisco. . . . So she just barged into the Hotel St. Francis, herself, and asked the orchestra leader for an audition. He must have liked her looks, because he gave her an audition, even when she admitted she hadn't had any experience. . . . He didn't know how young she was. . . . She sang at the St. Francis, and other swank San Francisco resorts, for several months." This period presumably preceded Carole's steady job at the Royal Hawaiian.

" 'The Way You Look Tonight' ": This item is found in John Franchey's January 1944 *Movies* article, "Love Would Come First! Carole Landis on Marriage and Career," one of Carole's more thorough biographical interviews, which, along with the usual information about the Royal Hawaiian, Kay Ellis, Carl Ravazza, and so on, includes a few unique details, including the name of her other song, "My Man," mentioned later, as well as the quote below about the effect of Carole's singing. Franchey appears to have interviewed the Royal Hawaiian bandleader, perhaps Ravazza himself, for this article.

"Kamokila": Information on this singular institution is taken from the *Oakland Tribune* issues of June 1 and November 23, 1933, and those of January 27, 31, March 2, 9, 16, April 9, 25, June 21, 27, December 12, 1935. Kay Ellis's association with the Cairo Club is referred to in the *San Francisco News-Call Bulletin* Newspaper Photograph Archive in the Online Archive of California; the death of Major Charles Ross on February 4, 1935, is described in various newspapers, notably the *Reno Evening Gazette* the following day. We can surmise that Kay left the Cairo after this unpleasant incident, which occurred not long after Carole's arrival in San Francisco.

"Carl Ravazza": In "I Don't Want to Be an Angel" in the December 1942 *Silver Screen,* Carole says it was the owner/manager of the Rio Del Mar who saw her perform (and that she tried out for the new job on her day off without telling her boss about it). Information on Ravazza is from his biographical sketch at nfo.net/usa/r1.html.

"As for Carole's activities other than singing": Franchey's article ("Love Would Come First!") also includes the following: " 'I was out of my head when I gave up that soft touch,' says Carole. 'I sang twice a night and slept the rest of the time when I wasn't lying on the beach. If I made a million bucks a week in pictures I still wouldn't have a better life than that.' " That room and board were included is found in Judith Banner's "Lucky Landis," *Hollywood,* May 1941.

"memoirs of Jimmy Starr": *Barefoot on Barbed Wire* (Lanham, Md., and London: Scarecrow Press, 2001), 153–155. (Thanks to Laura Wagner for the reference.) The location of the incident in the St. Francis Hotel suggests that it took place early in Carole's stay in San Francisco. Starr's implication that he had no contact with Carole before she became a star for Fox in 1941 is belied by at least three mentions of her in his daily columns, the first of which is dated November 18, 1937. However, this does not cast doubt on the authenticity of the St. Francis incident.

"a graphic description": Details aside, the young woman in Starr's narrative engages in sexual relations without either shame or perversity, in a spirit of friendly cooperation. She enjoys giving pleasure to her partner and is proud of her ability to do so.

"Ehrlich, who had served as Alice Kamokila Campbell's attorney": Ehrlich successfully defended Alexander Pantages in his notorious 1929 rape trial, assisted by young Jerry Giesler, who would represent Carole in her 1948 divorce case. See John Wesley Noble and Bernard Averbuch, *Never Plead Guilty: The Story of Jake Ehrlich* (New York: Farrar, Straus and Cudahy, 1955).

"blackmailer referred to by Florabel Muir": In her "What's behind the Carole Landis Tragedy?" *Motion Picture*, October 1948.

"Among Carole's acquaintances in San Francisco": See Reid's "No Advice to the Lovelorn." The article specifies that "one girl, in particular, had done considerable film work, and didn't like Hollywood, but she was willing to give Carole the names of some Hollywood people who might be able to help her." That Carole "took the train" comes from the *Colliers* article by Crichton, "Determined Lady."

"this was almost certainly Evelyn O'Brien": Thanks to fellow film researcher Scott O'Brien for this information about his great-aunt. The death of her sister Thelma is announced in the July 14, 1936, *Ogden Standard-Examiner*. Scott also pointed out an article in the *Utica Observer-Dispatch* dated October 22, 1941, which states, "Miss Landis has long been a close personal friend of the beautician [O'Brien] and according to her is as genuine as she is beautiful."

"Probably in late 1936": The date of 1937 for Carole's arrival in Hollywood can be found in the June 17, 1940, *Life* spread "Carole Landis Does Not Want to Be Ping Girl" that introduced the world to Carole. Interestingly enough, the year is seldom given explicitly in her other bios, where she typically says only that she came to Hollywood when she had saved enough money. Crediting Carole's unverifiable appearance as an extra in *A Star Is Born* places her arrival no later than January 1937; the film was completed on December 28, with retakes in January. If, as Kirk Crivello states in *Fallen Angels*, Carole was in the chorus of the Warner film *The King and the Chorus Girl*, this would place her arrival in Los Angeles no later than December 1936, since this film was in production between November 5 and December 30 of that year.

"by her own account": There are a number of similar versions; in at least one, the amount mentioned is $150 rather than $100. The fullest account by a small margin was in the Fox publicity magazine *Dynamo* in the fourth quarter of 1941: " 'I saved up

$100 . . . and one sunny day I hied myself southward, this time on a train. . . .' The movie scouts, though, didn't beleaguer her $5-a-week apartment and the weeks added up to months."

"$5 a week": This detail is mentioned in various Fox publicity releases as well as in a note in the October 1941 *Movie Life*: "Carole almost starved in a $5-a-week room before she got movie job as chorus girl."

"in July 1937": Clara's article misdates the contract on July 4, 1935.

Chapter 3. First Years in Hollywood (1937–1939)

"Carole's anonymous friend": "The Truth about Carole Landis," *True Confessions*, November 1948: "Carole got desperate as the weeks and months went by without work. When Carole asked to stay with my husband and me, we were both delighted to have her. We didn't have an extra bed for Carole, but she insisted that she was perfectly happy to sleep on a couch in our living room. As long as her money lasted, she also insisted upon paying a fair price for her board. When her money ran out completely she said she would stay only if we would let her help take care of the house."

"Carole tells the story": "The Man Upstairs," *American Magazine*, October 1942.

"According to Kirk Crivello": In *Fallen Angels* (p. 87), Crivello quotes chorine Beth Renner as recalling Carole's presence in the chorus line, stating that Carole was a favorite of director Mervyn LeRoy as well as Busby Berkeley.

" 'He never made anyone dance' ": Lois Lindsay, speaking to John Kobal in his *People Will Talk* (New York: Knopf, 1986), 197. Concerning Carole in particular, we have this exchange, with Madison Lacy, a photographer, speaking, "She'd go on the interview, and when Carole started swinging, [Berkeley] said, 'Oh, we want her!' . . . She had on a tight sweater, and when Carole started to swing and to dance, why, she was a cinch" (ibid., 198). That Carole was a friend of Evelyn O'Brien may also have played a role.

"a court judgment": In Carole's file at the Warner Brothers archives.

"According to her mother": Clara Ridste Landis, "The True Story of Carole Landis," *True Story*, October 1948. Kenny Morgan, a trade-paper journalist and publicity man whom we will meet again as Carole's main boyfriend in 1939, also took credit for engineering the move; this attribution is found in Elgar Brown's Carole series in the *Chicago Herald-Examiner*, July 8–14, 1948.

"Kirk Crivello recounts": In *Fallen Angels*, Crivello speaks to an eyewitness: "Busby Berkeley did ask Carole to marry him. Claire James was Miss California of 1938, the year Berkeley selected her for the chorus of *Gold Diggers in Paris* with Carole. . . . 'Carole was bitterly disappointed when Buz said he couldn't marry her,' Claire said. 'His mother, Gertrude, had heard rumors that Carole had once been a call girl and persuaded Buz to break off their engagement' " (p. 88). The story is also repeated in Mart Martin's *Did She or Didn't She?* (Secaucus, N.J.: Citadel Press, 1996).

"Gossip columns refer": Ed Sullivan in the November 1, 1937, *Hollywood Citizen News*: "Carole Landis and Busby Berkeley are running a temperature"; Jimmy Starr on November 18: "Carole Landis and Busby Berkeley have 'That Old Feeling' "; *Los Angeles Times*, January 1, 1938: "Most recent patch-ups . . . at Sardi's were spotted Busby Berkeley and Carole Landis"; *Hollywood Reporter*, May 7, 1938: "The Busby Berkeley–Carole Landis romance is definitely cold."

"The evidence suggests the contrary": Louella Parsons's May 28, 1938, column claims Carole hadn't even heard from Wheeler in three years until she found out about the suit and that she would testify for Busby "simply because she thinks it is the right thing to do." The *Los Angeles Times* story on May 21 says Carole "indignantly denied" Wheeler's story. It strains credibility, although not to the absolute breaking point, to assume that this was all an act.

"Wheeler was reported attempting": This appeared in the gossip column of the November 1940 *Modern Screen*, which also reported in February 1942 that Wheeler was being employed as a stand-in in Carole's Fox film *A Gentleman at Heart*. Although columnists at the time of Wheeler's suit gave his stage name as "Jack Roberts," this is probably a careless hearing of "Robbins."

"a small gold cross": An article by Sara Hamilton about the romance between Guy Madison and his future wife, Gail Russell, in the November 1947 *Photoplay* suggests that, perhaps in memory of Diana Lewis's gift, Carole often gave similar crosses to her friends in Hollywood: "He [Guy Madison] gets such a kick when you [Gail Russell] open that fat wallet of yours to reveal . . . [t]he card that accompanied the tiny cross sent you as a gift from Carole Landis, and mate of the one Guy wears."

"As Carole described": In *"Turnabout* girl goes straight," *Screen Guide*, August 1940, which also makes the point that both Landis and Lombard "got their start by posing for 'cheese cake' pictures."

"circumstances of her departure": This incident is retold in almost every biographical account. One of the earliest, Kyle Crichton's "Determined Lady," in the May 10, 1941, *Colliers*, states that "Warners gave her . . . the air." In a movie magazine piece written when she was more established, Kay Proctor's "I Don't Want to Be an Angel!" in the December 1942 *Silver Screen*, the story is a bit different: "Carole had an offer of the feminine lead opposite Bob Hope in a Los Angeles stage production of *Roberta*. The studio said no dice, so Carole tore up her contract and did the play anyway. That, in turn, brought two more offers—a Paramount test and the lead in a Broadway production of *Once upon a Night.*"

"Carole usually claimed": For example, in a Fox publicity release dated May 1, 1941: "She appeared in a Broadway play, *Once upon a Night* . . . but the play misfired. It closed after two nights." In Kay Proctor's "I Don't Want to be an Angel!" the story is a bit different: "For the first time in my professional life my conduct was absolutely above reproach. I worked like the dickens, did exactly as I was told, and fairly killed myself being sweetness and light all over the place. . . . So what happened? At the end of two weeks I was fired!"

"this new relationship inspired a columnist": Erskine Johnson, June 17, 1939, and Jimmie Fidler, November 23. Information on Morgan is taken from Michael Karol, *Lucy A to Z* (Lincoln, Neb.: iUniverse Star, 2001).

"By her own account": In Kay Proctor's article "I Don't Want to Be an Angel" (*Silver Screen*, December 1942), Carole claims that she went to a 1938 Republic Studios Christmas party and that "two days later she was signing a contract for three pictures." It seems likely that both the party and the contract were real, but that the timing was not, since William Witney was introduced to Carole by her agent in March.

"her actual introduction to the studio": William Witney, *In a Door, into a Fight, out a Door, into a Chase: Moviemaking Remembered by the Guy at the Door* (Jefferson, N.C.: McFarland, 1996), 145–146. Elsewhere, Witney says of Carole, "She had the most beautiful figure I'd ever seen on a girl, and she was a swell person with a hell of a sense of humor" (quoted in Tom Weaver's *Monsters, Mutants, and Heavenly Creatures*, 234).

"one of the best serials ever": For example, Gary Johnson in his "The Serials: An Introduction" in the on-line journal *Images* 4 (www.imagesjournal.com/issue04/infocus/introduction5.htm), puts *Daredevils* fifth in his list of the nine "best serials."

"Carole's acting in this serial": Kirk Crivello in his Landis bio in *Film Fan Monthly*, November 1973, says, "She was featured in . . . the memorable serial *Daredevils of the Red Circle* as an unmemorable leading lady," 5.

"Witney tells the story": Ibid, 151.

"In another anecdote": "One morning the wardrobe girl came to me. 'Billy, I can't get Carole to wear a brassiere.' 'She says it's too hot.' I laughed, 'Great. She needs one like a hole in the head.' The wardrobe girl didn't laugh. 'But the motion picture code!' she said. . . . I knew the code of decency would probably make us cut out any scenes of Carole without a brassiere. . . . I sighed. 'Carole, go put on a brassiere.' She protested, 'It's too hot.' I asked her, 'Have you ever heard of the code of decency that governs what you can and can't do in order to release a picture?' She shook her head no. 'Well, you will. Carole, close your eyes a moment and visualize me walking down the road, holes in my shoes and a bundle on a stick over my shoulder, all because of a brassiere.' She laughed and said, 'You win' " (ibid, 151–152).

Chapter 4. Ping Girl: At Roach Studios (1939–1940)

"Hal Roach tells the story": In Bernard Rosenberg and Harry Silverstein's *The Real Tinsel* (New York: Macmillan, 1970), 28–29.

"In sister Dorothy's words": D[orothy] Ross, "The True Story of My Sister," *Photoplay*, November 1948. Thanks to Lyn and Henry Saye for the photograph of Carole on the movie set.

"a gossip columnist": *Hollywood Reporter*, May 24, 1940.

" 'lovely, shapely and lightly clad' ": *Hollywood Reporter*, September 10, 1940; the May 4 *Film Bulletin* calls Carole a "marcelled beauty" while stating that she and Mature "do as well as could be expected as the primitive lovers."

"Jean Porter": Personal interview, May 5, 2004.

"perhaps on the initiative of Kenny Morgan": Elgar Brown's post-mortem series on Carole in the July 1948 *Chicago Herald American* gives Morgan credit not only for Carole's nose job but for the "Ping Girl" slogan that elsewhere is attributed to Hal Roach: "To further the Landis profile, Morgan decreed a slight nasal adjustment. Carole meekly had her nose straightened."

"The reviewers called *Turnabout*": "far-fetched comedy" and "Hubbard very capably handles the dual role," *Daily Variety*, May 1; "winning and alluring," *Film Daily*, May 7; "shows most attractive promise," *Hollywood Reporter*, May 1; "This cast extracts maximum comedy," *Moving Picture Daily*, May 3.

"Hal Roach invited Hollywood correspondents": The full story is found in an article in the May 27, 1940, *Edwardsville* (Illinois) *Intelligencer* entitled "Girl Declares She Isn't 'Ping.' " This article is the source of several following details concerning the reception, including Carole's letters to newspaper editors and the leftover meals and Scotch.

"according to at least one source": In John Morris's *Get the Picture: A Personal History of Photojournalism* (Chicago: University of Chicago Press: 2002), 47, we read, "A *Life* story could lift a young woman out of obscurity and into the limelight overnight. Carole Landis . . . a buxom cavewoman in Hal Roach's *One Million B.C.*, succeeded in catching Pollard's eye. When Peter Stackpole's pictures of her appeared in *Life*, her pay went from $75 a week to $750. Landis called Pollard to ask what she could do to repay him. Dick thought for a moment and then answered, "I've always wanted a Swiss army knife." Given that Carole's Fox contract starting January 1941 called for a starting salary of $400, the $750 figure should probably be cut in half.

"which book one reads": We have just read Morris's account; Stackpole himself, writing in his photo book *Life in Hollywood, 1936–1952* (Livingston, Mont.: Clark City Press, 1992), 72, although he disparaged Carole's acting ability and saw only that "she had no hang-ups about showing her attributes," tells the story differently: "When my photographs ran, Carole's studio was so pleased that they asked our office head if he would like to have a date with her. He politely refused, but he said he would like to have a red Boy Scout knife."

"an Internet dictionary": *Urban Dictionary* (www.urbandictionary.com/define. php?term=ping&page=2) has thirty-one definitions for *ping*, of which the thirteenth is this: "A crude onomatopoeia used to indicate that one has an erection. . . . More broadly,

the term is used as an exclamation upon the sighting of a very attractive female, implying that the sighting has the potential to induce instant erection, or has already done so."
    "a term of Hollywood slang": Kyle Crichton, "Determined Lady," *Colliers*, May 10,
1941. Crichton, himself surely "up on Hollywood slang," is rather arch on the subject:
"It will be recalled that Miss Landis, in a tragic moment, was dubbed The Ping Girl. . . .
After the damage was done she discovered to her horror that the world was not fully
up on Hollywood slang. Some people were certain that Ping referred to a tong hitherto
inhabited exclusively by Anna May Wong; others were certain it had to do with a certain
indoor game [presumably ping-pong]." E. J. Fleming (*Carole Landis*, 67) gives the
same interpretation of "ping," although without any confirming reference.
    "the Hollywood press corps": For example, "Carole Landis' supposed rebellion
against being the 'ping' girl, was a stunt from first to last," Harrison Carroll, May 28; "The
Hal Roach publicity department which had arranged the party didn't feel cheated. They
acted as if everything happened as planned, including Miss L's advertisement," Sidney
Skolsky, June 1.
    "As further proof that Carole meant business": The Calcraft suit is described in the
Nebraska State Journal on June 12, but the only source I have located for its resolution is
Frank Smoot's formerly online Carole biography at www.carolelandis.net.
    "Indeed, Roach was so insistent": The details of Carole's contract are to be found
in her Fox legal file in the UCLA Fine Arts Special Collections.
    "two Roach films for which she had been mentioned": in the May 14, 1940,
Los Angeles Times and the July 17, 1940, *Hollywood Citizen-News*, respectively.
    " 'I think sex is definitely here to stay' ": J. Reid, "No Advice to the Lovelorn,"
Silver Screen, March 1941.
    "to customary Landis see-level": Erskine Johnson, October 4, 1945.
    "A review of *Having Wonderful Crime*": by Lee Mortimer, facetiously dubbed Carole's
"best friend," in *The Hollywood Reporter*'s summary of reviews of the film on April 16, 1945.
    "distractingly desirable": "Ping Girl Gets Conked," *Life*, August 19, 1940.
    "In his autobiography": Alfred Zukor, *The Public Is Never Wrong* (New York: G. P.
Putnam's Sons, 1953), 151. "[Mabel Normand] was one of those rare comediennes—like
Gloria Swanson, Clara Bow, Carole Landis, and Jean Arthur after her—lovely to look at
and able to play dramatic roles."
    "fairly well received": *Variety*, rather critical as befits a New York publication, com-
plains about Dmytryk's direction and limits its comment on Carole to "Miss Landis has a
few moments"; in contrast, *Weekly Variety* compliments Carole's "growing naturalness
and progress"; and for *The Hollywood Reporter*, "Carole Landis registers as the heroine and
manages to display a goodly share of 'Oomph,' 'Ping' or whatever other name is applied
to that out-dated expression, 'Sex Appeal.' " All these articles appeared on July 31, 1940.
    "described by the always-friendly Louella Parsons": In her column of May 20, 1940.
    "pilot Mendelssohn Mantz": "Hollywood Sound-Track," *Movie-Radio Guide*, January
25, 1941.

"a credible gossip item": *Screen Romances*, January 1941.

"less often in the gossip columns": Hedda Hopper, column of September 27, 1940: "Carole Landis' and Willis Hunt's split wasn't so much due to incompatability [*sic*] as it was her desire for more publicity. Seems she got more space in national magazines and papers before her marriage and doesn't want anything to interfere with it."

"Another columnist, writing much later": Gene Coughlan, "Hollywood Heartbreak: The Story of Carole Landis," *Los Angeles Examiner*, September 16, 1948, quotes Carole as saying, "When an actress marries, then comes a divorce, the public always blames the girl. . . . It might be the husband's fault, you know. In this case, I was ex-wifed to death."

"in a perceptive autobiographical article": "I Am Carole Landis," *Life Story*, August 1943, one of Carole's most revealing autobiographical writings.

"Jimmie Fidler claimed": Fidler's and Hopper's columns are both dated March 5, 1941.

"knitted him a pair of woolen socks": "Carole Landis is knitting socks for none other than her ex, Willis S. Hunt, who is going into training at Bakersfield, preparatory to leaving for England to join the RAF," Louella Parsons, column of August 21, 1941.

"a gossip columnist's warning": in Cal York's December 1940 *Photoplay* column "Gossip of Hollywood."

"Carole met Franchot Tone": Their connection was first noted by Louella Parsons on October 30; on November 4, Sidney Skolsky asserted, "They have time for no one else"; further mentions occur on November 6, 11, 18, 25, 28. Carole was seen with Ryan at Ciro's on November 23 (*Hollywood Reporter*, November 25) and then in January and February. She had dated Cedric Gibbons in October, just before meeting Tone, then was seen with him in late December (Louella Parsons, December 23) and frequently in January. She was seen with Gene Markey on November 30 (Harry Crocker, *Los Angeles Examiner*, December 3), then on New Year's Eve (*Hollywood Reporter*, January 2).

"It seems unlikely that Tone actually proposed marriage": Walter Winchell's column of January 11, 1941, claims rather cryptically that Tone "wickered Carole Landis' denial," meaning that he tossed into his wastebasket her (false) denial that she had told her friends Tone had proposed. On December 30, Winchell himself had spoken of "Franchot Tone's proposal to Carole Landis and their rumored plan to elope New Year's Day."

"The October 1941 *Screenland* article": Drafts of "What Carole Landis Demands of Men!" and "Glamour Girls Are Suckers" (mentioned below) are found in Carole's file at the Herrick library; they are dated June 13 and August 23, respectively.

"Apparently, Tone liked Carole very much": Thanks for this information to Lisa Burks, who is working on a book on Tone and has had access to Tone's surviving family. Lisa also suggested that Tone was "very sexual."

"'boom, boom, crash!'": Carole's reaction to meeting Tom Wallace, as recorded in her *Four Jills in a Jeep*, 44.

"an article written shortly after Carole's death": Crawford Dixon, "The Carole Landis Tragedy," *Movieland*, October 1948.

"Spencer Tracy and Charles Boyer": A "side affair" with Tracy is mentioned in Darwin Porter's Hepburn biography, *Katharine the Great* (New York: Blue Moon Productions, 2004), 459; the book also recounts that Tracy and Carole "arrived at the [summer 1946 Irene Mayer Selznick] party drunk." Natasha Fraser-Cavassoni's biography, *Sam Spiegel* (New York: Simon & Schuster, 2003), 75–76, refers to one of Spiegel's assistants "escorting Carole Landis to meet Boyer."

"Jack Benny": Jack Benny and [daughter] Joan Benny, *Sunday Nights at Seven: The Jack Benny Story* (New York: Warner Books, 1990), 157.

"this film received tepid reviews": "Here is such a slather of slapstick farce as the screen has dished out but seldom since the old neo-Sennett days. . . . It is screwball from the first turn of the camera, and keeps up the pace most of the way to spell joyous and welcome entertainment for the mob. . . . Miss Landis is decorative as the show owner and sings very pleasantly a swell song," *Variety*, February 6, 1941. The same day's *Hollywood Reporter* mentions "haphazard direction" and a "badly-constructed script"; it adds that "Carole Landis, who plays the show owner, rarely has been photographed so badly, but is lovely when the camera does give her a break and, despite miscasting, handles her role competently enough."

"The press praised *Topper Returns*": *Weekly Variety* on March 12, 1941, calls the film a "superb and masterful directorial job" in which Carole and O'Keefe "come through with satisfactory portrayals"; the same day's *Hollywood Reporter* says that "Carole Landis gives pretty presence to an [*sic*] harassed heroine."

Chapter 5. "Sex-Loaded": At Twentieth Century-Fox (1941)

"Louella Parsons tells us": In her column of December 26, 1940. There is no other information about Clara's accident, in which, Louella said, perhaps with some exaggeration, that Clara was "seriously injured."

"Carole's Fox contract": The material in this paragraph is taken from Carole's Fox legal file in the UCLA Fine Arts Special Collections.

"bars on the windows": See, for example, the June 1941 *Silver Screen* "Topics for Gossip": "When someone commented on the bars on all the windows, Carole said, 'I didn't put them there. I like people coming in. Miss Oliver put them there.' "

" 'usually [had] an assortment of pooches' ": Louella Parsons, June 16, 1940.

"four that annoyed her neighbors": On February 11, Jimmy Starr noted that the neighbors objected to the dogs, citing zoning restrictions requiring an owner of more than three dogs to obtain a kennel license; Carole had instructed her lawyer to fight the charge. On April 9, the *Hollywood Reporter* gossip column reported that Carole was "in a jam because of her barking dogs."

"photographed with dogs": The main photograph in the June 29, 1943, *Look* spread on Carole is a two-page shot of her on the beach with Donner; they are looking into each other's eyes in a mock lovers' pose. Carole (in uniform) made the cover of *Our Dogs* magazine in July 1942.

"On Donner's death": Carole's article "My Dog is Dead" appeared in *Motion Picture* in April 1944; along with a full-page shot of Carole and Donner, the magazine also shows three photographs of her holding Donner's much smaller toy-terrier successor—which the *Hollywood Reporter* on July 16, 1943, reported stolen.

"By Carole's own account": As given in Kay Proctor's December 1942 *Silver Screen* article "I Don't Want to Be an Angel."

"a third-party article": Dudley Early, "Carole Landis," *Family Circle*, January 2, 1942.

"To sum it up": *Hollywood Reporter*, December 27, 1940.

" 'Teaming blondes' ": Louella Parsons, January 10, 1941.

"Tierney is cited for her title role": Gene Tierney, in her *Self-Portrait* (New York: Wyden Books, 1979), speaks of being one of the "Fox girls" without once mentioning Carole.

"the January papers": Articles to this effect appeared in *The Hollywood Reporter* (January 6), the *Los Angeles Times* (January 8), and the *New York Times* (January 30).

"A contemporary source": The Starr column referred to in the text was unearthed by the tireless research of Gary Hamann of Filming Today Press.

"most writers on either Rita or Carole": For example, Kirk Crivello claims (*Fallen Angels*, 93) that Mamoulian wanted Hayworth and that Fox held a press conference; John Kobal (*Rita Hayworth: The Time, the Place, and the Woman*, [New York: Norton, 1978], 124) writes that Mamoulian was unsatisfied with Carole; both authors falsely assume that the dye job requested was red rather than black.

"This act of rebellion": Fleming (*Carole Landis*, 101–104) uncritically repeats the canard that Carole's refusal of this role was directly linked to her minor part in *Sal*. Although the dates are readily available, Fleming follows earlier unreliable accounts—notably the biographical data on Frank Smoot's old carolelandis.net Web site—in moving the casting of this role from its actual date at the beginning of 1941 to August, after Carole's first Fox films.

"Carole's warm personal relationship with Mamoulian": Carole's name was associated with Mamoulian's four times between March 1 (Louella Parsons on March 3 had Mamoulian escorting Carole to the Ciro's opening) and April 29, 1942 (*The Hollywood Reporter*). With unconscious irony, on March 16, during the filming of *It Happened in Flatbush*, the *Reporter* depicted Carole as "debuting new hair shade, with Rouben Mamoulian escorting."

"Carole had become the brunette": The studio publicity release on *It Happened in Flatbush* (in the Herrick library files) states, "After several weeks of insisting, Carole finally won studio approval to darken her tresses to a golden-brown, her real shade."

"The following allegation": Leonard Mosley, *Zanuck: The Rise and Fall of Hollywood's Last Tycoon* (New York: Little Brown, 1984), 242–243. In subsequent writings the allegation is often attributed to Kenneth Anger's *Hollywood Babylon II*, also published in 1984, but clearly relying on Mosley.

"a later writer": Rex Harrison's normally circumspect biographer Alexander Walker in *Fatal Charm: The Life of Rex Harrison* (New York: St. Martins Press, 1992), 134.

"for six years running": Walker also informs us sententiously that actresses hired for sex are customarily limited to occasional minor roles, blissfully or deliberately ignoring the many films Carole starred in at Fox and elsewhere. A nearly opposite story, graphically illustrated in the 1998 E! Entertainment Television *Mysteries and Scandals* documentary on Carole by showing "Carole" pushing away "Darryl's" hand, is that Carole did well early in her Fox career but was blocked after she refused to continue her 4 p.m. meetings with Zanuck. Exactly what is supposed to have motivated this sudden reluctance is not made clear. Such naive attempts to explain public acts by hypothetical private motives forget that the public world has motives of its own—in particular, that Zanuck was only able to indulge his sexual fantasies at Fox because his box-office decisions made Fox a great deal of money.

"but delegated Lilli": Louella Parsons, January 22, 1948.

"In Lilli's autobiography": Lilli Palmer, *Change Lobsters—and Dance* (New York: Macmillan, 1975), 181. Lilli's reactions to the Rex-Carole affair will be discussed in chapters 9 and 10.

"attested elsewhere": See, for example, the graphic account in Corinne Calvet's *Has Corinne Been a Good Girl?* (New York: St. Martin's, 1983, 195–97), where the author describes Zanuck exhibiting his penis in his office. The impression this leaves is that Zanuck was demanding oral rather than genital intercourse.

"Both Kirk Crivello and E. J. Fleming": Crivello quotes Fox stock player Claire James, "The story around Fox was that Carole was Darryl F. Zanuck's mistress" (*Fallen Angels*, 94). But he also says that James "had minor roles in a number of Carole's films," although the record shows that James was in only two Fox films, both with Grable but without Carole. Fleming, whose book is full of inaccuracies, cites an interview with Col. Barney Oldfield as an independent source of Carole's relationship with Zanuck, including the story, adhered to in *Mysteries and Scandals*, that it was because she eventually refused to sleep with him that she was relegated to B films in 1942. Since Oldfield was a radio personality with no professional connection with Fox, his reports could only be secondhand. Oldfield also purportedly told Fleming that Carole herself had turned down the lead role in *My Gal Sal* after Zanuck "pulled *Blood and Sand*" (Fleming, *Carole Landis*, 104); the near absurdity of this statement, which follows the pseudo-chronology that puts *Blood and Sand* at the end rather than the beginning of 1941, weakens the credibility of Oldfield's other information. Unfortunately, neither Oldfield nor James is still alive.

"described in April 1943": gossip column, *Modern Screen*, April 1943.

"A more complex variant": Akins's play had been filmed in 1932 as *The Greeks Had a Word for Them*. According to the IMDb (but not the AFI catalog), this play was itself an uncredited source of the film *Three Blind Mice*.

" 'Carole Landis makes the most' ": *Hollywood Reporter*, June 16, 1941. " 'Miss Landis makes a fair vision' ": *New York Times*, July 5, 1941.

"the list of Fox's twelve highest-grossing films of 1941": The appendix of Aubrey Solomon's *Twentieth Century-Fox: A Corporate and Financial History* (Metuchen, NJ: Scarecrow Press, 1988) includes lists of the highest-grossing and most costly films for each year; future references to these figures derive from these lists.

"more than one columnist": Louella Parsons, August 31, 1941: "The Betty Grable–Carole Landis feud isn't a gag." *Movie–Radio Guide*, November 22: "Betty Grable is shedding real tears over her feud with Carole Landis." See also *Hollywood*, December 1941; *Photoplay*, January 1942; *Silver Screen*, January 1942 ("When George Raft wants to tease Betty he calls her 'Carole' ").

"As for assigning blame": Fleming's source is his standby Col. Barney Oldfield, whose questionable reliability I remarked on above; the dressing-room incident is from Jimmie Fidler's column of April 9: "Fox 'execs' may be chagrined to know Carole Landis' sneezes were an act; she wanted the deluxe new dressing room she got!"

"the Production Code Office issued a ban": Both Erskine Johnson and Walter Winchell in their April 9, 1941, columns refer to the ban, the latter stating that "Will Hays and his staff of censors have banned all 'sweater shots' from films and 'stills' in advertising of movies." The text, as reported in *Modern Screen*, July 1941, read, "Breasts may not be exposed, or outlined and emphasized." The first indication that the ban was in the works appeared on March 26 in the *Los Angeles Evening Herald Examiner* and elsewhere.

"public dismay": "Betty and Carole spoke about the Hays' Office edict to ban sweater photos, and these two sweater girls spoke about it as if it almost meant the end of their dramatic careers," Sidney Skolsky, April 11, 1941.

"As Sidney Skolsky would put it": Skolsky, November 16, 1945.

"a writer claimed later that year": *Movie–Radio Guide*, November 8, 1941.

"A-level publicity": "Fox upgrades *Dance Hall* to 'A' advertising budget and release," *The Hollywood Reporter*, May 14, 1941. According to Fox historian Aubrey Solomon (personal communication), *Dance Hall* only made about $200,000 at the box office, somewhat under its production cost of $220,000.

" 'play their parts in the jerky fashion' ": *Weekly Variety*, July 23, 1941.

" 'Neither of the characterizations' ": *Variety*, July 1, 1941; "neither Cesar Romero," *Weekly Variety*, July 23, 1941; "deep-throated," "likeable," *The Hollywood Reporter*, July 1, 1941.

"ex-hubby Willis Hunt": "Could Carole Landis and Bill Hunt be talking reconciliation? It certainly looked like it over the week-end," Hedda Hopper, March 5, 1941.

" 'swam all Sunday afternoon' ": *The Hollywood Reporter*, February 4, 1941.

"whom it appears Carole took seriously": A two-page photo spread entitled "Love, Laughter, and Landis," in the July 1941 *Movie Stars Parade* includes a picture of Carole and George in an amorous pose, calling him "her new heartthrob."

"told a Hollywood writer": Boze Hadleigh, as reported in his *Hollywood Gays* (New York: Barricade Books, 1996, 52).

"*Modern Screen* published an extract": In April 1942.

"Carole reported ill with the 'flu' ": I refer above to Jimmie Fidler's report on Carole's "illness" in his April 9 column. The November collapse was reported in the November 6 *Los Angeles Times*; by the following day, Louella Parsons could report that Carole "was reported some better yesterday after collapsing on the set with the flu." Reference to the September spell in New York is found in an unpublished letter to "Bill" dated October 20, 1941, where Carole claims she "had to go to bed for three days."

"most-dated starlet": *Movie–Radio Guide*, April 19, 1941.

"Carole gives it a cynical spin": "suspicion lingers that she is not averse to publicity about her many dates," *Movie–Radio Guide*, April 19, 1941. "Charles Chaplin, Gene Markey, Matty Fox, Kenny Morgan, Cedric Gibbons, George Montgomery, Bill Marshall—they've all developed flash-bulb squints playing the casual Landis swain. And Hollywood's legion of gossip-vendors chorus one question weakly: 'Who's next?' Like the smart girl she is, Carole . . . won't say," "It's Out-Landis!" *Modern Screen*, October 1941. See also the discussion below of "What Carole Landis Demands of Men!" *Screenland*, October 1941.

" 'a terrific eater' ": "The Truth about the Stars' Night Life," *Photoplay*, February 1945.

"her mother apparently got on her nerves": Jimmie Fidler's column on June 6, 1940—before Carole's marriage to Hunt—reads, "Carole Landis wants moma [*sic*] to live elsewhere—but moma likes Hollywood."

"Carole's oft-recalled phrase": "She Won't Depend on the Landis Line," again told to Gladys Hall, *Motion Picture*, October 1940.

"An 'anonymous admirer' ": "I Fell in Love with Carole Landis," *Screen Guide*, May 1942.

" 'Hollywood wives' ": John Austin's insistence on the "ladies of Hollywood" and "Hollywood wives" in his chapter on Carole in *Hollywood's Babylon Women*, originally *More of Hollywood's Unsolved Mysteries*, 31–32, cited by Frank Smoot in the biographical pages of his (no longer available) carolelandis.net Web site, is echoed in Fleming's book, *Carole Landis*: "[Carole] was becoming a target of an even more powerful industry group [than her co-workers]—the studio wives" (47). Whatever the effect of these ladies' gossip and innuendo on Carole's film career, there is little doubt that they inflicted emotional damage.

"Jerome Charyn's obsessively counterfactual portrait": Charyn, *Movieland: Hollywood and the Great American Dream Culture* (New York: Putnam, 1989), 139–140.

" 'always pleasing and appealing' ": *Variety*, October 17, 1941; "properly hard and brittle," *New York News*, January 17, 1942; "Carole Landis does a grand job," *The Hollywood Reporter*, October 17, 1941; "Miss Landis is given every opportunity," *Los Angeles Herald*, November 13, 1941.

"Gene Tierney said": Tierney's *Self-Portrait* with Mickey Herskowitz (New York: Wyden Books, 1979), 132. "People remember me less for my acting job than as the girl in the portrait." The "portrait" in *Laura* was really a photograph retouched to look like a painting. See Michelle Vogel, *Gene Tierney: A Biography* (Jefferson, NC: McFarland, 2005)—a movie biography without footnotes.

"There are a number": *The Hollywood Reporter*, November 14, 1941; "will have no appreciable meaning," *Weekly Variety*, November 19, 1941. The latter review continues: "Picture employs a sundry cast topped by Carole Landis and George Montgomery, both of whom are subjects of a buildup at the Twentieth Century studios. This is a tearer-downer for them, however. . . . Both Miss Landis and Montgomery struggle valiantly against great odds. They make a nice team, incidentally."

" 'No actress is doing more for the war effort' ": Walter Winchell, "Hollywood's War Effort," *Motion Picture*, August 1942. The remainder of the long passage about Carole in Winchell's article, by far the longest devoted to any star, reads as follows:

> She donates several nights each week to studious activity with the Aerial Nurse Corps. . . . This group, functioning under the supervision of the Sheriff's Aero Squadron, studies first aid, radio transmitting and receiving, as well as clerical work. They keep radio charts, stand by at air bases during alerts. They are on 24-hour call.
>
> . . . Carole's labors on behalf of Bundles for Bluejackets include long nights spent at one of their four canteens where she serves coffee and doughnuts to the men on duty, washes dishes or dances with them. . . .
>
> . . . [S]andwiched between these duties are personal appearances at Army and Navy benefit shows and at free shows for the men in uniform. . . . Carole has two nights a week at home. . . . On these two evenings, she and her mother invite service men to dinner at her rambling SM beach home. (35)

"autobiographical material to movie magazines": The first article devoted to Carole in a major publication was *Life*'s photographic write-up, "Carole Does Not Want to Be Ping Girl," on June 17, 1940; the first substantive article in a movie magazine was *Screen Guide*'s "*Turnabout* Girl Goes Straight" in August 1940, followed by the more developed "She Won't Depend on the Landis Line [i.e., measurements]," by Gladys Hall in the October *Motion Picture*. The title of Carole's last confessional article, which appeared in *Silver Screen* under her own byline in September 1947, was a self-doubting question to her readers, "Do You Think I Was Wrong?"

"one credible witness": Robert Dahdah, who was in the chorus of Carole's Broadway play *A Lady Says Yes* in 1945, in a personal communication, December 2004. Dahdah also told me the amusing fact that Carole always adjusted her breasts before being photographed.

" 'She gave so much of herself' ": D[orothy] Ross, "The True Story of My Sister," *Photoplay*, November 1948.

Chapter 6. B Actress and Patriot (1941–1942)

"Carole attended the marriage": Heller-Lary wedding, *Los Angeles Times*, September 11; American Legion, Hedda Hopper, September 24; Eddie Cantor show, *New York Times*, September 24; Meredith, *Hollywood Reporter*, September 29 ("Carole Landis' most frequent date during her Gotham stay was Burgess Meredith"); Martin, Winchell, October 10; Donner, *Los Angeles Examiner*, October 16 (which also mentions the World Series); Fight for Freedom, *Life*, October 15; Charlie Foy's, Louella Parsons, October 31.

"Production on the first of these": The November 6 *Los Angeles Times* reported that Carole had collapsed on the set the day before while working with Cesar Romero; Edwin Schallert's column on the third put the beginning of production "within about 10 days." This suggests that on the fifth Carole and Cesar were rehearsing rather than shooting.

"very amusing, exciting and unpredictable yarn": *Variety*; "sleepers," "charming dignity," "the most lady-like role," *The Hollywood Reporter*, both on January 6, 1942.

"stranded in Los Angeles": Louella Parsons, December 12, 1941.

"grounded in Wichita": See "War Train to Hollywood," *Screen Guide*, March 1942. In "The Courage of Carole Landis," *Stardom*, February 1943, Carole specifies that "we were set down in Wichita, Kansas, December ninth."

"invited for meals and weekends": Carole's family collection includes a guest book, many pages of which have been torn out, containing about thirty entries from July and August 1943 with fifty-odd names of different servicemen. Revealingly enough, not one of the comments refers to Carole's status as a movie star; they are all focused on the hospitality they received. A number of them give the Landis ladies the highest compliment of comparing their hospitality favorably with that of their own home town. A GI from Brooklyn says, "The hospitality here exceeds that of the people of Greenpoint in Brooklyn that wonderful city"; one from Georgia says, "Really the best afternoon I've spent since coming into the army; this is the nearest thing to 'southern Hospitality' I've run across since I left Georgia"; another, "This is the only place I have ever been where the hospitality exceeded that of New England; nearest thing to home!"

"Throughout the year": In April, Carole visited Fort Bliss in Texas; in June, she attended a bond rally in Kansas City; later that month, she toured the South; in late July and August she toured army camps in Texas. On July 26, she participated in the auction held at Tyrone Power and Annabella's house in Brentwood. This list, based on data from newspaper columns, is by no means exhaustive. Carole's family collection contains a detailed itinerary of the Texas trip, which included stops at Brownwood, Galveston, Blessing, Corpus Christi, San Antonio, the Alamo, and El Paso, along with nearby military installations.

"including a $1,500 opal ring": Louella Parsons, on September 30, 1942, wrote, "Carole Landis removed her ring and auctioned it for $1500 in bonds. She then took off her stockings and sold them—all for Uncle Sam."

"a movie writer described the change": Carl Schroeder, *Movie–Radio Guide*, June 1, 1943.

"An exemplary moment": The Wide World news service reported the request as coming from "H. F. Pennington, Jr., a sailor at Pearl Harbor: 'Heard your broadcast of April 23 and was so impressed I thought I would send you my one request and desire. Now I admit I want PLENTY, but it won't take much of the program's time. Soo-oo, if you could have Miss Carole Landis just step up to the microphone and SIGH—that's all, brother, just SIGH—I'll be happy.'" A retyped copy of the letter in Carole's family collection differs from this only in unimportant detail.

" 'The single most famous request' ": *Transmitter* (online journal of the Library of American Broadcasting), 2nd quarter, 2000. Fortunately, this unique moment was preserved on film; the film clip of Carole's sigh is available in various compilations, for example, *D-Day Remembered* (St. Clair Entertainment Group, 2004).

"Carole's sigh embodied 'what they were fighting for' ": Although we all remember the iconic pinup of Betty Grable as the embodiment of World War II womanhood, the following passage from Colin Briggs's article "Lynn Bari," in the February 2007 *Classic Images*, adds a new perspective: "Once, Lynn told me an interesting story about how servicemen became aware of the machinations of the Fox publicity department. *In response to their requests for photos of Carole Landis, the men were being sent Betty Grable pictures instead*, because Betty was Fox's biggest asset" (6, my emphasis).

" 'ardent' radio commentator Robert Arden": The gossip column in the May 1942 *Silver Screen* describes the following exchange: "When Victor Mature asked Carole Landis about her new romance with Robert Arden, the famous news commentator, Carole quipped, 'Well, his name is just a little off the beam. It should be ardent.'"

"several newspapers erroneously claimed": For example, the *New York Times* on April 1, 1942, wrote, "Carole Landis to Be Wed: Flies from Coast to Capital to Be Bride of Gene Markey."

" 'smokescreen' ": The Winchell column is dated April 16.

"a loyal member of the Screen Actors Guild": Thanks to Valerie Yaros of the Screen Actors Guild for this information.

" 'wasted on a part' ": *The Hollywood Reporter*, April 16, 1942.

"Carole and her fans were upset": For example, an aspiring Hollywood writer, in 1942, wrote, "Carole I don't know what kind of publicity man you have, but if I were you I would plant a bomb under him!!!!" Another fan, a photo dealer, wrote on October 2, 1942, that the "part of *My Gal Sal* is not right for your talents and even the minor roles of late [probably a reference to *Orchestra Wives*] . . . is [*sic*] hurting your popularity." Both letters are from Carole's family collection.

"this staging of her defeat": A similar situation arose in the career of French actress Isabelle Corey, who got her start as the sexy young girl in Jean-Pierre Melville's 1955 classic *Bob le flambeur*. The following year, Corey effectively destroyed her French film career by accepting against the advice of her mentor a secondary role to Brigitte Bardot in Roger Vadim's smash hit *And God Created Woman* (1956).

"Carole asked her fans": On September 24, 1942, Carole wrote to L. Allen Smith, a devoted member of her fan club: "Since I should like in the future to avoid roles as minor as that of Mae in *My Gal Sal*, I would be very grateful if you would write me a note, addressing it to me at 20th Century Fox Studios, expressing your personal dissatisfaction with this particular part. I feel that if I can get letters of this sort from all the club members it will help me to secure stronger parts in future pictures." Similar letters must have been sent to other club members, because there are replies to these letters among Carole's family materials.

"a screen magazine asked": "My Most Thrilling Love Scene," *Movies*, October 1942. Given the lead time and postdating of these publications, the questions were probably put to the stars (or their studio) in May or June at the latest.

"one of Carole's more perceptive admirers": James Pattarini, a regular correspondent, a partial collection of whose letters from Carole at the New York Public Library is her only publicly available correspondence, writes on October 18, 1943, "Two suggestions: 1. Please become and stay blonde again. When I saw you in person, your hair was blonde and I could hardly believe that one person could be so beautiful. 2—select one hair style and stick to it. I think you should let the public get used to one 'face.' You look very different with each new hair style." Included in the letter was a picture of Carole with the recommended hairstyle. Another critic was less analytic in reference to Carole's later 1942 roles: "You changed for the worse, too. You got too thin, hard, even your voice got harsh [probably a reference to *Orchestra Wives*]. Then, on top of all that, you dyed your pretty blonde hair to brown. I don't like you half as well now as I did the way you were before." Both letters are from the family collection.

" 'box-office natural,' " " 'batting 1000 percent' ": *Film Daily*; "does well," *Weekly Variety*; "displays advanced poise," *The Hollywood Reporter*; "complements persuasively," *Variety*; all dated May 28, 1942.

"veteran Archie Mayo": John Brahm directed the film for about two weeks in April 1942 before being replaced by Mayo. In Jeff Gordon's exhaustive discussion of the film, "Orchestra Wives: The Legendary Big-Band Musical," *Films of the Golden Age* 46 (fall 2006): 18–42, Lynn Bari explains that Brahm, whose direction of the musical numbers she preferred to Mayo's, was replaced because he was "behind schedule and way over budget." Bari's remarks are taken from an interview with the author in 1989; she died on November 20 that same year.

"Miller's plane mysteriously disappeared": On December 31, 1985, the *New York Times* published a story by Jo Thomas with the headline "R.A.F. Bombs May Have Downed Glenn Miller Plane" that lends plausibility to the claim of Fred Shaw and Victor Gregory, navigator and pilot, respectively, of a Royal Air Force bomber, that bombs jettisoned from their aircraft struck Miller's plane.

"Carole's 'catty' performance": *Variety*, August 11, 1942. The full sentence reads, "Orchestra wives of catty trickiness, even with one another, all turning in excellent performances, are Carole Landis, Virginia Gilmore, Mary Beth Hughes."

"A recent article": Bari's remarks about Carole are found in Gordon, "Orchestra Wives: The Legendary Big-Band Musical," 34–35.

"as one of her fans pointed out": James Pattarini, in a letter of September 26, 1942, wrote, "Please, don't ever accept any more 'cat' roles." In more general terms, another fan in his October 2 letter suggested Carole avoid playing the "wise cracking smart girl type who knows all the answers."

"the controversial story of a massacre of black soldiers": Geoffrey F. X. O'Connell's story "Ghosts of Mississippi" in the online Detroit weekly *metrotimes* (www.metrotimes. com/editorial/story.asp?id=1790) gives what appears to be a fair account of the facts of the case involving the 364th Negro Infantry Regiment.

"A reviewer remarked": "That Miss Landis is acceptable in an all-male story that really has no place for a woman is to her resounding credit. Somehow she never gets in the way of the plot that could have done without her," *The Hollywood Reporter*, September 18, 1942.

"Production Code admonitions": Code Administration chief Joseph Breen writes to Fox publicity director Colonel Joy on June 1, 1942, "We cannot approve the present characterization of Eddie as a woman of loose morals."

"'unusually good'": *Film Daily*, September 18, 1942.

"Carole looked forward to playing this title role": Letter to Nick Glod, August 27, 1942, "'The Powers Girls' [*sic*] is now in production and will be for a month or so. I am very happy about my role and about the picture, and hope it will be a BIG success" (from collection of Gwen Serna). In a letter to her frequent correspondent James Pattarini dated August 16, Carole refers to Priscilla Lane's casting in what would become Anne Shirley's role as her sister.

"one source credits for persuading producer Charles Rogers": "The reason Carole Landis gets the lead in the Rogers-Schaff *Powers Girl* is because Joan Bennett, herself unable to accept the part, did an all-out job of selling her," *The Hollywood Reporter*, July 15, 1942.

"makes her an extremely unsympathetic figure": In the "Analysis Chart" that accompanied the submission of the film script to the Production Code Office, Carole's character is listed as "unsympathetic."

"a 1943 news service article": "Miss Landis portrays an ambitious youngster who is determined to get out of the rut of modeling in a basement department store, and into the fame of being a Powers girl. Her own career has been somewhat similar," *Syracuse Herald Journal*, February 24, 1943.

" 'Carole Landis nevertheless is well cast' ": *Variety*, December 17, 1942.

Chapter 7. The Gift of Beauty: Carole at War (1942–1944)

"As Carole tells us": "Even before Pearl Harbor, I had wanted to get to England to offer my services wherever they might be useful. . . . When the call for entertainment finally came, I volunteered at once. I wanted to get in the first troupe going over, along with Merle Oberon and George Murphy. But George and I were working in a picture at the time and we couldn't get clearance," Landis, *Four Jills in a Jeep* (New York: Random House, 1944), 3.

"columnists were less reticent": The "Tattler" columnist in the May 1943 *Motion Picture*, one of the more reliable screen magazines, puts this in no uncertain terms, although it mentions no names: "Now that Kay Francis, Carole Landis, Martha Raye, and Mitzi Mayfair have returned home from their sensationally successful trip abroad to entertain our soldiers, it came to light how unpopular the first unit was over there. It was headed by a certain lady [presumably Merle Oberon] who wouldn't co-operate—always wanting a room and bath, while the four girls mentioned above went days without having one or changing their linen, while doing as many as fifteen shows a day."

"while the ladies were still abroad": Louella Parsons reported on February 18, 1943, that Fox intended to produce a movie of the trip entitled "Four Girls and a Jeep." Two days later, *The Hollywood Reporter* gave the correct title, as well as its original source in Mitzi Mayfair's rather than Carole's account: "The original idea for Four Jills was sold to Fox by Lou Irwin, who called it 'Bomber Girls,' and had already signed Mitzi Mayfair for it. In fact, much of her day to day diary of that North African jaunt will be in the picture."

"*Time* called their five-month trip": "Stars over the Front," *Time*, March 8, 1943.

"According to Frank Rosato": In *Passing in Review* 7, no. 2 (September 2004), the online newsletter of the 33rd Army Band of Heidelberg, Germany (www.rt66.com/ ~obfusa/33rd/nlsep04.htm).

"originally from small-town Oakdale, Pennsylvania": The 1920 census lists Tommy as an only child of two years and three months living with his parents in Oakdale.

"snooty movie actress": Landis, *Four Jills* . . . , 44.

"crystallized": The term, referring to the moment when the lover suddenly becomes conscious of his love, comes from *De l'amour*, Stendhal's classic 1826 analysis of romantic love.

"In an article written after her trip": "Carole Landis and Her Meditations in a Fox-Hole" (introduced by Gladys Hall), *Movie Show*, November 1943. In a scrapbook at the University of Southern California there is an undated newspaper photograph of Carole with thirteen Royal Air Force flyers and the caption, " 'Three weeks after it was taken,' she explains, 'five of them were dead.' "

"On returning from England": In the June 1943 *Movie Story* gossip column.

"The marriage took place": The most thorough account of the wedding is found in "A Film Star Marries," in the January 23, 1943, issue of the British magazine *Picture Post*.

"Articles appeared in movie magazines": These 1943 articles appeared, respectively, in *Screen Guide* (January), *Stardom* (February), *Movieland* (June), *Movie-Radio Guide* (June), *Photoplay* (June), *Screen Guide* (June), *Look* (June 29), *Screenland* (July).

"In an interview": Interview with Frederick C. Othman, in his column of March 21, 1943.

"she continued to appear": Carole appeared in at least seven different movie magazine fashion displays in 1946 as well as one in the October 1947 *Movie Life* and one in the January 1948 *Screen Guide*, although she had been in England since August. These totals are based on an extensive but by no means exhaustive survey of film publications.

"christened a Liberty Ship": The *Los Angeles Times* reported on July 16, 1943, that "Actress Carole Landis gave bond talks at each shift and christened the S.S. *Vernon Kellogg*."

"sang at the Harvest Moon Ball": "Ran into Phil [Baker] at Harvest Moon Ball, also Carole Landis, whose husband was so tired he went to bed while she performed for 20,000 people," Hedda Hopper, September 15, 1943.

" 'Former Governor Alfred E. Smith's' ": *New York Times*, January 5, 1944. Jerome Charyn (*Movieland*, 140) bizarrely makes this address a sign of Carole's "wildness," describing her as "admonish[ing] a crowd that was fleeing from the rain," although the *Times* describes the crowd as "brav[ing] cold rain to hear and see her" (ibid.).

"her mother's riveter salary": A number of movie magazines noted Clara's participation in the war effort alongside her daughter; for example, this gossip note in the April 1944 *Screenland*: "Hot from Hollywood: Carole Landis & mom at war: Carole Landis and her mother are the fightin'est females in Hollywood. Everyone knows Carole's record entertaining the boys but Ma Landis has worked at one of our big defense plants—the swing shift, no less—riveting, for over a year now. What's more, she's got a top record for attendance with only two days' absenteeism, caused by illness."

"Carole asked for the first available assignment": "Carole Landis doesn't want to wait until a story's written for her. She wants to work at once, so she'll co-star with Sonja Henie in 'Winter Time,' which begins Monday," Hedda Hopper, March 11, 1943.

"the complex plot of *Wintertime*": As a sign of Carole's peripheral role in the story, the detailed plot description of *Wintertime* in the AFI database omits her character altogether.

"Carole received a few compliments": The September 9, 1943, *Hollywood Reporter*, after calling the film "too feeble to stand on its own feet," describes "I Like It Here" as "an engaging novelty as sold by Miss Landis and Romero." *Variety* on the same date says, "Miss Landis clicks as pursuer of Romero."

" 'Edwin Seaver' ": Curiously enough, Seaver confirmed this claim in testimony before the McCarthy Senate Subcommittee on Investigations on March 25, 1953, replying to a question from Senator Jackson: "I ghosted Carole Landis's *Four Jills in a Jeep*." The testimony is on line at a257.g.akamaitech.net/7/257/2422/06amay20030700/ www.gpo.gov/congress/senate/mccarthy/83870.html.

" 'I interrogated [Carole]' ": Earl Wilson, *I Am Gazing into My 8 Ball* (Garden City, NY: Sun Dial Press, 1945), 35–36.

"the American Film Institute catalog": The reference is in the *American Film Institute Catalog of Feature Films, 1941–1950*, 814: "According to information in the Twentieth Century-Fox Records of the Legal Department, . . . Landis and Edwin Seaver wrote a book about her travels while the film was in pre-production at the studio. Although Landis' material was not used in the screenplay, the studio agreed to let her use the film's title as her book title for the publicity value."

"whose contribution was already anticipated": *The Hollywood Reporter*, February 20, 1943.

"An additional segment": Thanks to Bryan Cooper for letting me see the outtakes from *Four Jills*.

"On express orders from Zanuck": In notes on a script conference on September 7, 1943, Zanuck ordered that the writers "must make all four girls equal."

"The critics savaged": Negative reviews were registered in New York papers such as the *Herald Tribune* (April 6), which called the film "a little musical farce" and noted that "the makeup was so poorly applied in this film that not even the celebrated pinup qualities of Miss Landis are able to brighten up the screen"; the *Sun* (April 6), which called the film "third-rate stuff"; and the *World-Telegram* (April 5), which declared that "the girls . . . who cheerfully face the tough going of a trip to battlefronts are entitled to more respect that this picture gives them."

"the reviewer for the *Los Angeles Times*": Norbert Lusk, *Los Angeles Times*, April 17, 1944, wrote, "At best it is shallow entertainment and is unworthy of the laudable mission that took Kay Francis, Martha Raye, Mitzi Mayfair and Carole Landis overseas. They do their utmost to raise the film above the structure of mediocrity on which it is built." Bosley Crowther's *New York Times* review is dated April 9.

"was inevitably described as its originator": For example, the *New York Daily News* (April 6) had this: "If 'Four Jills in a Jeep' had stuck closer to the record, as outlined in Carole Landis' book . . ."

"in the words of hostile reviewer Crowther": In his preliminary *Times* review on April 6, 1943, Crowther wrote, "And in an old barn somewhere in North Africa Miss Landis sings 'Crazy Me.' (This latter bit, incidentally, is the only one which rings remotely true.)"

"the army intended to produce for its own use": *The Hollywood Reporter* announced on April 30, 1943, "Army recreational officials want a film version of the routines which the three actresses . . . performed before American troops in England and N Africa. The short is to be exhibited only before Army groups, and is not for public showing."

"ex-husband Willis Hunt": Louella Parsons, January 15, 1944.

"After an exchange of correspondence": This material is found in Carole's Fox legal file at UCLA.

"first-rate reviews": The *Los Angeles Examiner*, August 26, 1944, read, "Carole Landis heads the roster of female players in the role of Jill McCann, and is a natural in the assignment." *The Hollywood Reporter*, May 26, 1944, read, "In many respects, Carole Landis' portrayal of the pseudo-wife is the best of her career, even though she was not always photographed to the best advantage. The role required acting and this she gave it gratifyingly."

"The critics weren't particularly kind to this silly comedy": Crowther of the *New York Times* (April 13, 1945) called it a "brainless little picture"; the *New York World-Telegram* (April 12) called it "one of the feeblest collections of jokes ever assembled." *Variety* on February 15 took a more nuanced view, calling the film a "rollicking 70 minutes of fun and nonsense. Trio of stars acquit themselves satisfactorily enough in roles which might have been fashioned more convincingly by scripter, Miss Landis being standout of the three with her somewhat insane approach."

"Edgar Rice Burroughs": The Burroughs family correspondence is online; the letter to Caryl is at www.erbzine.com/mag10/1026.html#Sept%2015%20Caryl; that to Jane, at www.erbzine.com/mag10/1026.html#September%2016.

"There is a photo": Published in *Motion Picture*, December 1944, along with a few others, including one of Carole putting flowers on a soldier's grave, in an article entitled "Helping Our Boys Forget."

"One of these pictures found its way to *Newsweek*": On October 16, 1944, in a brief article entitled "NG, Baby?" The magazine had no compunction in reproducing without comment the reference to the Papuan as a "coon."

"A letter to *Newsweek*": The letter with the photo appeared on January 29, 1945. Like other eastern publications, *Newsweek* was always happy to poke fun at Hollywood personalities. It reported with glee the understandably hostile reaction to Carole's ill-considered remarks by the president of the Australian United Women's Association, while publishing the proof that Carole herself had appeared in a skimpy two-piece outfit.

"'the gals wound up the best of friends'": *The Hollywood Reporter*, May 17, 1945, read, "Paulette and Buzz Meredith were sitting together at a party when Carole came bouncing over. . . . Carole denied ever having said those things (wanna bet she DID?) and Paulette gave her a *tres* snappy answer we wish we could print. There's really no point to this story because the gals wound up the best of friends."

"Carole contracted an illness that some have called malaria": Carole's "lifelong friend" makes this explicit in "The Truth about Carole Landis" in the November 1948 *True Confessions*: "Her illness has been labeled malaria, but it was really amebic dysentery, which usually responds favorably to medical treatment."

"again in April 1948": In a letter to Gisi Weise, April 23, 1948, Carole wrote, "I've not been very well lately and am still under doctor's care . . . an ailment picked up overseas on tour during the war alas. He hopes to clear it out soon & it's parasitic and that always means difficulties apparently." Carole writes much the same thing to James Pattarini on April 28.

"an incident that reached the columns of the *New York Times*:": Bernard Sobel reported the incident on September 16, 1945, calling it "one of the most thoughtful fan gestures ever accorded Carole Landis . . . at home or abroad." In its obituary article on Carole on July 6, 1948, the *Times* compressed the soldier's search for flowers and his walk to the hospital into the implausible "an enlisted man hacked his way through eighteen miles of jungle."

"*Photoplay* published a letter": The text of the letter, from Pauline Landry of Franklin, New Hampshire, reads: "After reading a paragraph in a letter from my brother in the Southwest Pacific regarding film star Carole Landis I just had the urge to have others read it. . . . 'Several days ago Jack Benny, Martha Tilton and Carole Landis paid our patients a visit. . . . Carole Landis was the one, though. A regular trouper and a wonderful person. She spent all of her time with the wounded speaking to each patient individually. Not just saying hello and passing on, but stopping and sitting on the edge of each patient's bed and chatting for some time. This was on a Saturday afternoon and as she hadn't the time to see each and every one of the battle casualties, before leaving she promised she would be back "tomorrow afternoon." Sure enough, Sunday noon she came—not with Benny and Tilton, but alone—and stayed until six o'clock talking, joking and doing all that she could, which was a great deal, to cheer up the blind, the limbless and the sick.' To come overseas to entertain the soldiers is doing a lot. To do what Miss Landis did is doing infinitely more," *Photoplay*, November 1944.

"As early as January 1944": *The Hollywood Reporter*'s Rambling Reporter on January 27, 1944, wrote, "Carole Landis denies any marital rift, but don't be surprised if she's really adrift soon."

"a lightning USO trip": According to the *Los Angeles Times* (January 7), Carole and George arrived in England on the sixth to "join the USO in entertaining American troops stationed here." On January 10, Walter Winchell reported Carole and Tommy at the Stork Club, presumably on the previous evening; thus the trip could not have lasted more than three days.

"beauty attracts but does not hold": Hedda wrote on March 6, 1940, "Can it be that beauty is passé? If you'll stop a moment and analyze our Hollywood stars you'll discover few of them could actually be called beautiful. 'Beauty attracts, but does not hold' still holds in Hollywood, and more important at the box office." One wonders what inspired this reflection, which one fond of melodrama might say cast an ominous pall over Carole's nascent career. Given the publicity accorded to the just-completed *One Million B.C.* at the time of Hedda's writing, might it have been the emergence on the Hollywood scene of Carole herself?

Chapter 8. Regrouping (1945–1946)

"The stage had never ceased to tempt Carole": When Carole signed with Fox in 1941, their publicity release (dated May 1941) stated that "at Carole Landis' request, 20th Century-Fox has written in an 'escape clause' in her contract to permit her to do a turn on Broadway whenever a suitable vehicle is offered." And on March 19, 1941, Louella Parsons claimed that the Shuberts wanted Carole to star in a Stevens Taylor play called *Blondes Are No Headache*: "If Carole can persuade Darryl Zanuck to let her have a fling on the stage she'll travel to Broadway. The Landis gal, whose figger [*sic*] has earned her as much publicity as did Dietrich's famous underpinnings, wants to prove she can act before the footlights." Yet Carole didn't go to Broadway, and this play, as far as I can tell, was never produced.

"Carole was reported to be dissatisfied": Hedda Hopper, on December 22, 1944, writes, under the subhead "Carole Unhappy," "Carole Landis unhappy about her part in play for Broadway. We could say she's unhappy—period. So is Capt. Wallace, the man she married."

"her physique": Hedda Hopper, on February 14, 1945, writes, "From New York comes word it isn't Carole Landis' singing that's bringing customers to see 'A Lady Says Yes'—it's her chassis."

"The *New York Times* review": By Sam Zolotow on January 11, 1945. The *Wall Street Journal* review by Richard P. Cooke appeared on January 12.

"Walter Winchell put it succinctly": On January 17. Winchell continued, "The ditties are so-so, the humor so-what and the aisle sitters were so sorry."

"*Brooklyn Heights Press*": By Francis Wright, January 31, 1945. The review continues: "If she just stands there and smiles and smiles and smiles . . . Carole Landis appears on the scene . . . [and] we say 'Oh' and 'Ah' . . . and the show goes on . . . and we relax and are amused and interested. . . . [W]e go home with a few laughs . . . with the memory of Carole."

"Carole was reported": Louella Parsons, January 24, 1945.

"Although Carole expressed her willingness": The *New York Times* reported on March 21, 1945, that the show's continuation at the Broadhurst depended on Carole's decision whether to go on the road. On the twenty-second, the *Times* clarified matters: "The notice to close *A Lady Says Yes* on Sunday night, rather than the preceding night, has been posted at the Broadhurst. That's so, because we saw it backstage. Carole Landis, the film actress, who has the chief role in the musical, wants it known she is not to be blamed for the closing. She is willing to continue in the show—here or on the road—. until May 1, when her contract expires. She has to be back in Hollywood after that date. Miss Landis, who is suffering from laryngitis, has been out of the cast since Friday night, but expects to go on tonight."

"Carole found time": A letter from Carole's secretary Nan Stuart to James Pattarini (in the collected correspondence at the New York Public Library) dated March 8, 1945, says that Carole is "working on a signal corps film in Astoria [Queens]." Vic Herman's book, *Winnie the Wac* (Philadelphia: David McKay Company, 1945), is mentioned by Lowell B. Redelings in the *Hollywood Citizen-News* on May 31 as "hitting the bookstands tomorrow"; since Carole's preface refers to events in 1945, it must have been composed during the first months of the year. Herman's widow reprinted *Winnie the Wac* (with an additional preface by herself) in 2002.

"told her biographer Barbara Seaman": In Seaman's *Lovely Me* (New York: William Morrow & Co., 1987). The relevant passage is the following: "For Jackie the months with *A Lady Says Yes* were doubly rewarding, despite the play's dismal reception by the press. Not only was her role a major featured part in a Broadway play but her association with Carole Landis turned into one of the most intense relationships of her life. Carole fell in love with Jackie and was not reticent about showing it. She sent flowers, followed by a tiny pair of perfect pearl drop earrings, even tried to present a mink coat from her personal wardrobe. And Jackie, no doubt flattered, reciprocated, later describing to her girl friends how sensual it had been when she and Carole had stroked and kissed each other's breasts. . . . The depth of Jackie's feeling for Carole, and the nature of their physical relationship, can be surmised from the tender lesbian affair described in *Valley of the Dolls*. In it, Jennifer North, the blond beauty based at least in part on Landis, has the only truly satisfying love of her life with a woman—a brunette like Jackie" (ibid., 153–154).

"an entire life of Sapphism": For example, Boze Hadleigh's *Hollywood Gays* (New York: Barricade Books, 1996), 52: "Landis was bisexual. Reportedly, one of her female lovers was co-star Martha Raye (whose final, far younger husband is now openly . . . bisexual)." One can't prove a negative, but aside from the fact that Carole roomed with Mitzi during the Four Jills tour, in photographs of the group Carole appears much more affectionate with Kay Francis than with Raye, and there is no record of any other contact between them. One wonders if Hadleigh isn't simply confusing Raye with Francis, both reported to have bisexual tendencies. The October 19, 1943, entry in Francis's diary has "Carole home with me for dinner and spent night." Lynn Kear, who kindly supplied me with this information, was unable to say whether this had sexual connotations; the same is true of Francis's more cryptic notation, on December 14, 1943, the day of the cast party for *Four Jills*, "6:30—fight Carole but good!" This covers the known extent of Carole's alleged "bisexuality."

"According to Seaman": On the same page quoted above, Seaman writes, "Later that year Jackie fixed [Carole] up with Schmidlapp" (*Lovely Me*, 154). Louella Parsons's March 13, 1945, column states, "Carole Landis has a new romance in her life, and girls, he's plenty rich." On March 28, the *Hollywood Reporter* gossip column reported, " 'A Lady Says Yes' is just about shuttered and Carole Landis will be headed this way pronto. If she can tear herself away from Horace Schmidlapp. They have marriage on their minds."

"wealthy Cincinnati distilling and banking family": Even today, the Charlotte R. Schmidlapp Fund is listed on the Ohio Grantmakers' Forum Web site as "the largest fund in [Hamilton] county dedicated exclusively to the needs of women and girls."

"The only other indication": Seaman refers to "[Susann's] constant recollection of a phone call she had gotten from Carole on V-J Day in Toronto. Her friend had been seriously depressed, wondering what would happen to her now that she would no longer be needed to entertain the troops and raise war bond money. Carole complained that she was getting too old for the sexpot roles but that no one would give her a chance to act, and she had told Jackie how lucky she was to be so smart, because maybe she could make it as a writer" (*Lovely Me*, 156).

" 'Her white dress, shimmering' ": Susann, *Valley of the Dolls*, 54.

"about the most beautiful girl in the world": Before this description of Jennifer (Susann, *Valley of the Dolls*, 49), Carole's name is mentioned on the second page of the novel, as a kind of discreet dedication; a receptionist is describing her problems to the heroine: "The fellows I know not only expect me to keep my job, but at the same time I should look like Carole Landis in a negligee while I whip up a few gourmet dishes" (ibid., 4).

"her concern that her bosom would not age well": Carole's quote on that subject from Jean Porter is in chapter 4 of this book.

"made plans for a tour": A letter in her personal collection dated March 27, 1945, from Carole to her New York representative, the William Morris Agency, gives it permission to negotiate for these dates; although there is no reason to assume the tour did not take place, I have no proof she actually performed in these cities.

"Carole refused the female lead": Edwin Schallert of the *Los Angeles Times* on May 24, 1945, wrote, "When 'The Spider,' famous mystery melodrama with comedy slants, comes to the screen Richard Conte will be playing opposite Carole Landis." *The Hollywood Reporter*, May 28, 1945, read, "Carole Landis won't be in 'The Spider.' She'll go to Reno in a week for a divorce instead."

"turning down the starring role": Louella Parsons on June 25, 1945, wrote, "Carole Landis has just told 20th that she cannot be among those present when *Doll Face* goes before the cameras. This is the second picture Carole has turned down—first

'The Spider,' and now the erstwhile Joan Blondell play 'The Naked Genius'—the same play that caused such an uproar when it opened on Broadway. Carole's busy getting her divorce so that she can marry Horace Schmidlapp, the New York producer, and probably she won't be working after she becomes Mrs. Schmidlapp. Vivian Blaine, who did a pinch-hit for both Alice Faye and Betty Grable when they were busy having babies, lands the job." Parsons was clearly better informed than Erskine Johnson, who wrote as late as August 12 that Carole would star in the film; but this is no proof that the role was really offered her.

"The movie role went to Vivian Blaine": Fleming has no basis for his claim that Blaine "could not handle the role that was easy for Carole" (*Carole Landis*, 196).

"she took time to entertain the troops": Louella Parsons remarked on July 21, 1945, "Carole Landis is getting herself in very solid with the Las Vegas Army Air Field entertaining them so often."

"it was reported that she intended to marry Schmidlapp": Once again, Louella Parsons had the most thorough version of the story, with an article on July 23, 1945, bearing the headline, "CAROLE LANDIS WILL WED N.Y. PRODUCER IN TWO WEEKS." Many other sources reported with less precision that the wedding would take place some time in August.

"On August 1": For *Captain Eddie*, see the Associated Press news items in the *Zanesville (Ohio) Signal* on August 1 and 2, 1945, and the *Piqua (Ohio) Call* on August 2; for the Edgewater story, see the AP article in the *Joplin (Missouri) Globe* on August 14; for Des Moines, the December 1945 *Silver Screen* has a photograph of Iowa Governor Blue presenting the pig to Carole and Haymes on the occasion of the *State Fair* premiere.

"Carole and Horace were reported to be arguing": In early August, several papers reported rumors of a "rift" between Carole and Horace. Jimmie Fidler wrote on August 11, 1945, that, "according to inside rumors, Horace Schmidlapp's family won't welcome Carole Landis as an in-law unless she agrees to give up her acting career and be 'just a housewife.'" By August 16, *The Hollywood Reporter* was claiming that "Carole Landis isn't even answering the phone when Horace Schmidlapp jingles these days in New York."

"Carole later explained to a columnist": Dorothy Manners on September 12, 1945, wrote, "Carole Landis says the reason she broke her engagement to stage Producer Horace Schmidlapp is 'he wanted me to give up my work and stay in New York. I wouldn't ask him to give up his career to come to Hollywood and just sit around while I make pictures.'" Considering that Carole's auction of household goods took place in early September, it is likely that the interview on which the column was based took place before that date; or perhaps Carole simply kept changing her mind.

"after telling reporters in mid-August": Hedda Hopper reported on August 17, 1945, that "Horace Schmidlapp, whose engagement to Carole Landis was recently announced as 'off by common consent,' spends his evenings with her in New York night spots."

"young Buffalo moneybags 'Courtney Kane'": Dorothy Kilgallen, August 16, 1945.

"Jan Rubini's house": Harrison Carroll, September 20, 1945, says, "Carole Landis is lucky. She not only was able to rent Jan Rubini's house but is getting back her Polynesian house boy."

"Jay Gould": Carroll reported him with Carole on September 24, 1945; Jimmy Starr, on October 4; Kilgallen, on October 20.

"Commander James Kimberly": *The Hollywood Reporter* (Edith Gwynn) declares him and Carole "positively soggy!" on September 25, 1945, sights them at La Rue on October 5, calls it a "bonfire . . . now furnishing enough heat to warm 1948576 homes come winter" on the tenth, and sights them again on the fifteenth and twentieth. Notwithstanding Gwynn's romanticism, the better-informed Louella Parsons revealed on October 12 that Kimberly was disturbed by the car story described in the text: "In fact, he's been on the telephone to his wife, who, naturally, was very upset over this complete falsehood." Car or no car, Mrs. Kimberly cannot have been very pleased to learn of the "1948576 homes" being heated by her husband's "bonfire."

"a number of parties": On housewarming, see Edwin Schallert and Florabel Muir, both October 11, 1945; more complete guest lists are found in the January 1946 gossip columns of *Movieland* and *Silver Screen*. Hedda Hopper, October 16, wrote, "Carole Landis gave a party recently at which men outnumbered women four to one." "A whingding of a party": *Screen Guide*'s "Hollywood Life" column, January 1946.

"a late confessional article": "Do You Think I Was Wrong?" *Silver Screen*, September 1947. The relevant passage is the following: "After reading [the script] I . . . told the director and producer that I had no intention of doing the picture. . . . I . . . agreed to do the film providing certain changes were made. When the picture got under way, I discovered to my horror that not one of the promised changes had been made. I was so mad that I merely walked through the whole thing, not even attempting to do a good job. I hated it so much that I didn't even bother viewing the final results . . . until a few months ago. . . . I looked as though I'd simply stuck out my tongue and pouted my way through it—which is just about what I'd done."

"In a humorous article": Virginia MacPherson, "Carole's Curves Covered," *Hollywood Citizen-News*, October 9, 1945. The reporter makes a number of semi-humorous references to Carole's figure, noting that her "silhouette from neck to waistline is enough to make all would-be sweater girls give up."

"As one reviewer remarked": *The Hollywood Reporter*, January 16, 1946, in a review entitled "The Lights Burn Out," reads, "It is almost as though she were a school child being punished." *Daily Variety* on the same date reads, "Gargan does well as the copper, and Miss Landis, who spends most of the film sitting in Gargan's anteroom . . . looks decorative"; while the *New York World-Telegram* noted on February 15, "Nothing much happens in that back room, but nothing much develops in the rest of the picture's setting, either, so maybe Miss Landis is as well off in her seclusion as she might have been out in front of the camera with the actors."

"Carole's 'junior leaguer' role": Doug McClelland, *The Golden Age of "B" Movies* (Nashville, TN: Charter House, 1978), 28.

"doctors wanted Carole to put back some weight": Harrison Carroll, September 28, 1945, wrote, "Overseas tours are out for Carole Landis for a while. If she wants to preserve those curves, say doctors, she must take it easy after the finish of *Behind Green Lights*. Star dropped from 124 to 106 pounds but has gained some back."

"as early as September 20": The *New York Times* on this date reported her as having signed.

"Jean Renoir's *Diary of a Chambermaid*": *Chambermaid*'s production dates were from early July to early September; it starred Paulette Goddard, was produced by the Camden Production Company and distributed by United Artists. Renoir, exiled by the German occupation of France, spent the war years in the United States, where he made five films between 1941 and 1947. Curiously, Renoir, whose first Hollywood work was at Fox, had been Zanuck's original choice to direct *I Wake Up Screaming*.

"a spread in *Life*": "Speaking of Pictures: *A Scandal in Paris*," with ten photographs, *Life*, January 7, 1946. The brief text points out that Carole's "Flame song" as well as her costume were almost banned by the Production Code office, now headed by Eric Johnston; it also refers to Carole's garter stunt and the Gramlich incident, both described below.

"Carole gave this movie sequence some advance publicity": This was first reported on November 8, 1945, in *The Hollywood Reporter*; since the story refers to "the first guy to go over and get his second garter, in answer to that Carole Landis garter gag John del Valle cooked up for Arnold Pressburger's *A Scandal in Paris*," Carole's invitations must have gone out the previous week. On November 14, Bob Thomas reported in the *Hollywood Citizen-News* that "ten of the old wolves showed up in one afternoon. And a young one."

"as a critic pointed out mockingly": Erskine Johnson's "Talk of the Town" on February 2, 1946, remarks on "Carole Landis and Gene Lockhart, who play man and wife in the film 'A Scandal in Paris,' occupying twin beds in a period almost 100 years before twin beds were invented."

"'the best part [she] ever had'": The "Cheering Section" in the September 1946 *Screen Romances* calls Carole "elated" about the role: "'It's the best part I ever had,' she says. 'I hope I did it justice. It would be very pleasant to find myself graduated for good from 'B' films.'"

"she was the recipient of an obscene letter": On February 28, 1940, the *Los Angeles Herald* reported that one Stanley Campbell had been sentenced to three years in prison for this crime.

"a complaint of 'attempted rape'": this charge and Gramlich's arrest are described most fully in the November 17, 1945, *Traverse City (Michigan) Record-Eagle*, available through the ancestry.com newspaper files. The *Hollywood Citizen-News*, *Los Angeles Times*, and numerous out-of-town papers printed photographs of Carole identifying Gramlich at the police station on November 17. On December 5, the *Citizen-News* reported that Gramlich, "who had been treated in two Ohio mental hospitals," "was committed today to the state Mental Hospital at Norwalk, Calif."

"the reviewers were generally appreciative": The *New York Times* review appeared on September 16, 1946; *The Hollywood Reporter* reviewed *Scandal* on July 10. The *Los Angeles Examiner* wrote that "Carole Landis injects a bit of umph into the role of woman spurned." The *Los Angeles Times*, on October 5, read, "And for an ersatz Dietrich (in her 'Flame Song' she gives a pretty good imitation of the star, gams and all) Carole does all right, too." On the same date, the *Hollywood Citizen-News* wrote of "exciting Carole Landis."

"Carole received an order to report to Fox": Carole's Fox legal file in the UCLA Fine Arts Special Collections contains a telegram dated November 23 threatening her with suspension for missing her appointment, then another telegram, dated the twenty-sixth, ordering her to report the following day. That same day, Carole wrote Fox turning down the role.

" 'wed in green satin' ": Dorothy Kilgallen, December 21, 1945.

"a spokeswoman for a policewoman's association": The Fox publicity release accompanying the film mentions that the International Association of Policewomen "greeted the casting of Miss Landis as a lady cop with delight, and sent Mrs. Irma Buwalda, former regional director of the association, to assist Miss Landis as technical adviser on her police work in the film."

"The reviewers, for their part": "dresses and steps" is from *Variety* on May 22, 1946, which added that "her name won't hurt on the marquee"; the "movie queen" quote is from *The Hollywood Reporter* on the same date.

"Ironically, the eight hundred thousand dollars": See the tables appended to Aubrey Solomon, *Twentieth Century-Fox: A Corporate and Financial History* (Metuchen, NJ: Scarecrow Press, 1988); the 1946 table is on page 221.

"go on with [her] career": For example, in the *Los Angeles Times* on December 9, 1945.

"Louella Parsons claimed": Parsons, December 14, 1945, wrote: "Carole Landis's groom, Horace Schmidlapp, says he's through with stage production, but it's said he has plenty of money invested in Associated Filmakers, Inc. In New York this company is building a studio in Yonkers where movies will be made. The first productions will be commercial films, but Schmidlapp is planning feature pictures within a year. And what do you bet he doesn't star his bride? She's on suspension from 20th, and I doubt very much if she'll make another picture there." On December 30, Jimmie Fidler chimed in, "Carole Landis' new husband, Horace Schmidlapp, is going to produce entertainment pictures as well as commercial films, and Carole wants to star in them if she can get out of her 20th Century-Fox contract." A United Press article in the *Traverse City (Michigan) Record-Eagle* on February 20, 1946, entitled "Plenty of Money Being Invested in Television," mentioned Schmidlapp among "a few lively fellows with money to invest." The article goes on to report that "up in Yonkers . . . W. Horace Schmidlapp is putting some of his Cincinnati fortune into the building of a $500,000 movie and television studio at Central and Tuckahoe avenues. . . . Associated Filmmakers hopes that the studio will be ready for operation by July 1."

"As part of a strategy": Elizabeth Wilson's "Landis without Leopard Skins," *Liberty*, July 19, 1947, describes Carole's efforts to reinvent herself on the occasion of the pending release of *Out of the Blue*: "Now, gentlemen may prefer blondes, but the members of the Academy of Motion Picture Arts and Sciences apparently prefer brunettes. And what Carole wants most right now is an Academy Award. So as her first 'new personality' step, she had her blonde hair turned a lovely brownette overnight."

"Carole spent most of the year in the East": Most of the activities listed were reported in the *New York Times*: Hotel St. George, June 14, 1946; Cancer Society, April 3, April 19; United Jewish Appeal, October 22; Skymaster, July 24; exceptions are the Cancer Society plaque, which is in her family collection; the Cleveland visit, in the June 3 *Coshocton (Ohio) Tribune*; and the radio shows and the Earle Theater appearance, for which her (required) permission from Fox is in her legal file. The authorized radio programs took place on March 16, March 20, April 3, and July 11.

"Edith Gwynn's *Hollywood Reporter* column": On December 10, 1946, Gwynn wrote, "Whether or not Carole Landis and her rich mate are arguing about her 'career,' fact is, she is shopping for a press-agent—meaning she means to take another fling at the flickers."

"some writers' reports to the contrary": For example, Kirk Crivello, in his November 1973 *Film Fan Monthly* bio of Carole that would form the basis for his chapter on her in his *Fallen Angels*: "Carole's position in the studio hierarchy was definitely falling. She returned to Fox for two minor murder mysteries, BEHIND GREEN LIGHTS and IT SHOULDN'T HAPPEN TO A DOG. The latter title speaks for itself. *With that, the studio ended her contract*" (emphasis mine). In the book chapter, Crivello modifies the italicized sentence to "Carole was now free of her 20th Century-Fox contractual obligations." The Wilson article in *Liberty*, July 19, 1947, referred to above, describes her departure thus: "She had been off the screen for over a year: ever since Twentieth Century-Fox had handed her a little stinker called *It Shouldn't Happen to a Dog*. It shouldn't. But she made it. Then she picked up her salary check, told Twentieth Century-Fox what they could do with her contract, and took herself to New York."

"the warm tone of her correspondence": On October 30, 1947, Horace's mother, Jean Sturgis, wrote Carole in London a letter that ends, "Ever so much love and if you return for Xmas, do come to us. Take care of yourself—and don't stay away too long! fondly Mommie." The Handsaker column is dated February 24, 1946.

"rumors of a 'rift' ": "Carole Landis in town with a new hairdo . . . reports that the characters who rumored her rifting with Horace Schmidlapp are just dreaming." Dorothy Kilgallen, June 20, 1946.

"to answer a columnist's query": The quote is from the Elizabeth Wilson article in *Liberty*, which is the source of a good deal of often-repeated—and often-distorted—material: "When her New York millionaire-producer-bridegroom did not join her immediately, the columnists and commentators busied themselves with divorce rumors. 'What's keeping you apart?' asked a snoopy reporter at Ciro's one night. 'Distance,' replied Carole sweetly, and couldn't have spoken a truer word." No doubt Carole's intention was to defuse the divorce rumors, not to encourage them.

"Carole was hospitalized": On October 23, 1946, the *Los Angeles Times* reported that "Carole Landis, film actress, yesterday was admitted to St. John's Hospital, Santa Monica, with what was described as 'an acute abdominal condition.' Her condition was reported serious, but not critical. Her physician, Dr. W. L. Marxer, said she probably can leave the hospital within 10 days 'if all goes well.' " Another piece of evidence of Carole's health concerns scarcely two months before her death is her complaint of a parasitic illness in her April 1948 letters.

"co-hosting a dinner at the Waldorf": The *New York Times* reported on December 17, 1946, that "Joe Louis was guest of honor at a dinner held last night by the Southern Conference for Human Welfare at the Waldorf-Astoria Hotel. . . . Frank Sinatra was chairman of the dinner committee, which included Duke Ellington, Carole Landis, . . ." There is a photograph showing Carole standing next to Frank as Louis receives his award.

"a two-film contract": Carole's family papers include a copy of Carole's Eagle-Lion contract (as well as copies of her British film contracts).

"Eagle-Lion Films": This British-financed operation entered the American market by acquiring the assets of the Poverty Row studio Producers Releasing Corporation (PRC) in 1947; its last films were released in 1951.

Chapter 9. Anglophilia (1947–1948)

"the *Liberty* article that recounts it": Carole's interview article with Elizabeth Wilson, "Landis without Leopard-Skins," *Liberty*, July 19, 1947. Alexander Walker and others cite this incident, almost certainly at secondhand.

"*liveliest* in a nightgown": The ancestry.com newspaper database contains as of this writing one example of the misprint: the *Statesville (N.C.) Record Landmark*, also on January 6. The correct text of the article can be found in the January 6 *Mansfield (Ohio) News Journal*.

"columnists were retailing rumors": Sheilah Graham on February 5, 1947, wrote, "Carole Landis, also at Palm Springs, was billing and cooing—mostly billing (it's expensive this year) with husband Horace Schmidlapp. And the day before I had been told that they were on the verge of splitting up. If they are, they are hiding it very well." Walter Winchell on February 12, after Horace's return East, wrote, "Those nasty old gossips are saying that, despite denials, the Horace Schmidlapps (Carole Landis) have phooffft."

"Carole was observed to be house-hunting": Hedda Hopper on February 19, 1947; Hedda also reported that the separation rumors "are just that—rumors."

"Horace paid seventy-eight thousand dollars": Sheilah Graham, March 7, 1947, wrote, "Carole Landis paid $78,000 for her new 15-room house in the Pacific Palisades—or rather that is what her husband, Horace Schmidlapp, is going to pay when he arrives here on Sunday!" Hedda's column was on April 26.

"Another columnist claimed": Jimmie Fidler, April 12, 1947.

"One story is that": This is found in Fleming (*Carole Landis*, 239, where he misleadingly presents it as discovered at Carole's autopsy), whose source may be Carole's grandniece Tammy Gates, Sharon's daughter, who gave me this explanation in September 2003. Endometriosis is a congenital condition whose cause remains unknown. I have found no evidence to support speculations that Carole's infertility was the result of either childhood sexual abuse or a botched abortion at an early age.

"Carole's often-expressed hope": For example, in "Should War Wives Have Babies?" (*Photoplay*, December 1943), Carole states, "It is a great disappointment to me that I am not expecting along with several other of my married friends." Having just recovered from a serious attack of amoebic dysentery while touring in the Pacific, Carole told the Sydney, Australia, *Daily Mirror* on August 12, 1944, "I want a baby—before the war is over if the war lasts that long. Either a boy or girl will suit me. I'll love whichever comes along."

"Carole's family papers": The letter is addressed to Carole at 232 S. Mapleton Drive in Brentwood; Horace expresses satisfaction that the Eagle-Lion deal has gone through.

"to the general approval of reviewers": The August 26, 1947, *Hollywood Reporter*, which called Mayo "physically a dream," wrote that "Carole Landis does well what little she has as the vacationing wife." *Weekly Variety* on the same date reads, "Brent . . . scores in his comedy, and Miss Landis fetchingly follows in line." Less enthusiastically, the August 27 *Daily Variety* tells us that "Miss Landis, in a neutral role, remains merely decorative."

"Don Loper's 'slipper party' ": Hedda Hopper, April 14, 1947. Confiscated watches: *The Hollywood Reporter*, April 21.

"speculations about Horace's projects": For example, Jimmie Fidler on April 25, 1947, mentioned Horace's intention to make "a minimum of 12 features in the next few years." Fidler also mentions Carole's intention to handle all offers from her husband through her agent, perhaps one of those clever ideas the agent conceived to supply copy for the columns.

"The papers reported": For example, the *Los Angeles Times*, June 21, 1947. On June 27, the *Times* reported Oakes's first victory under Carole's colors; and on July 2, the second. The information from Oakes is courtesy of racing researcher Denny Miller, who conducted a personal interview with Oakes in 2004.

"a professional opportunity": Sidney Skolsky on July 2, 1947, writes, "Carole Landis will play a lead in 'The Play's the Thing' when Ross Hunter presents it at his Tent

Theater." Alexander Walker (*Fatal Charm*, 140) speaks of Carole as so unbalanced by her relationship with Harrison that she was "unable to take direction" in Hunter's staging of a different play, *Dream Girl*, after Carole's return from England in March 1948; despite these differences, considering the absence of any published reference to this second play, it is conceivable that both writers are referring to the same production.

"In March 1947": Bautzer's letter to Frank Angell, the investigator, dated March 25, 1947, is found in Carole's family collection. Clara's "marry a rich man" quote was reported in various places after the suicide, for example, the *Hollywood Citizen-News*, July 7, 1948.

"the loss of weight noted by Sidney Skolsky": Skolsky vied with Earl Wilson for honors in the infantile breast humor department. On February 15, 1947, Skolsky complained that Carole "has taken off so much weight that she doesn't resemble Carole Landis, especially in the best and familiar places." Then on March 5, like Walt Whitman untroubled by self-contradiction, he recycled the same quip by inverting it: "Carole has taken off plenty of weight, looks fine, and it might be difficult for you to recognize her if it weren't for a couple of things that haven't changed."

"Westmores' beauty book": Ern and Bud Westmore, *Beauty, Glamour, and Personality* (Sandusky, Ohio: Prang Co., 1947).

"Much of an unflattering nature": I will have occasion to refer below to Harrison's biographers, particularly to Alexander Walker (*Fatal Charm: The Life of Rex Harrison* [New York: St. Martins Press, 1992]) and Roy Moseley (with Phillip and Martin Masheter, *Rex Harrison: A Biography* [New York: St. Martin's Press, 1987]), and to Rex's own autobiography (*Rex: An Autobiography* [New York: William Morris & Co., 1975]). Despite his disparaging account à la Sperling of Carole's career, Walker remains Rex's most thorough biographer.

" 'got a raw deal' ": An actor who knew both Rex and Carole was Henry Wilcoxon, her costar in *Mystery Sea Raider*: "A lot of unkind things have been said about Carole over the years. . . . I liked her very much. She was a very pretty blond. She was a competent actress. She was a tireless worker on the set, and, okay, now I'll say it: considering that I knew both Rex Harrison and Carole, I think she got a raw deal." *Lionheart in Hollywood: The Autobiography of Henry Wilcoxon* (Metuchen, NJ: Scarecrow Press, 1991), 131.

"Cesar Romero did not hesitate": In his conversation with Boze Hadleigh in *Hollywood Gays*, where Romero also says that he had thought of marrying Carole to protect her from "abusive and two-timing men," husbands and lovers both. Kreuger's views were expressed in a personal interview held at his home in 2004.

" 'had secretly been meeting' ": Walker, *Fatal Charm*, 131. Walker mentions that it was only after Rex had finished *The Foxes of Harrow*, that is, in late July, that "he could relax with Carole in reasonable security" (ibid., 135).

"At the party": Betty Garrett, with Ron Rapoport, *Betty Garrett and Other Songs: A Life on Stage and Screen* (Lanham, MD: Madison Books, 1998), 247–248: "The party was at John [Huston]'s ranch in Tarzana and it was to celebrate his anniversary. . . . It was a formal evening that just about everybody in Hollywood seemed to be going to. . . . Later in the evening, Rex Harrison, who was rather drunk, danced with Carole Landis and was leaning all over her while Lilli Palmer, whom he was married to, stood in the doorway with her coat on, tapping her foot and waiting for him to finish so they could go home." Ms. Garrett confirmed this story in a personal communication in 2004. Keyes's book is entitled *Scarlett O'Hara's Younger Sister* (Secaucus, NJ: Lyle Stuart, 1977) in honor of her best-remembered role in *Gone with the Wind*; the party is described on page 124 as "the best goddamn party I ever went to."

"a supper party on or about June 14": On June 16, 1947, *Hollywood Reporter* columnist Edith Gwynn reports seeing the couple at "the big cocktail-through-dinner-through-midnight-through-everything party that Johnny Gibbs tossed for Elyse Hunt."

"Harrison's biographers": Allen Eyles, in *Rex Harrison* (London: W. H. Allen, 1985), treats the whole affair with Carole as a minor incident of interest only because of the ensuing scandal that affected Rex's career; Nicholas Wapshott, in *Rex Harrison* (London: Chatto & Windus, 1991), is equally perfunctory. Roy Moseley includes a brief, not unsympathetic bio of Carole, although it includes the mandatory quote from Sperling. Moseley's account, more nuanced than Walker's, takes the position that "Rex, knowing Carole to be a carefree girl, had not entered into the affair with her with any serious intent, and could not have expected this intensity to surface in Landis" (*Rex Harrison*, 107), which is reasonable if understood as not denying Rex's own attachment to the affair despite his disinclination to destroy his marriage for it. Walker, whose account of the suicide is the most thorough, spends less time on Carole herself, whom he tends to depict in near-pathetic terms: "[what] Rex tragically underestimated was how seriously Carole Landis took the affair. She knew him as a lover, yes, but also as a means of renewing her career. . . . A despondent Carole fell back on Rex for consolation and advice about her future" (*Fatal Charm*, 141). But both Moseley and Walker see Carole's tragedy from a Rex-centric viewpoint, as a moment of Rex's life, rather than treating their affair as a full-fledged human relationship. And although both were able to talk with Harrison as well as others involved in the affair, their insights into Rex's thoughts are sometimes dubious. For example, Walker claims that in February 1948 "[Rex] believed that Lilli still knew nothing of the affair. He hoped so" (ibid., 140), although the Keyes party alone, which had taken place several months earlier, would certainly have dispelled that illusion.

"Alexander Walker mistakenly explains": It is hard to understand how this generally careful writer could be so inaccurate as to confuse Carole's Eagle-Lion contract for two films (*Out of the Blue* was to be followed by *The Amazing Mr. X*) with the two separate contracts she signed with two different British production companies for *Brass Monkey* (Diadem Films) and *Noose* (Edward Dryhurst Productions). There is no apparent basis for Walker's reference to "a deal for two low-budget movies to be shot in England back to back—that is to say, using the same crew on each and with scarcely an interval between them—for the Eagle-Lion company, the overseas distribution arm of British Lion" (*Fatal Charm*, 138). A possible reason for this confusion is that the Dryhurst contract was formally drawn up with Eagle-Lion Studios in the United States, to whom Carole was still under contract; but this is just the inverse of the relationship described by Walker.

"On July 18, Louella Parsons": The July 18, 1947, Parsons column read: "Carole Landis who married a husband in England during the war, and then unmarried him after the war, goes there in August for a personal appearance tour. She will also talk over a picture offer and may stay to do one film."

"That summer, most likely in mid-July": Edith Gwynn's July 2, 1947, *Hollywood Reporter* gossip column records Carole and Horace hosting a luncheon-swimming-cocktail party with forty guests, but the guest lists don't appear to overlap and the Christmas motif is lacking; the Christmas party appears to have been an Eagle-Lion affair.

"On August 4": Louella Parsons, August 4, 1947: "Carole Landis flies East today for a week of personal appearances at the Hippodrome Theater in Baltimore and then on for a week in Boston."

"Horace was supposed": Louella Parsons on September 25, 1947: "Horace Schmidlapp plans to join Carole Landis in London in two weeks, so you can just throw those rumors that they are separating right out the window." But less than two weeks later, on October 8, she wrote: "Carole Landis writes to say that her husband, Horace Schmidlapp, will take the Katherine Dunham show to London and that he'll join her there the last part of this month."

"he had arrived on August 21": Walker, *Fatal Charm*, 138.

"Meanwhile, Lilli Palmer": Sheilah Graham writes on September 20, 1947, that Lilli is returning "to make another movie for boss Milton Sperling." Lilli's previous film, *My Girl Tisa*, produced by Sperling, had been shot from May to August 1947; it was released in February 1948. As it turned out, her next film, *No Minor Vices*, was made for MGM beginning in March 1948; she would never make another film for Sperling.

"the film's British release": See David Marlowe's "Is the Brass Monkey Now a Lucky Mascot?" *Picturegoer*, February 3, 1951.

"In a December 1947 letter to her fan club": The letter is in Carole's file at the Herrick Library. Unfortunately, it bears no date; it was written after the November 25 command performance and some time before Christmas, since she speaks of plans for a Dublin trip before a projected trip to Germany, which would presumably have been made several days before December 25.

"When we do have news of his sailing": Harrison Carroll on December 19, 1947, states that Horace sailed on the sixteenth "to join Carole Landis."

"Donald Bogle's biography": Bogle, *Dorothy Dandridge: A Biography* (New York: St. Martin's Press, 1997), 139–140. Hedda Hopper, April 28, 1948, reported on her conversation with Don Hearn, "with Special Services in the European sector," who praised

Rita's trip in 1947, when she "entertained 20,000 troops in eight days," then, after mentioning some other stars, made his comment about Carole without further explanation.

"Lilli, according to Louella": On December 5, 1947, Louella reported that Lilli was in St. Moritz "and will spend Christmas in Switzerland." This is, of course, no proof that Lilli and Rex did not spend the holidays together. They left England together on the *Queen Elizabeth* and were to have arrived in New York (says Louella, writing on January 22) on the twenty-third.

"in the light of Roy Moseley's statements": Moseley, *Rex Harrison*; Hunter's statement is on 105; Carole's shrine to Rex is mentioned on 106. Hunter, we recall, was obliged to drop Carole from a dramatic production because she was too distracted with Rex to remember her lines.

"Hedda claimed Carole would return": On November 7, 1947. On January 13, 1948, Hedda claimed that "June Lockhart won't know until she reads this that her next picture at Eagle-Lion is all set." In reality, June turned her attention to television and never made another picture for Eagle-Lion. Harrison Carroll's column is dated November 14. Louella's November 12 column gives some details about *Noose*, but confuses Carole's two British films by referring to Levis as the lead. Skolsky's Broadway idea dates from November 18.

"*Out of the Red*": Edwin Schallert writes in the November 20, 1947, *Los Angeles Times*, "Eagle-Lion . . . has purchased a Vera Caspary story called 'Out of the Red' in which Ann [Dvorak] will be starred. . . . [It] is about a young woman who goes to Las Vegas to obtain a divorce and who has adventures at the gaming tables."

"she told a movie journalist": Reported by Dolores Gilbert in "Carole Landis n'est plus," *Ciné Revue*, July 16, 1948: "She had thought [avait songé] of buying a country home in England and establishing herself there" (my translation). The pluperfect tense implies that Carole had no present intention of pursuing this idea.

"the one available American review": The review appeared in the *Los Angeles Times* on February 5, 1953; it says nothing specific about Carole's acting, but seems impressed with her character and persona; under the heading "Smart Newshen," it reads, "There have been a lot of smart newspaper girl heroines in movies, and Carole Landis plays one of the smartest."

" 'Her leading man in *Noose*' ": Moseley, *Rex Harrison*, 101.

"After finishing *Noose*": On March 4, 1948, Harrison Carroll reports Carole back in New York "and Horace Schmidlapp remains in Europe. What gives?" Yet the March 9 *Los Angeles Evening Herald Examiner* had Horace in New York. In her March 10 column, Louella Parsons reports Carole as saying that she "only learned yesterday" that Horace was back in New York; this suggests that Carroll's information on Schmidlapp's whereabouts probably came from Carole rather than a more knowledgeable source.

"On the ninth, she spoke through an agent": The *Herald Examiner*'s March 9, 1948, article reports that the couple "may hold a conference here within a short time over their marital status." This article also cites Carole's agent as the source of the quote about Horace's three-month stay in Europe. The reference to the attorney is from an Associated Press article in the March 11 *Dixon (Illinois) Evening Telegraph*.

"in the lead item of his widely read column": Walter Winchell, March 16,1948. The complete text reads: "Carole Landis's statement (that she was splitting from her husband) is a belated confirmation. She denied it often to me and now declares 'she hasn't seen him for months and that he doesn't respond to her phone calls' . . . [ellipsis in text] The fact is that her next husband (if and when) will be Rex Harrison, the British star. Mrs. Harrison (Lilli Palmer) knows all about the romance, which started only recently in London." On March 18, Hedda Hopper, after quoting Carole's—far from sincere—statement, "This waiting is rough. It's not fun," about waiting for Horace to "[show] some interest in ironing out their differences," adds maliciously, "I hear Carole did have fun in England."

" 'The hardest part of Zanuck's reprimand' ": Walker, *Fatal Charm*, 142–143.

"Lloyd Shearer": "Why Actresses Try Suicide," *Parade*, November 6, 1960.

"a divorce settlement with Schmidlapp": Details of the settlement appeared in Kilgallen's column on April 24, 1948 (which includes the detail of the $30,000), and in Louella's on May 17. Horace's refusal is discussed in the *Hollywood Citizen-News*, July 19, 1948.

"Despite being under a doctor's care": Letters to Gisi Weise (April 23, 1948) and James Pattarini (April 28, 1948).

"usual star turns": Both the April 30 and the May 3 dates are reported in the *Los Angeles Times* on the day of the respective events.

"According to Louella": On May 13, 1948, Louella reported that Gréville had arrived in Hollywood the previous Sunday (the ninth) for this purpose.

"According to her secretary Nan Stuart": Nan Stuart, whose real name was Jan Singer, had worked for Carole since 1941. This information comes from a letter on Carole's stationery dated August 3, 1948, in Carole's file at the AMPAS library; the addressee is Shirley Baxter, the president of Carole's fan club. Nan's recollection is partially confirmed by Crawford Dixon's sighting of Carole entering a store in Beverly Hills on that same Friday, as reported in his October 1948 *Movieland* article, "The Carole Landis Tragedy."

"Carole had plans to go to east": New York–based columnist Earl Wilson wrote on July 8, 1948, that she was expected in New York "this week." Carole's family collection contains a copy of a telegram dated May 30 from Harold J. Kennedy in New York City that reads, "Absolutely delighted. Please phone me immediately collect . . . regarding play and dates," and almost certainly refers to this trip.

"And in an April 28 letter": This is the same letter to James Pattarini where Carole spoke of being under a doctor's care for a recurrence of her illness. Her language is very definite: she had a "wonderful time in England making the Brass Monkey and Noose, and am returning there this summer to make another picture." It is unclear what if any connection this project had with Gréville's May visit.

Chapter 10. The Good Die Young (1948)

"hints were dropped": On October 22, 1949, Dorothy Kilgallen, who had followed Carole's career sympathetically in her columns, claimed that "California" police had found a new clue; on the thirtieth, Jimmie Fidler made the same claim, referring correctly to the Los Angeles Police Department. I have found no further information about this tantalizing "clue." The LAPD claims the files on the case have been destroyed, since they only permanently maintain the files of murder cases.

"Rex and Carole had been together": Both Walker (*Fatal Charm*) and Moseley (*Rex Harrison*) had access to interview material that is no longer accessible; much of what they say appears objective, but needless to say, they interpret the affair from Rex's perspective and their discussion of Carole's motives reflects this bias. The material in this paragraph derives largely from Walker, *Fatal Charm*, 143–144.

"hiring a private detective": It is also possible that Walker is inadvertently referring to the 1947 investigation conducted by Bautzer into Horace's finances referred to in the preceding chapter.

"Horace's apparent interest in a number of other women": After Carole filed for divorce in March, Horace was connected to no fewer than four women in the next two months: "Showgirl Gene Courtney" (Dorothy Kilgallen, March 29, 1948, six days after the filing); "Rusty Reagan, an actress" whom Horace was expected to marry "immediately following his divorce" (Erskine Johnson, April 8); "singer Nan Wynn" (Kilgallen, April 30; *Hollywood Reporter*, May 11); "Doris Lilly" (Louella Parsons, June 17).

" 'Carole and I continued to meet' ": Rex Harrison, *Rex: An Autobiography*, 104–105.

"In his deposition": "Jury May Act in Mystery," *Los Angeles Evening Herald Examiner*, July 9, 1948.

"her regular maid, Susie Smith": In a letter in Carole's file at the Herrick Library, her secretary Nan Stuart gives this information. The family collection contains a condolence letter from Smith to Carole's mother, dated July 17, 1948, which says, "Am only grieved that I was not with her, perhaps she would not have been so despondent."

"Carole's delicate financial situation": There is evidence in Carole's personal papers of dealings with a bankruptcy referee (an empty envelope from U.S. District Court, David B. Head, Referee in Bankruptcy, dated May 27, 1948); Carole's quest a year earlier to discover Horace's sources of income is already an indication that she was pressed for funds. After the suicide, there was much discussion of Carole's financial status, although, given her film offers and prospects, this can have been at most a contributory cause of her depression.

" 'Suzie,' as a code": Walker, *Fatal Charm*, 143.

"Moseley quite plausibly suggests": Moseley writes: "Rex found it increasingly difficult to extricate himself. . . . Not only was [*Anne of the Thousand Days*] a marvellous acting opportunity, but it also seemed to offer the chance to step back and draw breath in order to consider what he should do next regarding the Landis affair. It would be a convenient enforced separation as it would mean his going to New York for a considerable period of time" (*Rex Harrison*, 107–108). Walker writes: "It is reasonable, in view of later events, to conjecture that Rex left Carole Landis without having been able to convince her that their coming separation—on which he was determined—was in the best interests of both of them. They had reached the end of the affair—which was all it ever had been, or so he later swore to his intimates" (*Fatal Charm*, 145).

"Chicago journalist Michael Sheridan": In one of a series of "Breathless Moments," apparently dealing with Hollywood suicides and the like, entitled "What Carole Landis Told Me" in the October 8, 1949, *Chicago Herald American Home Magazine*.

"Tennessee senator Estes Kefauver": "Let's stop sleeping-pill suicides," *Los Angeles Times*, March 20, 1949.

"Esther Williams specifically recalls": See Esther Williams with Digby Diehl, *The Million Dollar Mermaid* (New York: Harcourt, 1999), 164–165. Williams was waiting to discuss a script she thought Rex would like to do with her: "I gave up waiting for Rex when the clock struck 2 a.m."

" 'A lawyer came to tell us' ": Palmer, *Change Lobsters—and Dance* (New York: Macmillan, 1975), 176. The story is repeated by Moseley but curiously does not appear in Walker. Might suspicion that Palmer lied about her whereabouts on the evening of July 4 have led Walker to doubt her veracity on this subject as well? The July 10, 1948, *Los Angeles Examiner* had a story by Harry Lang, "Two Other Death Tries by Carole Bared by Police." Lang claims his source was "intimate friends" and that the attempts, in New York and Hollywood, were "quite recent." For what it is worth, Carole's secretary in her letter mentioned above denies any previous suicide attempts.

"two previous attempts": There is also an incident related by Walter Winchell on July 12, 1948: "Insiders hear Carole Landis planned suicide by driving her car off a west coast cliff in 1946. . . . A kitten dashing across the path of the car changed her mind. . . . Carole then drove to the home of Dick Haymes' mother (the story goes) and while holding the kitten in her lap—Mrs. Haymes and Carole talked out the problem" (ellipses are in Winchell's text).

"When Fannie May Bolden arrived": This material, apparently from an interview with Bolden, is in Moseley, *Rex Harrison*, 108.

"at Maxwell Anderson's house": This generally accepted statement is contradicted by bizarre testimony from Anderson's daughter, Hesper, in her memoir *South Mountain*

Road (New York: Simon & Schuster, 2000): "It was the summer that Carole Landis killed herself over Rex Harrison. He was at our house that day, talking with my father about *Anne of the Thousand Days*, when the police arrived and told him that Carole Landis, a young actress who was his mistress at the time, had committed suicide. I'd watched from my window as Harrison, shaken, left with the police" (133). There is no obvious way to reconcile this statement with Rex's declaration, confirmed by Fannie May, that he discovered Carole's body.

"Fannie May stated at the inquest": "Jury May Act in Mystery," *Los Angeles Evening Herald Examiner*, July 9, 1948.

"the correct name": In a letter to James Pattarini dated May 8, 1947, Nan Stuart mentions the presence of "Two kittens. Miss A. and Miss C. don't stand for anything."

"Carole's mother examined the cat": Dorothy Ross's article, "The True Story of My Sister" (*Photoplay*, November 1948), states, "Miss C. picked up stickers [splinters?] in her paws around the place. But Mother checked and found her feet were all right."

" 'it contained something highly compromising' ": Palmer, *Change Lobsters—and Dance*, 178–179.

" 'a three-line lover's farewell' ": Walker, *Fatal Charm*, 156.

"Another account refers to a note": In Roland Culver's *Not Quite a Gentleman* (London: William Kimber & Co., Ltd., 1979), 120.

" 'shortly before his death' ": Moseley, *Rex Harrison*, 113.

" 'a package' that Carole deposited": Walker, *Fatal Charm*, 152.

"Walker goes overboard": Walker, *Fatal Charm*, 154.

" 'curious, inexplicable statement' ": Moseley, *Rex Harrison*, 116.

" 'peculiar natural condition' ": *Los Angeles Evening Herald Examiner*, July 7, 1948. The name of the examining physician was Irving Madoff, who reported to Coroner Ben Brown; see "Star's Suicide Bares Love Tangles," *Chicago Herald-American*, July 9.

"A reporter mentions": Harry Lang of the *Los Angeles Examiner*, on July 8, 1948. Walker writes: "Then, for the very first time . . . since the discovery of Carole Landis's corpse, a name cropped up . . . that had been . . . conspicuously absent up to now. . . . It was the name of Rex's current employer: the studio that had him under contract and stood to be harmed by any unpleasant developments such as a grand jury hearing or a subsequent trial" (*Fatal Charm*, 156). Walker's dramatic tone leads Fleming (*Carole Landis*, 240) to misinterpret the expression "the name of Rex's current employer," without noticing the apposition, "the studio," as referring to Zanuck himself.

"any sign of foul play": Nan Stuart, in a second letter to Shirley Baxter, president of Carole's fan club, expresses suspicion about the fact that the lights were off. (Does this confirm Walker's idea that Carole took the pills after sunrise? Or did Rex, or Fannie, simply turn them off?) Stuart wondered if Carole took the pills by mistake, or if "she may not have been talked into what happened." Whatever one thinks of Rex, one would have to have a good deal more evidence before accusing him of "talking" Carole into committing suicide!

"Carole's funeral attracted": The most complete contemporary account was written by James Lindsley for the Associated Press and appeared in the *Lima News* (Ohio) on July 11, 1948. Only portions of Bishop Pyman's seven-minute sermon were reported; my version is a synthesis of the AP, UP, and INS accounts.

"delayed by bad weather in Chicago": *Los Angeles Times*, July 11, 1948.

"Carole's purported reaction to Lupe Velez's suicide": *Los Angeles Examiner*, July 16, 1948: "When Lupe Velez ended her life with an overdose of sleeping pills, Carole told a friend: 'I know just how she felt . . .' "

"one movie writer even suggested": Arno Johansen, "Will Rex Harrison Survive Scandal?" *Movieland*, November 1948.

"anonymous 'lifelong friend' ": This article, "The Truth about Carole Landis," which dealt in part with Carole's childhood, was cited extensively in chapter 1. The friend's analysis of the Harrison affair and the suicide is also noteworthy, although it has generally been ignored by other writers: "What could Carole do? Try to persuade him to give up his wife and marry her?. . . If she succeeded in taking this man from his wife, would he, later on, hate her for breaking up his marriage? By nature Carole was a warm-hearted person without a bit of malice in her system. Knowing how much she loved this man, she could guess how dear he was to his wife. She didn't want to hurt her. She loved this man deeply, but in her heart she was sure that he did not return this love with the same ardor. He judged her by the record she had made before the world—a record of success in her career but of too many quick-dying loves."

"it may even be that Carole herself wanted to do so": This information is from Carole's grand-niece Tammy, who told me she had it from her grandmother Dorothy Ross, Carole's sister. One need not assume any decision was made to find it useful to know that she was considering this step.

"an undated poem in typescript": there are also some handwritten drafts and a typed final version I was not able to examine in detail.

"to show Earl Wilson her slightly bowed legs": Wilson recounts this incident in his book *I Am Gazing into My 8-Ball* (Garden City, NY: Sundial Press, 1945), 34; he repeated it in a post-mortem column on July 10, 1948.

"Fox actress Martha Stewart": Telephone conversation with author, January 15, 2005.

"Carole left over $51,000 in obligations": This data is from the "Estate Statement" in her family papers.

"under contract with Eagle-Lion": June Lockhart told me in 2004 that she had persuaded the Eagle-Lion studio chief to give Carole an advance in 1947 against her future performance in *The Amazing Mr. X*, which she needed because of her debts. After Carole's death, Eagle-Lion sued her estate for a $7,500 reimbursement for this advance, as reported in the *Los Angeles Times*, April 23, 1949.

"proceeds of the sale of their home": The *Los Angeles Times* on February 16, 1949, reports the approval of a reduction of the sale price of the house from $67,500 to $66,000, but the estate evaluation in March still lists the proceeds as $67,500.

"Florabel Muir's post-mortem article": *Motion Picture*, October 1948. The same story is found in *Rave* magazine ("Seven Who Killed Themselves: Why?") in June 1953, but it is unlikely that *Rave* had an independent source.

"Crawford Dixon's explanation": In "The Carole Landis Tragedy," *Movieland*, October 1948, referred to in chapter 4.

"Biographer Frank Smoot": In his online biography of Carole, "A Small-Town Midwestern Beauty" (www.carolelandis.net), Smoot states in reference to Carole's hospital stay, "Some writers have attributed this stay to an overdose of sleeping pills, an attempted suicide. But, no. Her physician, Dr. W. L. Marxer wrote Landis a prescription for fifty seconal sleeping pills on October 26, 1946, four days later." Smoot's text is no longer available but he is a credible source.

"Carole herself suggests": Landis, *Four Jills in a Jeep*, 79.

"Carole's personal physician": *Dixon Evening Telegraph*, July 7, 1948.

" 'have a very wonderful marriage' ": In "A Film Star Marries" (January 23, 1943), the British weekly *Picture Post*'s version of Carole's "official biography" reads, "She wants to 'have a very wonderful marriage and children whom I may love and make a fuss over long after the movies are gone.' " According to Carole's Fox mid-1944 publicity bio, "Carole says that she wants to . . . have children she can love and fuss over long after the movies have forgotten her."

"her attorney Jerry Giesler": *Los Angeles Evening Herald Examiner*, July 7, 1948.

"her estate was estimated at a mere $20,000": The July 19, 1948, *Hollywood Citizen-News* estimated that the "Everything" Carole left her mother in her suicide note, "even with Schmidlapp's $30,000 [which he was no longer offering]—came to not more than $50,000." This is amazingly close to the final figure of about $19,000. Figures in the following paragraph are from Carole's personal papers.

"Republic is an exception": Carole is not included among James Robert Parish's *Fox Girls* (New Rochelle, NY: Arlington House, 1971), nor does she figure among his *Glamour Girls* (ibid., 1975) or *Hollywood Beauties* (ibid., 1978); she is barely mentioned in William Everson's *The Films of Hal Roach* (New York: Museum of Modern Art, 1971) and Richard Lewis Ward's *A History of the Hal Roach Studios* (Carbondale: Southern Illinois University Press, 2005), and not at all in Daniel Bubbeo's *The Women of Warner Brothers* (Jefferson, NC: McFarland, 2002); admittedly, her Warner Brothers roles were hardly worthy of note. Although Carole made individual films at Paramount, RKO, Columbia, and Eagle-Lion, she cannot be said to have left her mark on any of these studios. Only Thomas Burnett Swann's *The Heroine or the Horse: Leading Ladies in Republic's Films* (South Brunswick, NJ: A. S. Barnes, 1977) contains a sympathetic sketch of Carole.

"accounts of Hollywood's contribution to the war effort": The most thorough account of Carole's war activities is found in Roy Hoopes's *When the Stars Went to War: Hollywood and World War II* (New York: Random House, 1994). Hoopes relies heavily on Carole's own memoir of the Four Jills trip, to which he adds biographical details unrelated to the war; he fails even to mention Carole's service in the Pacific. Maxene Andrews of the Andrews Sisters, in her book (written with Bill Gilbert) *Over Here, Over There: The Andrews Sisters and the USO Stars in World War II* (New York: Zebra Books, 1993), speaks admiringly of the Four Jills tour.

"Carole goes unmentioned": Molly Haskell, *From Reverence to Rape* (New York: Holt, Rinehart and Winston, 1974); a second edition, which also fails to mention Carole, was put out by the University of Chicago in 1987. Marjorie Rosen, *Popcorn Venus* (New York: Avon, 1973).

"several active Web sites": Aside from my own Web site, www.carolelandis.org, Gwen Serna's www.carolelandis.com and Liz Nocera's www.carolelandisonline.com are sites exclusively devoted to Carole; there are also many Carole Landis pages on multi-person sites.

BIBLIOGRAPHY

A Lifelong Friend. "The Truth about Carole Landis." *True Confessions*, November 1948.

Adams, Marjorie. Interview with Carole Landis. *Boston Globe*, [late 1944].

An Anonymous Admirer. "I Fell in Love with Carole Landis." *Screen Guide*, May 1942.

Anderson, Hesper. *South Mountain Road*. New York: Simon & Schuster, 2000.

Andrews, Maxene, and Bill Gilbert. *Over Here, Over There: The Andrews Sisters and the USO Stars in World War II*. New York: Zebra Books, 1993.

Anger, Kenneth. *Hollywood Babylon*. San Francisco: Simon & Schuster, 1975.

———. *Kenneth Anger's Hollywood Babylon II*. New York: E. P. Dutton, 1984.

Arce, Hector. *Groucho*. New York: Putnam, 1979.

———. *The Secret Life of Tyrone Power*. New York: Morrow, 1979.

Astor, Mary. *A Life on Film*. New York: Delacorte Press, 1971.

———. *My Story: An Autobiography*. Garden City, N.Y.: Doubleday, 1959.

Austin, John. *Hollywood's Babylon Women*. New York: SPI Books, 1994.

Banner, Judith. "Lucky Landis." *Hollywood*, May 1941.

Behlmer, Rudy. *Memo from Darryl F. Zanuck*. New York: Grove Press, 1993.

Benny, Jack, and his daughter Joan. *Sunday Nights at Seven: The Jack Benny Story*. New York: Warner Books, 1990.

Benny, Mary Livingstone, and Hilliard Marks, with Marcia Borie. *Jack Benny*. Garden City, New York: Doubleday, 1978.

Berle, Milton, with Haskel Frankel. *Milton Berle: An Autobiography*. New York: Applause Theatre & Cinema Books, 2002.

Billman, Larry. *Betty Grable: A Bio-bibliography*. Westport, Conn.: Greenwood Press, 1993.

Bogle, Donald. *Dorothy Dandridge: A Biography*. New York: St. Martin's Press, 1997.

Boller, Paul, and Ronald Davis. *Hollywood Anecdotes*. New York: William Morrow, 1987.

Bordman, Gerald Martin. *American Musical Theatre: A Chronicle*. New York: Oxford University Press, 2001.

Briggs, Colin. "Lynn Bari: A Much Titled Lady." *Classic Images*, February 2007.

Brown, Elgar. "The Life Story of Carole Landis." *Chicago Herald-American*, July 8–14, 1948.

Bubbeo, Daniel. *The Women of Warner Brothers: The Lives and Careers of 15 Leading Ladies*. Jefferson, N.C.: McFarland, 2002.

Calvet, Corinne. *Has Corinne Been a Good Girl?* New York: St. Martin's Press, 1983.

Cassini, Oleg. *In My Own Fashion: An Autobiography*. New York: Simon and Schuster, 1987.

Cecil, Vera. "Screen Beauty: Carole Landis Tells Intimate Details of Her Life." *National Police Gazette*, December 1944.

Chaplin, Charles, Jr., with N. and M. Rau. *My Father, Charlie Chaplin*. London: Longmans, Green and Co., 1960.

Charyn, Jerome. *Movieland: Hollywood and the Great American Dream Culture*. New York: Putnam, 1989.

Clarke, Thurston. *Searching for Paradise: A Grand Tour of the World's Unspoiled Islands*. New York: Ballantine Books, 2002.

Coffey, Frank. *Always Home: 50 Years of the USO*. Washington: Brassey's, 1991.

Coughlan, Gene. "Hollywood Heartbreak: The Story of Carole Landis." *Los Angeles Examiner*, September 16, 1948.

Crichton, Kyle. "Determined Lady." *Colliers*, May 10, 1941.

Crivello, Kirk. "Carole Landis." *Film Fan Monthly*, November 1973.

———. *Fallen Angels: The Lives and Untimely Deaths of 14 Hollywood Beauties*. Secaucus, N.J.: Citadel Press, 1988.

Culver, Roland. *Not Quite a Gentleman*. London: William Kimber & Co., Ltd., 1979.

Dallinger, Nat. *Unforgettable Hollywood*. New York: William Morrow, 1982.

Darrell, Kirk. "Carole Landis' War Diary." *Screenland*, July 1943.

Davis, Ronald. *The Glamour Factory*. Dallas: SMU Press, 1993.

———. *Hollywood Beauty: Linda Darnell and the American Dream*. Norman: University of Oklahoma Press, 1991.

De Leo, Edward, with David Sheldon and Joan McCall. *Al Pacino . . . and Me*. Philadelphia: Xlibris, 2002.

Dick, Bernard F. *Engulfed: The Death of Paramount Pictures and the Birth of Corporate Hollywood*. Lexington: University Press of Kentucky, 2001.

Dixon, Crawford. "The Carole Landis Tragedy." *Movieland*, October 1948.

Dmytryk, Edward. *Hollywood's Golden Age*. Boalsburg, Pa.: BearManor Media, 2003.

———. *It's a Hell of a Life, but Not a Bad Living*. New York: NYT Times Books, 1978.

Drew, William M. *At the Center of the Frame: Leading Ladies of the Twenties and Thirties*. Lanham, Md.: Vestal Press, 1999.

Dudley, Fredda. "All That a Woman Loves: Carole Landis' Wartime Romance." *Movieland*, June 1943.

Dunne, John Gregory. *The Studio*. New York: Farrar, Strauss & Giroux, 1968.

Dunning, John. *Tune in Yesterday*. Englewood Cliffs, N.J.: Prentice-Hall, 1976.

Dyer, Richard. *Only Entertainment*. London and New York: Routledge, 2002.

Dynamo [Fox publicity organ]. "Zanuck Names Six Players Sure of Stardom in 1941–42," 4th quarter, 1941.

Early, Dudley. "Carole Landis." *Family Circle*, January 2, 1942.

Eells, George. *Hedda and Louella*. New York: Putnam, 1972.

Etcoff, Nancy. *Survival of the Prettiest: The Science of Beauty*. New York: Doubleday, 1999.

Evans, Delight. "Open Letter to Betty and Carole." *Screenland*, February 1942.

Everson, William. *The Films of Hal Roach*. New York: Museum of Modern Art, 1971.

Eyles, Allen. *Rex Harrison*. London: W. H. Allen, 1985.

Faith, William Robert. *Bob Hope, a Life in Comedy*. New York: Putnam, 1982.

Farber, Stephen, and Marc Green. *Hollywood Dynasties*. New York: Putnam, 1984.

Fein, Irving. *Jack Benny: An Intimate Biography*. New York: Putnam, 1976. With introduction by George Burns.

Feinman, Jeffrey. *Hollywood Confidential*. Chicago: Playboy Press, 1976.

Film Fun, July 1938 (photos of Carole).

Finch, Christopher, and Linda Rosenkrantz. *Gone Hollywood*. Garden City, N.Y.: Doubleday, 1979.

Fisher, Steve. *I Wake up Screaming*. New York: Dodd, Mead, 1941.

Flagg, James Montgomery. "Carole Landis, Silhouette Girl" (drawing and commentary). *Los Angeles Evening Herald Examiner*, November 7, 1941.

Fleming, E. J. *Carole Landis: A Tragic Life in Hollywood*. Jefferson, N.C.: McFarland, 2005.

———. *The Fixers: Eddie Mannix, Howard Strickling, and the MGM Publicity Machine*. Jefferson, N.C.: McFarland, 2005.

Flynn, Errol. *My Wicked, Wicked Ways*. New York: Putnam, 1959.

Ford, Selwyn. *The Casting Couch*. London: Grafton Books, 1990.

Fortin, Noonie. *Memories of Maggie*. San Antonio, Tex.: Langmarc Publishing, 1995.

Franchey, John. "Love Would Come First! Carole Landis on Marriage and Career." *Movies*, January 1944.

Fraser-Cavassoni, Natasha. *Sam Spiegel*. New York: Simon & Schuster, 2003.

Gabrial, Jan. *Inside the Volcano: My Life with Malcolm Lowry*. New York: St. Martin's Press, 2000.

Gargan, William. *Why Me? An Autobiography*. Garden City, N.Y.: Doubleday, 1969.

Garrett, Betty, with Ron Rapoport. *Betty Garrett and Other Songs: A Life on Stage and Screen*. Lanham, Md.: Madison Books, 1998.

Gehring, Wes D. *Romantic vs. Screwball Comedy: Charting the Difference*. Lanham, Md.: Scarecrow Press, 2002.

Gibson, Clare. *The Wedding Dress*. London: Courage Books, 2001.

Giesler, Jerry, as told to Pete Martin. *The Jerry Giesler Story*. New York: Simon and Schuster, 1960.

Gilbert, Dolores. "Carole Landis n'est plus . . ." *Ciné Revue*, July 16, 1948.

Gilpatrick, Kristin. *Famous Wisconsin Film Stars*. Oregon, Wis.: Badger Books, 2002.

Glynn, Prudence. *Skin to Skin: Eroticism in Dress*. New York: Oxford University Press, 1982.

Gordon, Jeff. "Orchestra Wives: The Legendary Big-Band Musical." *Films of the Golden Age*, fall 2006.

Grams, Martin. *The History of the Cavalcade of America*. Delta, Pa.: M. Grams, 1998.

———. *Radio Drama: A Comprehensive Chronicle of American Network Programs, 1932–1962*. Jefferson, N.C.: McFarland, 2000.

Gubernick, Lisa Rebecca. *Squandered Fortune: The Life and Times of Huntington Hartford*. New York: Putnam, 1991.

Guild, Leo. *Hollywood Screwballs*. Los Angeles: Holloway House, 1962.

Guiles, Fred Lawrence. *Joan Crawford: The Last Word*. Secaucus, N.J.: Carol Pub. Group, 1995.

Gussow, Mel. *Don't Say Yes until I Finish Talking: A Biography of Darryl F. Zanuck*. Garden City, N.Y.: Doubleday, 1971.

Hadleigh, Boze. *Hollywood Gays: Conversations with Cary Grant, Liberace, Tony Perkins, Paul Lynde, Cesar Romero, Brad Davis, Randolph Scott, James Coco, William Haines, David Lewis*. New York: Barricade Books, 1996.

———. *Hollywood Lesbians*. New York: Barricade Books, 1994.

Hagen, Ray, and Laura Wagner. *Killer Tomatoes*. Jefferson, N.C.: McFarland, 2004.

Hall, Gladys. "Carole Landis and Her Meditations in a Fox-Hole." *Movie Show*, November 1943.

———. "She Won't Depend on the Landis Line." *Motion Picture*, October 1940.

———. "What Carole Landis Demands of Men!" *Screenland*, October 1941.

Hamilton, Sara. [Romance between Guy Madison and Gail Russell]. *Photoplay*, November 1947.

Hannsberry, Karen Burroughs. *Bad Boys: The Actors of Film Noir*. Jefferson, N.C.: McFarland, 2003.

———. *Femme Noir: Bad Girls of Film*. Jefferson, N.C.: McFarland, 1998.

Harris, Marlys J. *The Zanucks of Hollywood*. New York: Crown Publishers, 1989.

Harrison, Rex. *Rex: An Autobiography*. New York: William Morris & Co., 1975.

Headlines. "Suicide of a Sex Symbol." November 1972.

Hearn, Chester G. *The American Soldier in World War II*. Motorbooks International, 2001.

Henderson, Robert M. *D. W. Griffith: His Life and Work*. New York: Oxford, 1972.

Herman, Vic. *Winnie the Wac*. Foreword by Carole Landis. Philadelphia: David McKay Co., 1945. Reprint, enlarged ed. Carlsbad, Ca.: Virginia Herman: 2002.

Hill, Norman, ed. *The Lonely Beauties*. New York: Popular Library, 1971.

Hollywood. Hollywood News. December 1941.

Hoopes, Roy. *When the Stars Went to War: Hollywood and World War II*. New York: Random House, 1994.

Jacobson, Laurie. *Dishing Hollywood: The Real Scoop on Tinseltown's Most Notorious Scandals*. Nashville, Tenn.: Cumberland House, 2003.

Jessel, George, with John Austin. *The World I Lived In*. Chicago: Regnery, 1975.

Johansen, Arno. "Will Rex Harrison Survive Scandal?" *Movieland*, November 1948.

Johnson, Gary. "The Serials: An Introduction." *Images 4* (www.imagesjournal.com/issue04/infocus/introduction5.htm).

Joy, Dean P. *Sixty Days of Combat*. New York: Ballantine Books, 2004.

Karol, Michael. *Lucy A to Z*. Lincoln, Neb.: iUniverse Star, 2001.

Kear, Lynn, and John Rossman. *Kay Francis: A Passionate Life and Career*. Jefferson, N.C.: McFarland, 2006.

Keyes, Evelyn. *I'll Think about That Tomorrow*. New York: Dutton, 1991.

———. *Scarlett O'Hara's Younger Sister*. Secaucus, N.J.: Lyle Stuart, 1977.

Keylin, Arleen, and Suri Fleischer, eds. *Hollywood Album: Lives and Deaths of Hollywood Stars from the Pages of the* New York Times. New York: Arno Press, 1977–1979.

Kobal, John. *People Will Talk*. New York: Knopf, 1986.

———. *Rita Hayworth: The Time, the Place, and the Woman*. New York: Norton, 1977.

Kuniczak, W. S. *My Name Is Million: An Illustrated History of the Poles in America*. Garden City, N.Y.: Doubleday, 1978.

Lacey, Madison S., and Don Morgan. *Hollywood Cheesecake: 60 Years of Leg Art*. Secaucus, N.J.: Citadel Press, 1981.

Lamparski, Richard. *Lamparski's Hidden Hollywood*. New York: Simon & Schuster, 1981.

Landis, Carole. "Carole Landis Names Hollywood's Most Fascinating Men." *Movie Stars Parade*, February 1941.

———. "Do You Think I Was Wrong?" *Silver Screen*, September 1947.

———. "Don't Marry a Stranger." *Photoplay*, January 1945.

———. "Four Jills in a Jeep." *Saturday Evening Post*, December 18, 1943–January 15, 1944 (five installments).

———. *Four Jills in a Jeep*. New York: Random House, 1944.

———. "Glamour Girls Are Suckers, as Told to Gladys Hall." *Photoplay*, December 1941.

———. "Helping Our Boys Forget." *Motion Picture*, December 1944.

———. "How to Handle Wolves with Kid Gloves." *Modern Screen*, March 1941.

———. "I Am Carole Landis." *Life Story*, August 1943.

———. "I Don't Live in a Night Club!" *Screen Guide*, July 1941.

———. "I'm Glad I'm a Fighting Man's Sweetheart." *Screen Guide*, January 1943.

———. "If I Were Victor Mature." *Silver Screen*, July 1942.

———. "The Man Upstairs." *American Magazine*, October 1942.

———. "My Dog Is Dead." *Motion Picture*, April 1944.

———. "My Pal Pat." *Movieland*, November 1944.

———. "My Wartime Honeymoon." *Photoplay*, June 1943.

Landis, Clara Ridste. "The True Story of Carole Landis." *True Story*, October 1948.

Leaming, Barbara. *Bette Davis: A Biography*. New York: Simon & Schuster, 1992.

Lester, James T. *Too Marvelous for Words: The Life and Genius of Art Tatum*. New York: Oxford University Press, 1995.

Levin, Martin. *Hollywood and the Great Fan Magazines*. New York: Arbor House, 1970.

Life. "Carole Landis Does Not Want to Be Ping Girl." June 17, 1940.

———. "Pictures to the Editors." September 6, 1943.

———. "Ping Girl Gets Conked." August 19, 1940.

Look. "Carole Landis: Movie Star Finds Happiness in War Marriage." June 29, 1943.

Lynn, Kenneth. *Charlie Chaplin and His Times*. New York: Simon & Schuster, 1997.

MacPherson, Virginia. "Carole's Curves Covered." *Hollywood Citizen-News*, October 9, 1945.

Madsen, Axel. *The Sewing Circle: Hollywood's Greatest Secret: Female Stars Who Loved Other Women*. Secaucus, N.J.: Carol Pub. Group, 1995.

Marlowe, David. "Is the Brass Monkey Now a Lucky Mascot?" *Picturegoer*, February 3, 1951.

Martin, Mart. *Did She or Didn't She?* Secaucus, N.J.: Citadel Press, 1996.

Martin, Tony, and Cyd Charisse. *The Two of Us*. New York: Mason/Charter, 1976.

Marx, Samuel. *Mayer and Thalberg: The Make-Believe Saints*. Los Angeles: Samuel French, 1988 [1975].

Mayo, Virginia, as told to L. C. Van Savage. *The Best Years of My Life*. Chesterfield, Mo.: BeachHouse Books, 2002.

McDonald, Paul. *The Star System: Hollywood's Production of Popular Identities*. London: Wallflower, 2000.

McGee, Tom. *Betty Grable: The Girl with the Million Dollar Legs*. Vestal, N.Y.: Vestal Press, 1995.

McLellan, Diana. *The Girls: Sappho Goes to Hollywood*. New York: LA Weekly Books, 2000.

McLelland, Doug. *The Golden Age of "B" Movies*. Nashville, Tenn.: Charter House, 1978.

Meredith, Burgess. *So Far, So Good: A Memoir*. Boston: Little, Brown, 1994.

Miller, Don. *"B" Movies: An Informal Survey of the American Low-Budget Film, 1933–1945*. New York: Curtis Books, 1973.

Milton, Joyce. *Tramp: The Life of Charlie Chaplin*. New York: Harper-Collins, 1996.

Modern Screen. "Dear Diary." April 1942.

———. "Good News." November 1940, July 1941, February 1942, April 1943.

———. "It's Out-Landis!—Intimate Close-Up of That Gentlemen-Preferred Blonde." October 1941.

Montgomery, George, with Jeffrey Millet. *The Years of George Montgomery*. Los Angeles: Sagebrush, 1981.

Mordden, Ethan. *The Hollywood Studios: House Style in the Golden Age of the Movies*. New York: Simon & Schuster, 1988.

Morella, Joe, with Edward Z. Epstein. *Rita: The Life of Rita Hayworth*. New York: Delacorte Press, 1983.

Morley, Patrick. *"This Is the American Forces Network": The Anglo-American Battle of the Air Waves in World War II*. New York: Praeger Publishers, 2001.

Morris, John G. *Get the Picture: A Personal History of Photojournalism*. Chicago: University of Chicago Press, 2002.

Moseley, Roy, with Phillip and Martin Masheter. *Rex Harrison: A Biography*. New York: St. Martin's Press, 1987.

Mosley, Leonard. *Zanuck: The Rise and Fall of Hollywood's Last Tycoon*. New York: Little Brown, 1984.

Motion Picture. "Tattler." May 1943.

Movie Life. "Elemental, My Dear Watson" (raincoat fashions). October 1947.

———. "Tables for Two." October 1941.

Movie Show. "Movie Star and Millionaire." September 1946.

Movie Stars Parade. "Love, Laughter, and Landis." July 1941.

———. "Pride of the Yanks." January 1944.

Movie Story. "Gossip." June 1943.

Movie-Radio Guide. "Cupid over Hollywood." January 25, 1941.

———. "Spotlight on Carole Landis: Hollywood's Most Dated Starlet." April 19, 1941.

———. "This Week." November 8, 1941, November 22, 1941.

Movies. "My Most Thrilling Love Scene." October 1942.

Muir, Florabel. "What's behind the Carole Landis Tragedy?" *Motion Picture*, October 1948.

Murphy, George, with Victor Lasky. *"Say . . . Didn't You Used to Be George Murphy?"* New York: Bartholomew House, 1970.

Murray, William. *Janet, My Mother, and Me: A Memoir of Growing Up with Janet Flanner and Natalia Danesi Murray*. New York: Simon & Schuster, 2000.

Newsweek. Letters to the Editor. January 29, 1945.

———. "NG, Baby?" October 16, 1944.

Noble, John Wesley, and Bernard Averbuch. *Never Plead Guilty: The Story of Jake Ehrlich*. New York: Farrar, Straus & Cudahy, 1955.

O'Brien, Pat. *The Wind at My Back: The Life and Times of Pat O'Brien, by Himself*. Garden City, N.Y.: Doubleday, 1964.

O'Brien, Scott. *Kay Francis: I Can't Wait to Be Forgotten*. Boalsburg, Pa.: BearManor Media, 2006.

O'Connell, Geoffrey F. X. "Ghosts of Mississippi." *metrotimes* (online Detroit weekly: http://www.metrotimes.com/editorial/story.asp?id=1790).

O'Steen, Johnny. *Were These the Golden Years? Fifty Years of Warner Brothers, Hollywood, and Much More*. North Hollywood, Calif.: J. R. O'Steen, 1976 [reproduced typescript].

Our Dogs. Cover. 4th quarter, 1942.

Palmer, Lilli. *Change Lobsters—and Dance*. New York: Macmillan, 1975; also London: W. H. Allen, 1977.

———. *The Red Raven*. London: W. H. Allen, 1976.

Parish, James Robert. *The Fox Girls*. New Rochelle, N.Y.: Arlington House, 1972.

Parish, James Robert, and William T. Leonard. *The Funsters*. New Rochelle, N.Y.: Arlington House Publishers, 1979.

Parish, James Robert, and Don E. Stanke. *The Glamour Girls*. New Rochelle, N.Y.: Arlington House Publishers, 1975.

Parish, James Robert, with Gregory W. Mank and Don E. Stanke. *The Hollywood Beauties*. New Rochelle, N.Y.: Arlington House, 1978.

Parish, James Robert, with Steven Whitney. *The George Raft File*. New York: Drake, 1973.

Passing in Review (Online newsletter of the 33rd Army Band of Heidelberg, Germany). "33rd ABAA's Stirred by Frank Rosato's Talk." September 2004. (http://www.rt66. com/~obfusa/33rd/nlsep04.htm).

Photoplay. "Cal York's Gossip of Hollywood." December 1940, January 1942.

———. "Speak for Yourself: 'A Regular Trouper' " (letter from Pauline Landry of Franklin, N.H.). November 1944.

———. "The Truth about the Stars' Night Life." February 1945.

Pic. Cover. July 12, 1938.

Picture Post. "A Film Star Marries." January 23, 1943.

Pitrone, Jean Maddern. *Take It from the Big Mouth: The Life of Martha Raye*. Lexington: University Press of Kentucky, 1999.

Porter, Darwin. *Brando Unzipped*. New York: Blood Moon Productions, Ltd., 2006.

———. *Katharine the Great*. New York: Blue Moon Productions, 2004.

Proctor, Kay. "I Don't Want to Be an Angel." *Silver Screen*, December 1942.

Pyle, Ernie. *Here Is Your War*. New York: Henry Holt and Co., 1943.

Ragan, David. *Movie Stars of the '40s: A Complete Reference Guide for the Film Historian or Trivia Buff*. Englewood Cliffs, N.J.: Prentice-Hall, 1985.

———. *Who's Who in Hollywood, 1900–1976*. New Rochelle, N.Y.: Arlington House, 1976.

Rave. "Seven Who Killed Themselves: Why?" June 1953.

Reid, James. "No Advice to the Lovelorn." *Silver Screen*, March 1941.

Rice, Craig [Georgianna Craig]. *Having Wonderful Crime*. New York: Simon and Schuster, 1943.

Ringgold, Gene. *The Films of Rita Hayworth*. Secaucus, N.J.: Citadel Press, 1974.

Rosen, Marjorie. *Popcorn Venus*. New York: Avon, 1973.

Rosenberg, Bernard, and Harry Silverstein. *The Real Tinsel*. New York: Macmillan, 1970.

Ross, D[orothy]. "The True Story of My Sister." *Photoplay*, November 1948.

Rubin, Martin. *Showstoppers: Busby Berkeley and the Tradition of Spectacle*. New York: Columbia University Press, 1993.

Schatz, Thomas. *Boom and Bust: The American Cinema in the 1940s*. Vol. 6 of *History of American Cinema*. New York: Scribner's/Simon & Schuster Macmillan, 1997.

———. *The Genius of the System: Hollywood Filmmaking in the Studio Era*. New York: Henry Holt and Company, 1996.

———. *Hollywood Genres: Formulas, Filmmaking, and the Studio System*. Philadelphia: Temple University Press, 1981.

Schneider, G.W.S. *Don't Tell His Children*. Philadelphia: Xlibris, 2000.

Schroeder, Carl A. "Carole Landis, Fighting War Bride." *Movie-Radio Guide*, June 1943.

Schultz, Margie. *Ann Sheridan. A Bio-Bibliography*. Westport, Conn.: Greenwood Press, 1997.

Screen Book. Photo of "Carol Landis" in *Varsity Show* ensemble finale. October 1937.

Screen Guide. Photo of Carole on crutches with broken toes. February 1938.

———. "A Heroine Comes Home!" June 1943.

————. "Hollywood Life." January 1946.

————. "Hollywood Merry-go-round: Canine Companions to Match Their Coats!" January 1948.

————. "Make Up Your Mind: Carole Landis' Real-Life Movie." October 1944.

————. "Turnabout Girl Goes Straight." August 1940.

————. "War Train to Hollywood." March 1942.

Screen Romances. "Hollywood Sound-Track." January 1941.

Seaman, Barbara. *Lovely Me.* New York: William Morrow & Co., 1987.

Seinfeldt, Mark. *Final Drafts: Suicides of World-Famous Authors.* Amherst, N.Y: Prometheus Books, 1999.

Shearer, Lloyd. *Walter Scott's Personality Parade.* New York: Grosset & Dunlap, 1971.

————. "Why Actresses Try Suicide." *Parade,* November 6, 1960.

Sheridan, Michael. "What Carole Landis Told Me." *Chicago Herald American Home Magazine,* October 8, 1949.

Silver Screen. "Hollywood Earfuls." May 1942, December 1945.

————. "Topics for Gossip." June 1941, January 1942.

Silvers, Phil, with Robert Saffron. *This Laugh Is on Me: The Phil Silvers Story.* Englewood Cliffs, N.J.: Prentice-Hall, 1973.

Simon, George Thomas. *Glenn Miller and His Orchestra.* New York: T. Y. Crowell Co., 1974.

Skolsky, Sidney. "Tintype of Carole Landis." Syndicated column. March 18, 1941, March 10, 1942, July 22, 1943, November 23, 1945.

Smith, Thorne. *Turnabout.* Garden City, N.Y.: Doubleday Doran, 1931.

Smoot, Frank. *Carole Landis: A Small-Town Midwest Beauty.* Published on Web site www.carolelandis.net, circa 2003.

Solomon, Aubrey. *Twentieth Century-Fox: A Corporate and Financial History.* Metuchen, N.J.: Scarecrow Press, 1988.

Stackpole, Peter. *Life in Hollywood, 1936–1952.* Livingston, Mont.: Clark City Press, 1992.

Stallings, Penny, with Howard Mandelbaum. *Flesh and Fantasy.* New York: St. Martin's Press, 1978.

Stardom. "The Courage of Carole Landis." February 1943.

Starr, Jimmy. *Barefoot on Barbed Wire.* Lanham, Md., and London: Scarecrow Press, 2001.

Susann, Jacqueline. *Valley of the Dolls.* New York: Random House, 1966.

Swann, Thomas Burnett. *The Heroine or the Horse: Leading Ladies in Republic's Films.* South Brunswick, N.J.: A. S. Barnes, 1977.

Tapert, Annette. *The Power of Glamour: The Women Who Defined the Magic of Stardom.* New York: Crown Publishers, 1998.

Tierney, Gene, with Mickey Herskowitz. *Self-Portrait.* New York: Wyden Books, 1979.

Time. "Stars over the Front." March 8, 1943.

Tornabene, Lyn. *Long Live the King: A Biography of Clark Gable.* New York: G. P. Putnam's Sons, 1976.

Transmitter (online journal of the Library of American Broadcasting). "Command Performance." 2nd quarter, 2000.

Treadwell, Bill. *Give It to Me Easy: A Thousand and One Characters*. Cynthiana, Ky.: Hobson Book Press, 1944.

Turner, Lana. *Lana: The Lady, the Legend, the Truth*. New York: Dutton, 1982.

Twentieth Century-Fox Studios. Publicity bios of Carole. May 1941, January 1944, June 1944.

Vandour, Cyril. "Carole Landis: Love Is What You Make It." *Movies*, July 1941.

Vogel, Michelle. *Gene Tierney: A Biography*. Jefferson, N.C.: McFarland, 2005.

Vogel, Michelle, and Liz Nocera. *Hollywood Blondes: Golden Girls of the Silver Screen*. Shelbyville, Ky.: Wasteland Press, 2007.

Wagner, Walter. *You Must Remember This*. New York: G. P. Putnam's Sons, 1975.

Walker, Alexander. *Fatal Charm: The Life of Rex Harrison*. New York: St. Martin's Press, 1992.

Wapshott, Nicolas. *Rex Harrison*. London: Chatto & Windus, 1991.

War Activites Committee. *Movies at War*. New York: War Activities Committee, Motion Picture Industry, 1942–1945.

Warren, Doug. *Betty Grable: The Reluctant Movie Queen*. New York: St. Martin's Press, 1981.

Weaver, Tom. *Monsters, Mutants, and Heavenly Creatures: Confessions of 14 Classic Sci-Fi/Horrormeisters!* Baltimore, Md.: Midnight Marquee Press, 2001.

Westmore, Ern, and Bud Westmore. *Beauty, Glamour, and Personality*. Sandusky, Ohio: Prang Co., 1947.

Wilcoxon, Henry, with Katherine Orrison. *Lionheart in Hollywood: The Autobiography of Henry Wilcoxon*. Metuchen, N.J.: Scarecrow Press, 1991.

Wiley, Mason, and Damian Bona. *Inside Oscar: The Unofficial History of the Academy Awards*. New York: Ballantine Books, 1986.

Williams, Esther, with Digby Diehl. *The Million Dollar Mermaid*. New York: Harcourt, 1999.

Wilson, Earl. *Hot Times: True Tales of Hollywood and Broadway*. Chicago: Contemporary Books, 1984.

———. *I Am Gazing into My 8-Ball*. Garden City, N.Y.: Sundial Press, 1945.

———. *Let 'em Eat Cheesecake*. Garden City, N.Y.: Doubleday & Co., 1949.

———. *The Show Business Nobody Knows*. Chicago: Cowles Book Co., 1971.

Wilson, Elizabeth. "Landis without Leopard Skins." *Liberty*, July 19, 1947.

Winchell, Walter. "Hollywood's War Effort." *Motion Picture*, August 1942.

Wise, James E., and Anne Collier Rehill. *Stars in Blue: Movie Actors in America's Sea Services*. Annapolis, Md.: Naval Institute Press, 1997.

Witney, William. *In a Door, into a Fight, out a Door, into a Chase: Moviemaking Remembered by the Guy at the Door*. Jefferson, N.C.: McFarland & Co., 1996.

Wright, Cobina [Sr.]. *I Never Grew Up*. New York: Prentice-Hall, 1952.

Wright, Mike. *What They Didn't Teach You about World War II*. Novato, Calif.: Presidio Press, 2000.

Zukor, Adolph. *The Public Is Never Wrong*. New York: G. P. Putnam's Sons, 1953.

Supplemental Sources

In addition to the discrete items in the bibliography, the following sources were consulted (non-exhaustive list):

Family Materials: letters, photographs, newspapers, fan club bulletins, memorabilia. Legal records: birth, marriage, divorce, death, testament, name change.

Ancestry.com: census data, death index, historical newspaper collection.

NewspaperARCHIVE.com: historical newspaper collection.

Letters: Very few of Carole's thousands of letters have been assembled in any one place. I have had access to the few dozen letters collected by fellow Carole enthusiast Gwen Serna as well as a number that have appeared on the Internet in auction sales. Ken Richards provided me with copies of letters from Carole concerning his singing career. Phil Weiss kindly provided me with his transcriptions from the only extant library collection of Carole's letters, the "Letters to James R. Pattarini" at the New York Public Library, which also includes a number of letters from her secretary, Nan Stuart. Texts of letters are occasionally made available at on-line auction sites such as eBay and rrauction.com. Altogether, I have compiled the text of some 132 letters and fragments as of September 2007.

Correspondence/interviews: family members, Hollywood personalities, World War II veterans, others in entertainment industry.

Libraries

University of Southern California: Roach production files, Fox scripts, scrapbooks, movie magazines; Warner Bros. archive.

Academy of Motion Picture Arts and Sciences Margaret Herrick Library: Production Code Files, Special Collections.

University of California, Los Angeles: Fine Arts Special Collections, Fox legal files.

San Francisco News-Call Bulletin Newspaper Photograph Archive in the Online Archive of California (online).

Movie Columnists

References in the text or notes to syndicated columns do not include mention of specific newspapers.

Harrison Carroll
Harry Crocker
Jimmie Fidler

Sheilah Graham
Edith Gwynn
Gene Handsaker
Hedda Hopper
Erskine Johnson
Dorothy Kilgallen
Dorothy Manners
Frederick C. Othman
Louella Parsons
Lowell B. Redelings
Edwin Schallert
Jimmy Starr
Ed Sullivan
Earl Wilson
Walter Winchell

Selected Issues of Film Periodicals

Daily Variety
Film Bulletin
Film Daily
The Hollywood Reporter
Motion Picture Daily
Weekly Variety

Selected Issues of Los Angeles Newspapers

Hollywood Citizen News
Los Angeles Evening Herald Examiner
Los Angeles Examiner
Los Angeles Herald
Los Angeles Times

Selected Issues of New York Newspapers

Brooklyn Heights Press
New York Herald Tribune
New York News

New York Sun
New York Times
New York World-Telegram
Wall Street Journal

Other Newspapers Accessed through Online Databases

Coshocton (Ohio) Tribune
Dixon (Illinois) Evening Telegraph
Joplin (Missouri) Globe
Lima (Ohio) News
Mansfield (Ohio) News Journal
Nebraska State Journal
Oakland Tribune
Piqua (Ohio) Call
Reno Evening Gazette
San Bernardino Sun
Statesville (NC) Record Landmark
Syracuse Herald Journal
Traverse City (Michigan) Record-Eagle
Zanesville (Ohio) Signal

FILMOGRAPHY

Feature Films

Three Texas Steers, 1939. Dir. George Sherman; Prod. William Berke; Republic Pictures.

Daredevils of the Red Circle, 1939. Dir. John English, William Witney; Prod. Robert Beche; Republic Pictures (serial).

The Cowboys from Texas, 1939. Dir. George Sherman, William Witney; Prod. Harry Grey; Republic Pictures.

One Million B.C., 1940. Dir. Hal Roach Jr., Hal Roach; Prod. Hal Roach; Hal Roach Studios/United Artists.

Turnabout, 1940. Dir. Hal Roach; Prod. Hal Roach; Hal Roach Studios/United Artists.

Mystery Sea Raider, 1940. Dir. Edward Dmytryk; Prod. Eugene Zukor; Paramount Pictures.

Road Show, 1941. Dir. Hal Roach; Prod. Hal Roach; Hal Roach Studios/United Artists.

Topper Returns, 1941. Dir. Roy Del Ruth; Prod. Hal Roach; Hal Roach Studios/United Artists.

Moon over Miami, 1941. Dir. Walter Lang; Prod. Darryl Zanuck; Twentieth Century-Fox.

Dance Hall, 1941. Dir. Irving Pichel; Prod. Sol Wurtzel; Twentieth Century-Fox.

I Wake Up Screaming (aka *Hot Spot*), 1941. Dir. H. Bruce Humberstone; Prod. Milton Sperling; Twentieth Century-Fox.

Cadet Girl, 1941. Dir. Ray McCarey; Prod. Sol Wurtzel; Twentieth Century-Fox.

A Gentleman at Heart, 1942. Dir. Ray McCarey; Prod. Walter Morosco; Twentieth Century-Fox.

My Gal Sal, 1942. Dir. Irving Cummings; Prod. Darryl Zanuck; Twentieth Century-Fox.

It Happened in Flatbush, 1942. Dir. Ray McCarey; Prod. Walter Morosco; Twentieth Century-Fox.

Orchestra Wives, 1942. Dir. Archie Mayo; Prod. William Goetz; Twentieth Century-Fox.

Manila Calling, 1942. Dir. Herbert I. Leeds; Prod. Sol Wurtzel; Twentieth Century-Fox.

The Powers Girl (aka *Hello Beautiful*), 1943. Dir. Norman Z. McLeod; Prod. Charles R. Rogers; Rogers Productions/United Artists.

Wintertime, 1943. Dir. John Brahm; Prod. Darryl Zanuck; Twentieth Century-Fox.

Four Jills in a Jeep, 1944. Dir. William A. Seiter; Prod. Irving Starr; Twentieth Century-Fox.

Secret Command (aka *Pilebuck*), 1944. Dir. A. Edward Sutherland; Prod. Phil Ryan; Terneen Prods./Columbia.

Having Wonderful Crime, 1945. Dir. A. Edward Sutherland; Prod. Robert Fellows; RKO.

Behind Green Lights, 1946. Dir. Otto Brower; Prod. Bryan Foy; Twentieth Century-Fox.

A Scandal in Paris, 1946. Dir. Douglas Sirk; Prod. Arnold Pressburger; Arnold Productions/United Artists.

It Shouldn't Happen to a Dog, 1946. Dir. Herbert I. Leeds; Prod. William Girard; Twentieth Century-Fox.

Out of the Blue, 1947. Dir. Leigh Jason; Prod. Isadore Goldsmith; Eagle-Lion Films.

Noose (aka *Silk Noose*), United Kingdom, 1948; United States, 1950. Dir. Edmond T. Gréville; Prod. Edward Dryhurst; Associated British, Pathé/Associated British Film Distributors (ABFD) [U.K.], Monogram [U.S.].

Brass Monkey (aka *Lucky Mascot*), 1951. Dir. Thornton Freeland; Prod. Nat Bronstein; Alliance Communications (Calif.) and Diadem Films (U.K.)/Allied Artists.

Bit Parts

A Star Is Born, 1937. Dir. William Wellman; Prod. David O. Selznick; Selznick International, United Artists (uncredited performance).

A Day at the Races, 1937. Dir. Sam Wood; Prod. Max Siegel, Sam Wood; MGM (uncredited performance).

Fly-Away Baby, 1937. Dir. Frank McDonald; Prod. Bryan Foy, Hal B. Wallis, Jack L. Warner; Warner Bros. (uncredited performance).

The Emperor's Candlesticks, 1937. Dir. George Fitzmaurice; Prod. John Considine Jr.; MGM (uncredited performance).

Broadway Melody of 1938, 1937. Dir. Roy Del Ruth; Prod. Jack Cummings; MGM (uncredited performance).

Varsity Show, 1937. Dir. William Keighley; Prod. Louis F. Edelman, Hal B. Wallis, Jack L. Warner; Warner Bros. (uncredited performance).

Over the Goal, 1937. Dir. Noel M. Smith; Prod. Bryan Foy; Warner Bros. (uncredited performance).

Alcatraz Island, 1937. Dir. William C. McGann; Prod. Bryan Foy; Cosmopolitan, First National, Warner Bros. (AFI: offscreen credit).

Missing Witnesses, 1937. Dir. William Clemens; Prod. Bryan Foy; Warner Bros. (uncredited performance).

She Loved a Fireman, 1937. Dir. John Farrow; Prod. Bryan Foy, Hal B. Wallis, Jack L. Warner; Warner Bros. (uncredited performance).

Tovarich, 1937. Dir. Anatole Litvak; Prod. Anatole Litvak, Robert Lord, Hal B. Wallis, Jack L. Warner; Warner Bros. (in trailer only).

Hollywood Hotel, 1938. Dir. Busby Berkeley; Prod. Sam Bischoff, Bryan Foy; Warner Bros. (AFI: offscreen credit).

The Patient in Room 18, 1938. Dir. Bobby Connolly, Crane Wilbur; Prod. Bryan Foy, Hal B. Wallis, Jack L. Warner; Warner Bros. (uncredited performance).

The Invisible Menace, 1938. Dir. John Farrow; Prod. Bryan Foy, Hal B. Wallis, Jack L. Warner; Warner Bros. (uncredited performance).

Blondes at Work, 1938. Dir. Frank McDonald; Prod. Bryan Foy, Hal B. Wallis, Jack L. Warner; Warner Bros.

A Slight Case of Murder, 1938. Dir. Lloyd Bacon; Prod. Samuel Bischoff; First National, Warner Bros. (uncredited performance).

Love, Honor, and Behave, 1938. Dir. Stanley Logan; Prod. Louis F. Edelman; Warner Bros. (AFI: offscreen credit).

He Couldn't Say No, 1938. Dir. Lewis Seiler; Prod. Bryan Foy, Hal B. Wallis, Jack L. Warner; Warner Bros. (uncredited performance).

Over the Wall, 1938. Dir. Frank McDonald; Prod. Bryan Foy, Hal B. Wallis, Jack L. Warner; Warner Bros. (AFI: offscreen credit).

Women Are Like That, 1938. Dir. Stanley Logan; Prod. Robert Lord, Hal B. Wallis, Jack L. Warner; Warner Bros. (uncredited performance).

Torchy Blane in Panama, 1938. Dir. William Clemens; Prod. Hal Wallis, Jack L. Warner; Warner Bros. (uncredited performance).

Gold Diggers in Paris, 1938. Dir. Ray Enright; Prod. Samuel Bischoff, Hal B. Wallis; Warner Bros.

When Were You Born, 1938. Dir. William C. McGann; Prod. Bryan Foy; First National, Warner Bros. (uncredited performance).

Men Are Such Fools, 1938. Dir. Busby Berkeley; Prod. David Lewis, Hal B. Wallis, Jack L. Warner; Warner Bros. (AFI: offscreen credit).

Penrod's Double Trouble, 1938. Dir. Lewis Seiler; Prod. Bryan Foy; Warner Bros. (uncredited performance).

Boy Meets Girl, 1938. Dir. Lloyd Bacon; Prod. Samuel Bischoff, Hal B. Wallis, Jack L. Warner; First National, Warner Bros. (AFI: offscreen credit).

Four's a Crowd, 1938. Dir. Michael Curtiz; Prod. David Lewis, Hal B. Wallis, Jack L. Warner; Warner Bros.

Reno, 1939. Dir. John Farrow; Prod. Robert Sisk; RKO (uncredited performance).

Carole is sometimes credited with appearances in *The King and the Chorus Girl* (1937; Dir. Mervyn LeRoy; Prod. Mervyn LeRoy; Warner Bros.), in production in November and December 1936, and *The Adventurous Blonde* (1937; Dir. Frank McDonald; Prod. Bryan Foy, Hal B. Wallis, Jack L. Warner; First National, Warner Bros.), made in June and July 1937, although she is not visible in either film and does not appear in the production reports. She is also sometimes credited with *Girls on Probation* (1938; Dir. William C. McGann; Prod. Bryan Foy; First National, Warner Bros.), but the production reports show only that she tested for a part but was not chosen.

Documentaries (Partial List)

Meet the Stars #5: Hollywood Meets the Navy, 1941. Dir. Harriet Parsons; Republic Pictures.

Hedda Hopper's Hollywood No. 2, 1941. Dir. Herbert Moulton; Prod. Herbert Moulton; Paramount Pictures.

Show Business at War: March of Time IX, 10, 1943. Dir. Louis de Rochemont; Prod. Louis de Rochemont; Twentieth Century-Fox, Time Magazine.

For further information about Carole, please consult the Web site at www.carolelandis.org.

INDEX